BLOCKCHAIN
FOR BUSINESS LAWYERS

JAMES A. COX AND MARK W. RASMUSSEN, EDITORS

ABA SECTION OF
SCIENCE & TECHNOLOGY LAW

Cover by Mary Anne Kulchawik/ABA Publishing.

The materials contained herein represent the opinions of the author and editors, and should not be construed to be the views or opinions of the law firms or companies with whom such persons are in partnership with, associated with, or employed by, nor of the American Bar Association or the Section of Science & Technology Law unless adopted pursuant to the bylaws of the Association.

Nothing contained in this book is to be considered as the rendering of legal advice for specific cases, and readers are responsible for obtaining such advice from their own legal counsel. This book is intended for educational and informational purposes only.

Printed in the United States of America

22 21 20 19 18   5 4 3 2 1

Library of Congress Cataloging-in-Publication Data

Names: Cox, James A. (Jim A.), editor. | Rasmussen, Mark (Mark W.), editor.
Title: Blockchain for business lawyers / Jim Cox and Mark Rasmussen.
Description: Chicago : American Bar Association, 2018. | Includes index.
Identifiers: LCCN 2018023573 (print) | LCCN 2018025906 (ebook) | ISBN
    9781641051965 (e-book) | ISBN 9781641051958 (softcover: alk. paper)
Subjects: LCSH: Electronic funds transfers—Law and legislation—United
    States. | Blockchains (Databases)—United States. | Finance—Technological
    innovations.
Classification: LCC KF1030.E4 (ebook) | LCC KF1030.E4 C69 2018 (print) | DDC
    346.73/0821—dc23
LC record available at https://lccn.loc.gov/2018023573

Discounts are available for books ordered in bulk. Special consideration is given to state bars, CLE programs, and other bar-related organizations. Inquire at Book Publishing, ABA Publishing, American Bar Association, 321 North Clark Street, Chicago, Illinois 60654-7598.

www.ShopABA.org

Contents

CHAPTER 3
Smart Code and Smart Contracts   87

CHAPTER 4
Blockchain Technology, Security, and Privacy 117

CHAPTER 5
Antitrust Regulation and Blockchain Technology 135

CHAPTER 6
Cryptocurrencies and the Regulation of Money Transmission   **163**

CHAPTER 7
State Laws Addressing Blockchain Technology   **185**

CHAPTER 8
Disputes, Liability, and Jurisdiction in the Blockchain Era   215

About the Editors and Chapter Authors

Editors

Mark W. Rasmussen is a partner of Jones Day, resident in Dallas. Mark is a seasoned litigator and investigator with more than a dozen years of experience representing clients in complex commercial litigation, securities litigation, regulatory and internal investigations, and bankruptcy litigation. He also advises clients on regulatory compliance related to cryptocurrencies, initial coin offerings (ICOs), and blockchain technology and was recently appointed by Chief Judge Barbara Lynn, of the Northern District of Texas, to be the first receiver in an SEC enforcement action involving an ICO promoter.

James A. Cox is of counsel to Jones Day, resident in Dallas. With more than two decades of legal experience and a background in computer science, Jim has successfully advised clients on their most challenging and difficult matters in litigation and arbitration, including complex technology-related disputes, international disputes, class actions, and disputes involving corporate acquisitions. Jim is now applying that experience to the innovative fields of cryptocurrency and the blockchain, advising clients on Bitcoin, Ethereum, and other virtual currencies, as well as on broader applications of blockchain technology.

Chapter Authors

Dickson C. Chin is a partner of Jones Day, resident in New York. He represents investors, financial institutions, utilities, developers, energy marketers, commercial users, and other market participants in a wide range of energy transactions. His practice encompasses energy marketing and trading, renewable energy, project finance and development, construction, joint ventures, and mergers and acquisitions. Dickson also coordinates the global structured finance and derivatives lawyers of the Firm. In addition to advising clients on financial products and derivatives, intercreditor issues, bankruptcy, and regulatory considerations related to swap transactions, he is also actively involved with representing clients on blockchain and other distributed ledger technology, smart contracts, and initial coin offerings.

Kayla M. Davis is an associate at Jones Day, resident in Washington, D.C. Kayla advises banks, non-bank financial institutions, and financial technology companies with regard to strategic, regulatory, and transactional matters. Kayla provides strategic and regulatory advice on new business models, products, and services. She also advises on regulatory issues in connection with transactions and agreements and counsels clients on regulatory compliance matters. Kayla also has experience representing employers in a broad range of labor and employment matters.

Nicholas Dimitriou is an associate at Jones Day, resident in Singapore. Nicholas has more than ten years of experience advising on mergers and acquisitions, joint venture arrangements, and corporate restructuring. His extensive experience is in the energy, natural resources, and infrastructure sectors, with a particular focus on energy projects and transactions. He has represented renewable energy companies, oil and gas companies, energy providers, financial institutions, private equity firms, and insurance companies as a private practice lawyer and as part of a client secondment. Nicholas also has an in-depth knowledge of blockchain technology, including its specific application in the energy industry, and has hosted and moderated seminars on this topic. He is involved with representing clients on blockchain and other distributed-ledger technology and smart contracts and has contributed to a number of publications in this area, including articles and white papers from a Singapore perspective on digital tokens and ICOs and on the taxonomy of cryptoassets.

Emily O. Harris is an associate at Jones Day, resident in Chicago. Emily has more than a decade of experience representing investment advisers, private funds, broker-dealers, and operating companies on a broad range of regulatory and corporate matters. Her practice covers the formation, marketing, operation, and regulation of private funds (including hedge funds, funds of funds, hybrid funds, private equity funds, and venture capital funds); registration and compliance issues regarding investment advisers; broker-dealer "status" issues; sales of registered investment advisers; and investment company "status" matters. She also advises clients on forming investment entities for, and regulatory compliance with respect to, investments in cryptocurrencies and related assets.

Bradley W. Harrison is a partner of Jones Day, resident in Cleveland. Brad is a trial attorney who represents clients in courts and before arbitration panels throughout the United States. He is no stranger to the courtroom, having served as trial counsel in several jury trials and as a member of numerous other trial teams throughout the country. Brad devotes a large part of his practice to the defense of companies in product liability actions and often defends companies in class actions and multidistrict litigation. Brad also spends a considerable portion of his practice on commercial disputes, including complex business tort and contract litigation.

Gwendolyn R. Higley is a staff attorney at Jones Day, resident in Dallas. Gwen focuses her practice on issues of e-discovery. She has experience managing all stages of e-discovery projects, including data preservation, collection and processing, development of review and QC protocol, and document production. Gwen also has experience with matters concerning internal corporate investigations and government investigations.

Samir C. Jain is a partner of Jones Day, resident in Washington, D.C. Samir has more than twenty years of experience at high levels of government and in private practice working on cutting-edge legal and policy issues involving cybersecurity, privacy, national security, communications, and internet law. Prior to joining Jones Day in 2017, Samir was senior director for cybersecurity policy for the National Security Council at the White House. He led the team responsible for cyber incident responses, chaired the interagency body that reviewed proposed cyber operations, directed evaluation of legislative proposals concerning reform of the Electronic Communications Privacy Act, and regularly worked with international cyber counterparts, including leading an interagency delegation to India and coordinating the campaign to gain acceptance of U.S.-proposed international cyber norms. Samir also served as associate deputy attorney general at the United States Department of Justice (DOJ), where his responsibilities included overseeing the development of proposals to modernize the Computer Fraud and Abuse Act and other cyber-crime laws and supervising evaluation of telecommunications license applications for significant national security risks. In that role, he also represented the DOJ in White House cybersecurity meetings and international negotiations such as China's agreement not to engage in cyber-enabled intellectual property theft for commercial gain.

Richard J. Johnson is a partner of Jones Day, resident in Dallas. Jay is a former federal prosecutor with fifteen years of government and law firm experience in litigation, investigations, and regulatory compliance. Having

xii BLOCKCHAIN FOR BUSINESS LAWYERS

previously tried a number of cases to juries in federal court, he represents companies facing complex litigation and advises on regulatory compliance measures, with an emphasis on data privacy, cybersecurity, intellectual property, and white-collar issues. Jay also cofounded the Firm's Global Privacy & Cybersecurity Update, a bimonthly publication produced by a global thirty-attorney team. Prior to joining Jones Day, Jay was an Assistant U.S. Attorney in the Eastern District of Texas and the district-wide coordinator for computer hacking and intellectual property issues. In that capacity, he guided the district's preparation for and response to cyber and IP crime and counseled prosecutors on collecting electronic evidence. Jay led numerous trial and investigations teams involving fraud, identity theft, and other federal crimes. He received the Justice Department's Director's Award for Superior Performance as lead trial counsel in the prosecution of a large-scale mortgage fraud scheme. Jay also traveled to Bosnia and Herzegovina, Macedonia, and Croatia to train local judges and law enforcement personnel on effective investigation techniques.

Peter A. Julian is an associate at Jones Day, resident in San Francisco. Peter's practice focuses on representing companies in antitrust government investigations, enforcement actions, and private antitrust litigation. He has developed particular experience working on antitrust matters with technology clients. Peter also has experience in complex litigation, including briefing and motion practice, pretrial discovery, and trial preparation.

Jared R. Kelley is a project attorney at Jones Day, resident in Dallas. Jared Kelley focuses his practice on the defense of corporations and executives in securities fraud class actions, internal corporate investigations, and government investigations into alleged violations of the Foreign Corrupt Practices Act. He has extensive experience in e-discovery, including data processing, document review, and production.

Lisa M. Ledbetter is a partner of Jones Day, resident in Washington, D.C. Lisa advises domestic and international financial institutions in navigating complex and novel regulatory, transactional, and enforcement challenges. She provides strategic advice on commercial and retail bank regulation and financial technology. Lisa counsels financial institutions and non-bank companies on new business models, products, and services. Lisa represents several financial services trade associations, assisting with public positions, and comments on domestic and international issues. Lisa advises clients on strategic opportunities emanating from changes in federal and state laws and regulatory requirements. She advises on bank equity investments and activities, Volcker Rule limitations on trading and investments, liquidity, counterparty credit limits, derivatives, capital and business planning, fintech, cybersecurity, anti-money laundering, and credit and debit cards. Lisa is experienced in responding to civil investigative demands and defending agency enforcement actions. She is experienced as well in conducting internal investigations.

Margaret I. Lyle is of counsel to Jones Day, resident in Dallas. Margaret defends class actions and represents businesses in complex litigation and appeals, including intellectual property, data privacy, contract, and internet-marketing claims. She has successfully defended consumer and mass tort class actions claiming fraud, unjust enrichment, conspiracy, products liability, medical monitoring, and toxic exposure, as well as those brought under the Fair Credit Reporting Act, the Magnuson-Moss Warranty Act, the Driver's Privacy Protection Act, the Credit Repair Organizations Act, RICO, and state consumer statutes. Margaret serves as a cochair of the ABA's Woman Advocate Committee and is a past editor-in-chief of the ABA's *The Woman Advocate*.

Richard M. Martinez is a partner of Jones Day, resident in Minneapolis. Rick's practice focuses on technology and its impact on society. He has extensive domestic and international experience in technology and intellectual property matters and in cybersecurity, data privacy, and information law. Rick has been involved in patent licensing campaigns that have generated eight- and nine-figure settlements and has represented Fortune 100 corporations, leading educational institutions, technology start-ups, and individuals in privacy and cybersecurity matters, including wire transfer fraud, Wiretap Act claims, privacy torts, and disputes relating to the ownership of data. Rick is a technology lawyer with substantial experience in technological fields and computer-implemented inventions, including computer hardware and software, and network and web-based communications, including web browser technology, flash memory, automated systems, and consumer electronic devices. Rick has earned a powerful reputation for negotiating licenses with Japanese and Korean businesses and for his ability to work internationally and cross-culturally. Prior to joining Jones Day in 2016, he handled granting and acquisition of licenses with such companies as Toshiba, Samsung, LG, Panasonic, Sony, Sharp, and Phillips. He has had first-chair responsibility in high-stakes IP litigation in state and federal courts, representing plaintiffs and defendants, and practices actively in matters before the International Trade Commission.

Locke R. McMurray is of counsel to Jones Day, resident in New York. Locke's practice focuses on derivative products, secured transactions, and securitized products. Locke utilizes his deep knowledge of Fixed Income, Currencies and Commodities (FICC) markets to deliver innovative solutions to clients. He also has vast experience with the treatment of derivatives and other financial instruments in bankruptcy and the structuring and enforcement of credit mitigants such as close-out netting, financial collateral arrangements, and third-party credit support (e.g., guaranties, letters of credit, financial guaranty insurance, and credit default swaps). Locke is adept at structuring exotic transactions and has managed documentation teams during his more than fifteen years as in-house counsel at a variety of banks. Locke advises clients on the Dodd-Frank Act, particularly in relation to its extraterritorial application, margining for non-cleared swaps, the "end-user" clearing exemption, and the extent to which foreign exchange transactions are excluded from regulation. Most recently, he has advised clients on the regulatory status of cryptocurrencies and ICOs.

Joseph Melnik is a partner of Jones Day, resident in the Silicon Valley office in California. Joe's practice is focused on technology licensing, technology commercialization, and other technology-related transactions. Joe counsels clients on complex transactions related to a broad range of technologies including software, semiconductors, energy, data and network security, and consumer devices. He negotiates and structures license agreements, joint ventures, joint development agreements, strategic alliances, services, supply, and various other agreements for domestic and global projects. Joe also advises companies of all sizes on the development and implementation of strategies for maximizing the benefits of technology transactions; advising on intellectual property issues that arise in connection with corporate transactions, such as mergers and acquisitions; and assisting clients in developing domestic and international product commercialization strategies that utilize intellectual property positions to protect and expand market share. Joe also represents clients in patent litigation, license disputes, and post-grant proceedings. He has successfully represented companies in patent cases relating to a wide variety of technologies, including cryptography, smart cards, biometrics, cellular telephony, SMS, computer networking, wireless communications, semiconductors, database technologies, and financial transactions. In addition, Joe frequently represents companies in high-stakes licensing disputes in a broad range of technology areas and has been lead counsel on numerous IPR proceedings before the Patent Trial and Appeal Board.

Colin C. Richard is an associate at Jones Day, resident in Washington, D.C. Colin advises banks, non-bank financial institutions, and financial technology companies with regard to strategic, regulatory, and transactional matters. He has experience advising on issues related to the Federal Reserve, Office of the Comptroller of the Currency, Federal Deposit Insurance Corporation, Consumer Financial Protection Bureau, and Department of the Treasury. Colin has experience advising on issues arising from the Dodd-Frank Wall Street Reform and Consumer Protection Act, Bank Holding Company Act, National Bank Act, Federal Deposit Insurance Act, Gramm-Leach-Bliley Act, and Bank Secrecy Act and their implementing regulations. He counsels clients on regulatory compliance matters and provides strategic and regulatory advice regarding new business models, products, and services. He also advises on regulatory issues in connection with transactions and agreements.

Ryan C. Thomas is a partner of Jones Day, resident in Washington, D.C. With more than fifteen years of experience, Ryan represents companies in all aspects of competition law, including mergers, joint ventures, monopolization, pricing and distribution issues, and cartel investigations. He has worked across many industries, including semiconductors, optical components and modules, electronic sensors, medical devices, pharmaceuticals, and ophthalmic lenses and equipment.

Thomas D. York is an associate at Jones Day, resident in Dallas. Tom specializes in antitrust and competition matters, including antitrust litigation, merger review, civil and criminal antitrust investigations, and internal investigations. He works across a range of industries, including aviation, consumer products, emerging technology, health care, pharmaceuticals, oil and gas, semiconductors, and sports. Tom also regularly counsels on antitrust issues such as competitor collaborations, distribution, licensing, pricing, and single-firm conduct.

Foreword

In nearly every forum, blockchain has been described as one of the most transformative and disruptive technologies in decades.

- **MIT Technology Review:** "Many see the [blockchain] technology's rise as a vital new phase in the internet economy—one that is, arguably, even more transformative than the first." [Michael J. Casey & Paul Vigna (May/June 2018)]
- **Congressional Hearings:** "Blockchain technology has the potential to make game-changing transformations to our digital economy and financial security." [Rep. Elizabeth Esty (Feb. 2018)]
- **Government Auditor Forum:** The Comptroller General of the United States identified "cryptocurrencies and blockchain" as one of the top five emerging science and technology trends foreseeably transforming society. [Gene Dodaro (May 2018)]
- **Computer World:** Blockchain has been described as the "most disruptive tech in decades." [Lucas Mearian (May 2018)].

As one of its core missions, the Science & Technology Law Section dives into the most complex and transformative technology issues defining tomorrow's legal careers and challenges, ranging from the internet of things and artificial intelligence to cybersecurity and biotechnology. With our *Blockchain for Business Lawyers* book, we are proud to continue our proven leadership by introducing the legal profession to the hottest, freshest, and most dynamic intersections of law, science, and technology.

Like our other books and publications such as *The SciTech Lawyer*, the *Blockchain* book demanded visionary leadership and collaborative excellence. We owe this great work product to the cutting-edge foresight and driving dedication of our two co-editors, Mark W. Rasmussen and James A. Cox, without whom this book could not have landed on your bookshelf. As the Section Chair, I am privileged to thank them for their hard work, team leadership, and terrific expertise in bringing us this vital resource for practitioners needing a thoughtful and practical guide to the "disruptive" and "transformative" field of blockchain.

We also recognize the dedicated efforts of the chapter authors who shared their time and expertise to produce this great work:

- Chapter 1: "Introduction to Blockchain Technology" by James A. Cox
- Chapter 2: "Cryptocurrencies, Initial Coin Offerings, and Financial Regulations" by Mark W. Rasmussen, Emily O. Harris, Locke R. McMurray, and Nicholas Mimitriou
- Chapter 3: "Smart Code and Smart Contracts" by Dickson C. Chin
- Chapter 4: "Blockchain Technology, Security, and Privacy" by Richard C. Johnson, Samir C. Jain, and Richard M. Martinez
- Chapter 5: "Antitrust Regulation and Blockchain Technology" by Ryan C. Thomas, Thomas D. York, and Peter A. Julian
- Chapter 6: "Cryptocurrencies and the Regulation of Money Transmission" by Lisa M. Ledbetter and Colin C. Richard
- Chapter 7: "State Laws Addressing Blockchain Technology" by Margaret I. Lyle, Gwendolyn R. Higley, and Jared R. Kelley
- Chapter 8: "Disputes, Liability, and Jurisdiction in the Blockchain Era" by Joseph Melnik and Bradley W. Harrison

In addition, we thank our terrific SciTech Book Publishing team led by Michael Hawes and Bonnie Fought for keeping our Section at the forefront on a broad range of technology and law publications. In addition, we thank our ABA Publishing team, including Sarah (Sam) Forbes Orwig, for her continuing leadership and encouragement for publishing the *Blockchain* book. Finally, my special thanks go to our Section Staff Director, Caryn Cross Hawk, for keeping us on track on all of the SciTech Section initiatives, including our many publications.

David Z. Bodenheimer
Chair, Science & Technology Law Section
2017–2018

Preface and Editors' Acknowledgments

The preparation of a book on a legal topic like this one is a challenging endeavor. In this case, we faced a dual problem: the law is evolving quickly *and* the underlying technology is changing even faster; on a near-daily basis, we see new reports of decisions and guidance from regulators, blockchain initiatives, startup companies, novel applications, and many other developments of significance. The realities of book publishing mean that at some point, we had to call a halt to the writing. Accordingly, we have done our best as of the publication date to paint an accurate picture of the current law as applied to the technology, including, in some cases, our judgments as to where we think the law and the technology will go. Nevertheless, the one thing we can be certain about is that both law and technology will outstrip any effort to capture them in a single writing.

As the editors of this book, we owe a debt of gratitude to the authors, who have generously taken time away from busy practices to contribute their expertise, to the readers of this book. In addition, we thank our many other colleagues, within Jones Day and outside the firm, who are not listed as editors or chapter authors but without whom this book could not exist. Finally, we offer a special thanks to our London partner Harriet Territt and our New York partner Stephen J. Obie, who lead Jones Day's Blockchain & Digital Currencies team.

Mark W. Rasmussen and James A. Cox

CHAPTER 1

Introduction to Blockchain Technology

James A. Cox

Blockchain technology is a major technological innovation that promises to work significant changes to the way we do business in several different fields. Those changes, in turn, will bring new legal challenges that our laws, courts, regulatory agencies, and other institutions will need to address. Given what we see as the wide scope and lasting impact of blockchain technology, we cannot expect to discern (much less solve) all of these legal challenges now; nevertheless, we hope in this book to identify the principal challenges in seven separate fields of law, to review legal developments so far and then to suggest some possible resolutions in light of those developments.

Although we expect blockchain technology to bring great change in many fields, we do not see it as a panacea. Blockchain technology offers concrete benefits over prior approaches, but it also comes with real costs that can limit or preclude its use in some applications. To better assess the legal challenges facing existing and new applications of blockchain technology, it is important to understand the benefits and costs of the technology; that task, in turn, requires understanding what blockchain technology is at a deeper, more technical level than existing publications for lawyers on this subject usually attempt. We think achieving that level of understanding is worth the effort. For that reason, we include a more detailed discussion of the technology in this chapter.

Before getting started in our effort to understand blockchain technology, it is worth clarifying what we mean by the term. The starting point is clear: October 31, 2008, when Satoshi Nakamoto, the pseudonymous and still publicly unknown author, released his Bitcoin white paper.[1] On that day, he introduced blockchain technology for the first time along with a fully conceived platform for its use to implement digital cash. Since then, we have expanded our understanding of the scope of the term to include novel technologies that continue to employ Nakamoto's key insights but that differ in their approaches to certain issues. For example, one prominent "blockchain" project discussed below is unquestionably based on elements of Nakamoto's original work on blockchain technology but *does not actually use a blockchain*.[2] Some commentators have responded to these developments by proposing a new term—distributed ledger technology (DLT)—which is intended to apply more broadly to blockchain-inspired technologies even if they do not actually use blockchains. The broader term carries its own potential ambiguities,[3] and in this book, the term *blockchain technology* is intended broadly to include DLT and other related technologies that are derived in part from Nakamoto's original conception.

1. BITCOIN AND THE ORIGIN OF BLOCKCHAIN TECHNOLOGY

In his 2008 e-mail announcing Bitcoin to an online cryptography mailing list, Nakamoto noted his system's key achievements:

- The system was purely peer to peer and relied on "no trusted third party";
- The system solved the "double-spending problem";
- New coins were defined as "an ongoing chain of hash-based proof-of-work, forming a record that cannot be changed without redoing the proof-of-work";
- The system was resistant to attackers "as long as honest nodes control the most [hashing] power on the network."[4]

---

1 Satoshi Nakamoto, *Bitcoin: A Peer-to-Peer Electronic Cash System*, http://www.bitcoin .org/bitcoin.pdf.

2 *See infra* subsection 2(e)(ii).

3 For example, taken literally, DLT would seem to cover the well-established technology of distributed databases, which Oracle and other companies have been offering for decades. *See, e.g., Distributed Database Concepts*, ORACLE DATABASE ADMIN. GUIDE, ch. 29, https://docs .oracle.com/cd/B14117_01/server.101/b10739/ds_concepts.htm.

4 E-mail from Satoshi Nakamoto, Oct. 31, 2008, http://article.gmane.org/gmane.comp .encryption.general/12588/.

Although Nakamoto's goal in the Bitcoin paper was highly specific (a system of electronic cash with the features he described), he needed a key innovation that, we now realize, is far more generally applicable. Today, we call that innovation *blockchain technology*. To more fully understand the innovation of blockchain technology, including how that innovation can be put to uses other than Bitcoin, we need to explore Nakamoto's paper in more detail.

(a) The Role of Digital Signatures

One of Nakamoto's earliest ideas was that an "electronic coin" in his system could be defined as a "chain of digital signatures."[5] By the time Nakamoto wrote in 2008, digital signatures were a well-understood feature of public-key cryptography and had been in general commercial use for several decades.[6] In public-key cryptography, participants use a cryptographic algorithm to generate a key pair composed of a *public* key and a related *private* key. The public key is distributed to all participants while the private key is intended to remain a secret. The mathematical relationship between the two keys is such that a message encrypted using one of the keys in the key pair can only be decrypted using the *other* key in the key pair.

For example, a participant, Alice, digitally signs a message[7] by encrypting it with Alice's *private* key, which only she possesses. Then, anyone can read the message *and verify that Alice encrypted it* by successfully decrypting the message using Alice's *public* key, which is freely available. The fact that the message can be decrypted using Alice's public key proves that Alice—and only Alice—*digitally signed* the text with her private key, since only Alice possesses the private key.

Defining a coin as a chain of digital signatures solved a number of problems for Nakamoto. In his system, the original owner and each successive owner of a coin would use their private keys to digitally sign the transaction

---

5 Nakamoto, *supra* note 1, at 2.

6 The notion of digital signatures was first described in 1976. W. Diffie & M. Hellman, "New Directions in Cryptography," IEEE TRANSACTIONS on INFORMATION THEORY, IT-22(6): 644–54 (Nov. 1976). Three years later, Rivest, Shamir, and Adleman first described the "RSA" algorithm implementing digital signatures. R. Rivest, A. Shamir, & L. Adleman, "A Method for Obtaining Digital Signatures and Public-Key Cryptosystems," COMMUNICATIONS OF THE ACM 21 (2): 120–26 (1978).

7 In practice, to sign a message, Alice would encrypt only a "hash" of the message text. Hashing is discussed later in this chapter.

transferring the coin to the next person. A prospective recipient of a transaction could validate those signatures using the available public keys of the signers. That chain of digital signatures created a mathematically provable chain of ownership establishing the provenance of each coin.

(b) The Double-Spending Problem

Digital signatures did not solve all of Nakamoto's problems. For example, digital signatures alone could not prevent network participants from "spending" the same coins more than once by signing multiple, separate transactions. This is the *double-spending problem*. Stated more generally, an electronic cash system is confronted with a proposed transaction:

Proposed Transaction:

Alice sends 1 BTC to Bob

Payment System Response Query:

Did Alice previously receive 1 BTC?
Did Alice previously send that 1 BTC to someone else?

The system must have some way to determine whether the sender, Alice, owns a spendable coin that has not previously been sent to someone else. In the physical world of currency, the problem is solved by using hard-to-duplicate physical tokens such as coins and paper bills. In that world, physical possession of the tokens denotes ownership and the right to spend, and the spending transaction itself is accomplished through transfer of that physical possession to another person. In the electronic world, though, a different solution is needed.

Before the publication of Nakamoto's paper, electronic payment systems typically solved the double-spending problem by relying on a privileged intermediary—often a financial institution—which served as a trusted central party to validate the identities of participants and confirm the authenticity of transactions. Figure 1.1 illustrates the topology of such a system.

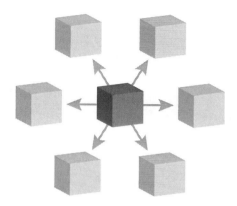

Figure 1.1: Centralized System

Each node is connected directly to the trusted central party. All network nodes must send proposed transactions to the trusted central party for validation, and no node may accept a proposed transaction until the central trusted central party confirms the transaction's validity. In such a system, the trusted central party typically keeps a ledger of all transactions, including the precise time they were received. Timing is important because the task of preventing double spending should only assess *earlier* transactions. We are confronted with the same new proposed transaction:

Proposed Transaction:

Alice sends 1 BTC to Bob

Centralized Payment System Response:

My authoritative records demonstrate that Alice previously received 1 BTC and has not previously sent that 1 BTC to someone else. Transaction validated.

The trusted central party validates the transaction by confirming that Alice previously received the coin she now wishes to spend *and* that there are no earlier transactions in which Alice already spent that coin. Because the trusted central party has authoritative records of all transactions and the time they took place, the central party has the means to authoritatively validate the new spending transaction.

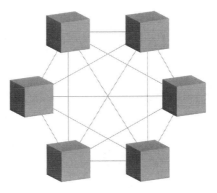

Figure 1.2: Peer-to-Peer System

In contrast to such a centralized system, Nakamoto sought a peer-to-peer system that did not assign trusted status to a special central party. In fact, Nakamoto's proposed network had no centralized nodes at all; he envisioned that each node would be connected directly only to neighboring nodes; connections to other nodes in the network would be indirect. Figure 1.2 illustrates the topology of a decentralized system.

A peer-to-peer system would confront the same kinds of proposed transactions as a centralized system:

Proposed Transaction:

Alice sends 1 BTC to Bob

Local Peer Response:

My own copy of the ledger of transactions demonstrates that Alice previously received 1 BTC and has not previously sent that 1 BTC to someone else. Transaction validated.

The local peer receiving the transaction could not rely on a centralized, trusted node to confirm that Alice had received but not spent that coin in earlier transactions. Therefore, Nakamoto reasoned, each node would need the means to evaluate for itself the validity of the transaction. Because "[t]he only way to confirm the absence of a transaction is to be aware of all transactions,"[8] each peer node, like the trusted party in a centralized system, would have to maintain *its own ledger of all transactions*, including the precise time they occurred.

---

8 Nakamoto, *supra* note 1, at 2.

(c) Achieving Consensus through Proof of Work

In Nakamoto's peer-to-peer system, each node receives all new publicly announced transactions and maintains its own separate ledger of these transactions. Without more, however, there could be no guarantee in such a system that the separate ledgers would remain consistent. Malicious nodes might refuse to pass on transactions or pass them on in a different order. (Of course, even malicious nodes could not alter digitally signed transactions without being detected.) In addition, even in the absence of malice, network delays, connection problems, and the variable topology of the network could cause transactions to arrive at different nodes at different times. Thus, Nakamoto needed a mechanism to achieve *consensus* among the nodes as to which transactions should be included and in what order.

Nakamoto decided to use *proof of work* to achieve consensus on the Bitcoin network. In the event of a conflict between nodes about which transactions to add to their ledgers, Nakamoto specified that nodes should make the choice that represents the largest amount of computational work put into the ledger overall. It is important to note that he could have made other choices, such as simple majority voting of nodes or *proof of stake* (voting weighted by coins held or escrowed). He chose proof of work because it best met the goals he set for his publicly available electronic cash system.

Nakamoto's proof-of-work mechanism begins when proposed transactions are publicly announced on the network. Nodes receiving these transactions validate their digital signatures, periodically collecting validated transactions into *blocks*. Then, network nodes perform "work" by competing to discover a special numeric value for the block that meets rules Nakamoto set down.[9] These rules involve the use of a widely accepted hashing algorithm, SHA-256. To discover the special numeric value for a given block of transactions, a node repeatedly increments a counter included in the block until the result of applying the hashing algorithm to the block is a value smaller than a target value. When a node discovers a value small enough, it has "found" a valid block that can be added to its own ledger and distributed to other nodes to be added to their ledgers as well.

Hashing algorithms like SHA-256 are mathematical functions that take as input a set of data of arbitrary size and produce as output a numerical value of a predetermined size—in the case of SHA-256, the output value is 256 bits.

---

9 Nakamoto, *supra* note 1, at 3.

Input	Hash Sum
"We the people of the United States"	1482a4775eefc767a7fa975971e6531c0b73e73c
"We the people in the United States"	6586a9712086a1a7288afc00dac7cfdcc07a08ab
"We"	b3780dbafddf7e06add542122118f38cc06884b5

Table 1-1: Hash Function—Similar Input, Different Output

Table 1-1 illustrates how a hashing function can take, as input, data of any length and can produce, as output, a specified number of a predetermined size. In this illustration, although the input texts are of different lengths, the resulting hash value (which is set out in hexadecimal base-16 notation) is always the same length. Hashing functions are also designed so that any changes to the input data—even the alteration of just one bit—will cause the output value to change in a way that is practically impossible to predict.

In Table 1-2, changes of just one bit in the binary input numbers lead to large and unpredictable changes in the resulting hash values.

This characteristic of hashing functions plays two important roles in Nakamoto's system. First, it secures the blocks against changes. None of the information in a block can be changed without causing an unpredictable change in the hash value. Second, it explains the difficult nature of the "work" in Nakamoto's proof-of-work system. Nakamoto's system requires nodes to find a block hash value that is smaller than a specified difficulty target. There is no practical way to do this except by repeatedly iterating the counter, recalculating the block's hash value, and then comparing that value against the difficulty target. Thus, when a node finds a small enough hash value and distributes the block to the network, the valid block itself constitutes proof that the node has put the required work into the calculation. If a competing node were to attempt to change

Input	Hash Sum
00000001 (binary)	bf8b4530d8d246dd74ac53a13471bba17941dff7
00000011 (binary)	9842926af7ca0a8cca12604f945414f07b01e13d
00000010 (binary)	c4ea21bb365bbeeaf5f2c654883e56d11e43c44e

Table 1-2: Hash Function—One Bit Differences in Input

any data in the block, it would have to redo the work and find a new valid hash value.

Finding valid blocks is hard work, but plainly essential to the functioning of the Bitcoin system. Nakamoto, along with later Bitcoin developers, therefore recognized that for finding a new block, the system would need to provide to the successful node an incentive payment in the form of newly created bitcoins, transaction fees offered by the sender, or both. Today, the work of finding valid blocks has become known as "mining." In recent times, for economic reasons, Bitcoin mining has become concentrated in a small class of businesses with access to specialized computing hardware and cheap electricity. As originally conceived, however, mining was practicable for any full node in the network.

(d) The Robustness of the Blockchain

With one additional fact, we can now see how Nakamoto's electronic cash system creates the robust structure of the blockchain: each block contains, in addition to collected transactions, the computed hash value of *the immediately prior valid block*. As additional valid blocks are found, they are linked together in the *blockchain*. As Figure 1.3 illustrates, each valid block now becomes proof of not only the work that went into finding the right hash value for that block alone but also the work that went into validating all the earlier blocks in the chain. If a malicious node tried to alter the transactions in a new valid block in the blockchain, the node would have to not only redo the work in the affected block but also simultaneously outcompete the entire remaining network as it found still more new blocks and added them to the blockchain linked to the original affected block. Thus, as valid blocks

Figure 1.3: The Blockchain

are added to the chain, older blocks become even more secure, protected by the work reflected in blocks subsequently added.

The resulting blockchain-based system now meets all of Nakamoto's design goals. It operates peer to peer without any special trusted party to validate transactions. The chain of digital signatures proves ownership and transfer of coins. Because each node maintains a ledger of all transactions, the system avoids the double-spending problem. The proof-of-work mechanism maintains consistency of the ledgers and prevents attacks on the blockchain, at least by actors who do not control a majority of processing power on the network.

(e) Pseudonymity

Bitcoin is frequently described as an "anonymous" payment system, but as the discussion in this chapter makes clear, that is not entirely correct. To prevent the possibility of double spending, transactions in the Bitcoin system are announced publicly and the public blockchain includes a complete record of all transactions. What can be anonymous about Bitcoin is the link between the digital signatures on the blockchain and the identities of the people actually involved in the transactions. A person's public key acts as a *pseudonym*. As Nakamoto explained in the original paper, this model allows for privacy even though all transactions are publicly posted on the blockchain because the public keys can be kept anonymous: "The public can see that someone is sending an amount to someone else, but without information linking the transaction to anyone."[10] Nevertheless, in today's environment, most Bitcoin holders need to use commercial exchanges and wallet services that impose detailed identification requirements through which their public keys can be directly linked to their identities;[11] thus, authorities can frequently track Bitcoin transactions just as they can with fiat-currency transactions.

(f) Forks

Like the internet itself, the Bitcoin network is not "owned" by anyone. As a consequence, Bitcoin has encountered several disputes among members of the Bitcoin community with respect to proposed changes, and some of these disputes have led to *forks* in the Bitcoin blockchain.

---

10 Nakamoto, *supra* note 1, at 6.

11 *See generally* Chapter 6 (discussing know-your-customer and similar requirements as applied to money transmitters).

A fork begins when a node adds a block to its copy of the block-chain that is not accepted by some other node on the network. The two nodes then have blockchains that are the same, except that they differ from each other in the last block. Ordinarily when that happens, Bitcoin's consensus mechanism causes one of the competing blocks—the *orphaned block*—to be rejected by the rest of the network because that version of the blockchain contains less proof of work. In some cases, however, nodes can keep working to add new blocks to the ends of both differing blockchains and the separation between the two chains can grow longer with time. When this separation between the two branches of the blockchain goes unresolved over time, the blockchain is said to have forked.

There have been several forks of the Bitcoin, some intentional and some due to programming errors. In August 2017, the developers of Bitcoin Cash intentionally forked the Bitcoin blockchain in an effort to increase the *scalability* of the network (its ability to handle a growing volume of transactions). These developers started out by proposing to change Bitcoin itself. When their proposals encountered opposition, they elected to simply release their own modified version of the Bitcoin software—a version that applied new validation rules for blocks. Some nodes on the network adopted the modified software and started validating blocks that were rejected as too large by the original software; at that point, the two chains forked. Today, both blockchains continue actively operating, and the two chains support what now are two separate cryptocurrencies.

2. BLOCKCHAIN BEYOND BITCOIN

There is nothing about blockchain technology that limits its application to Bitcoin. What are the other circumstances in which the technology, or a derivative of it, might apply? In answering this question, we look for guidance to the problems of Bitcoin and how blockchain technology solved those problems.

(a) Currencies and Payment Systems

The most natural use of blockchain technology is to implement other cryptocurrencies. At the time of the writing of this book, CoinMarketCap's comprehensive listing identified 1,384 separate currency coins and tokens with some identified market value.[12]

---

12 *Cryptocurrency Market Capitalizations,* https://coinmarketcap.com/all/views/all/#.

Many new cryptocurrencies are modeled on Bitcoin but with specific changes to meet developers' differing goals. This process has been aided by the decision of Nakamoto and the Bitcoin developers who followed him to release the Bitcoin Core software under an open-source license that (with certain limitations) allows it to be modified and used for other purposes. The easy availability of this code for modification makes it straightforward to design and implement a new cryptocurrency that is derived from Bitcoin.

Table 1-3 lists a few of the many Bitcoin-derived cryptocurrencies. Although each adds or changes elements in original Bitcoin, they all use a modification of the Bitcoin Core software.

Coin	Year Introduced	Selected Differences from Bitcoin
Litecoin	2011	Replaces Bitcoin's SHA-256 hashing algorithm with *scrypt*, an algorithm designed to be more resistant to the development of special-purpose hashing processors and, thus, the centralization of mining.
Peercoin	2012	Achieves consensus using a hybrid *proof-of-work* and *proof-of-stake* mechanism.[1]
Dogecoin	2013	Originally introduced as a joke currency based on a 2013 internet meme featuring the wry observations of a Shiba Inu; market capitalization of the currency today, however, exceeds $1B.
Dash	2014	Using a two-tier node system adds features for "private" transactions that cannot be traced by source and for "instant" transactions that do not have to await normal network consensus.
Bitcoin Cash	2017	Implemented as a fork of the Bitcoin blockchain and designed to add scalability improvements that some Bitcoin developers had resisted.

1 Proof of stake refers to a system that weights voting on consensus by coins held or escrowed.

Table 1-3: Bitcoin-derived cryptocurrencies

In recent months, the number of new blockchain-based tokens offered for sale has exploded due to the enormous interest in Initial Coin Offerings (ICOs).[13] Typically, the developers of a new coin attempt to describe its characteristics in a "white paper" modeled on Nakamoto's Bitcoin paper. These new coins can serve an enormous variety of purposes, such as representing physical or online assets or granting access to the features of some online platform, but in addition, they are intended to represent a store of value like Bitcoin and to be traded for other cryptocurrencies and fiat currencies in online markets. ICOs are discussed in more detail in Chapter 2.

(b) Distributing the Ledger

As discussed above, Bitcoin's peer-to-peer blockchain system was originally designed to replace the functionality of a traditional electronic-payment model in which a centralized party—a bank or other financial institution—maintained a single authoritative ledger on which all currency transactions were recorded. Network nodes then communicated with the centralized party to validate transactions. Nakamoto's distributed system eliminated the centralized ledger but, in effect, replicated that ledger at every node. That created a difficult problem of keeping the multiple ledgers consistent with each other, which Bitcoin solved through a computationally costly proof-of-work mechanism.

Many human activities are amenable to representation in a ledger system like the Bitcoin system's payment model.

- *Real property.* In most jurisdictions, governments maintain records of real property ownership such as deeds, leases, easements, and similar documents. Historically, the original paper records have been kept in archives, with manual or computer-based indexing available in some jurisdictions and, in some places, at least for recent years, computer-based imaging of records. Traditionally, real property transactions are complex affairs requiring multiple intermediaries and manual interventions. At base, real property records can be viewed as a ledger system amenable to significant, if not revolutionary, improvement through blockchain technology.

---

13 *See* Chapter 2. One important factor in the explosion of interest in ICOs is the functionality offered by the Ethereum platform, discussed in more detail below and in Chapter 2. The Ethereum platform makes it extremely easy to develop and offer new virtual currency coins—called "tokens"—with user-defined characteristics.

- *Other assets.* Businesses, government agencies, and most other organizations of any size maintain lists of physical assets of various kinds.
- *Identity.* Governments maintain ledgers of information on passports, drivers' licenses, Social Security records, and other kinds of identification documents.
- *Other government records.* Government agencies maintain a wide variety of databases covering regulated subjects, including tax assessments and payments, permits, and licenses.

Not all centralized ledgers are better replaced by distributed blockchain technology. As we have seen, blockchain technology brings discrete benefits, but it also brings significant costs. Later on, we will discuss the potential tradeoffs of these benefits against the costs in more detail.

(c) Blockchain Computing

The success of Bitcoin has also inspired new cryptocurrencies that do not use a modified version of the Bitcoin Core software and that seek to implement an entirely new kind of functionality. The most prominent of these is the Ethereum project. The Ethereum developers sought to radically improve the ability of blockchain-based systems to perform *on-chain computation*.

A rudimentary form of this kind of functionality is present in Bitcoin. The outputs of a Bitcoin transaction are defined not simply as the public-key addresses (or hashes) of the recipients, but as *scripts* written in a purposely limited scripting language. This simple scripting language allows implementation in Bitcoin of, among other things, multisignature transactions that allow or require a combination of different digital signatures to spend the output.

"Simple" Bitcoin Scripting	
Alice sends 1 BTC to Bob	The simplest kind of Bitcoin transaction—Bob has the sole right to spend the output by signing a transaction with his private key.
Alice sends 1 BTC to Bob *or* Carol	Either Bob *or* Carol may spend the output by signing with their private keys.
Alice sends 1 BTC to Bob *and* Carol	A transaction spending this output must carry the digital signatures of both Bob and Carol.
Alice sends 1 BTC to *two out of the three of* Bob, Carol, and Ted	A transaction spending this output needs to carry the digital signatures of least two of the three recipients.

2. *Blockchain beyond Bitcoin*

Scripting in Bitcoin allows automated implementation in software of business practices such as corporate signature authority rules and third-party escrows. But Bitcoin scripting was intentionally kept limited in functionality in comparison to traditional programming languages. There were at least two reasons for this decision. First, complex scripting could require significant computational resources from each blockchain node, delaying confirmation of transactions and creating additional burdens for network participants. Second, complex scripting created much greater security risks.

In 2013, Vitalik Buterin, at the time a Bitcoin developer, proposed a new system, Ethereum, that would implement a full Turing-complete programming language as part of a decentralized blockchain-based system of network nodes. Turing completeness means that the Ethereum programming language and its platform, the Ethereum Virtual Machine (EVM), can, in theory, perform any computation performable by any computer with modern architecture. After two years of development, the Ethereum platform went live in 2015. The Ethereum system also included a new cryptocurrency coin, Ether. Like Bitcoin, Ether was intended to represent a store of value to be traded for other currencies or for goods and services; indeed, a 2014 online crowdfunding sale of "pre-mined" Ether raised more than $18 million to support further development of the Ethereum platform. But Ether had a second and more important function: it provided a way to charge users for the computational costs of the programming steps executed by the Ethereum platform.

The Ethereum developers, like the Bitcoin developers before them, understood that there had to be a way to impose limits on the computational complexity of programming code executed by nodes on the blockchain. Instead of imposing preselected limits on program complexity and length, however, the Ethereum developers created a system, called "gas," to allocate these costs in a flexible way to the party submitting a transaction. "Gas" is a measure of the operational cost of performing operations on the EVM. When submitting a transaction, an Ethereum user specifies the gas limit and gas price (in Ether) she is willing to pay to complete the transaction. The Ethereum miner including the transaction in a successfully validated block is entitled to collect the gas, along with the transaction fee and mining reward.

Given the power of the EVM, there is virtually no limit *in principle* to the complexity of the programming code that an Ethereum transaction can execute. As a result, some users speak not of submitting transactions on Ethereum but of creating "smart contracts" or "distributed applications" (or dApps), which run on the Ethereum blockchain. Of course, there are limits *in practice* to the complexity of smart contracts or dApps due, in part, to the gas mechanism but also due to the underlying infrastructure of the platform. After all, the Ethereum platform, like the Bitcoin platform, is still made up of individual nodes on a network, each of which is charged with maintaining the entire blockchain, including validating newly found blocks and the transactions included within them. That means that *every full node on the Ethereum network must execute every programming instruction in every transaction (dApp) in every valid block processed by the global Ethereum network.*

The availability of smart contracts in a blockchain system makes it possible to envision autonomous, distributed functioning of a number of complex activities that cannot happen today without manual control and intervention or centralized bureaucracy.

- *Autonomous trading platforms.* Smart-contract code automatically matches buyers and sellers, and automatically executing blockchain transactions securely implement trades and ownership changes in securities, commodities, or other assets.
- *Supply chains.* Actors at each stage of a supply chain—purchasing, manufacturing, transportation, delivery, payment—enter secure transactions into a blockchain system, and smart contracts automatically track products and allocate appropriate resources at the next stage of the chain.
- *Peer-to-peer insurance.* The pooling of risks, the events documenting the losses and claims, and the submission and payment of claims, are represented in autonomous transactions on the blockchain.
- *Organizational decision making and voting.* Participants in an organization vote for new policies, investments, or candidates by recording secure transactions on a blockchain, and smart-contract code automatically tallies the results and effectuates the election results.

(d) Permissioned Blockchains

The Bitcoin and Ethereum blockchains are public. Anyone can operate a node on these networks, download the blockchain, and participate in validating new transactions and blocks. The information on these blockchains is fully available to all participants. To the extent any transactional privacy exists, it depends on keeping secret the link between a person's real identity and the public keys used on the network. Any node is equally entitled to perform any of the operations supported by the blockchain and network, and there are no nodes with greater permissions or privileges than other nodes.

A network of nodes running a blockchain, however, need not be publicly accessible. The operators of a network can choose to limit access to identified, authorized parties over private communication channels (dedicated lines or encrypted tunnels over the internet). They can keep private some or all information on the blockchain. Blockchain networks with limits on access or on the availability of information are called *permissioned blockchains*. Permissioned blockchains seem more appropriate than public blockchains when the functionality involves commercially or personally sensitive information, or operations that should be conducted only by designated organizations or individuals.

A permissioned blockchain simplifies some of the problems confronted by the developers of public blockchains. The Bitcoin blockchain, for example, consists of entirely untrusted nodes; accordingly, it employs a proof-of-work consensus mechanism that involves the expenditure of significant computing resources to prevent double spending. A permissioned blockchain, by contrast, may be defined to consist only of nodes vested with some degree of trust—at a minimum, the permission to connect to the network. As a result, permissioned blockchains typically achieve their security and consistency objectives through less costly means than a Bitcoin-like proof-of-work mechanism.

Although permissioned blockchains simplify some problems, they can create others. Governance is the most obvious example. As the example of Bitcoin demonstrates, public blockchains do not require a structured governance mechanism, and the Bitcoin network has, so far, succeeded by relying on nothing more than general community acceptance. Many other successful cryptocurrencies follow that example. A permissioned blockchain network, however, must have some governance structure, if for no other reason than to decide who can connect to it.

Most of the business-use cases for blockchains—proposed and existing—involve permissioned blockchains. Some blockchain purists have criticized this approach on what can only be described as philosophical grounds. After all, Nakamoto's original purpose was to *eliminate* the trusted third party as an element of online financial transactions, and many of the innovations of the blockchain involve mechanisms to deal with untrusted parties. Why, despite those facts, are commercial enterprises interested in using permissioned blockchain technology for business? The answer is that permissioned blockchains offer multifaceted benefits from an approach that takes selective advantage of the key insights developed by blockchain technology.

(e) Platforms for Permissioned Blockchains

The business interest in blockchain technology has led to the development of technology platforms for permissioned blockchains. In general, these platforms seek to take advantage of some of the key advantages of Bitcoin-based blockchain technology—for example, the immutable ledger of transactions, cryptographically secured authentication, and the ability to easily (and locally) validate transactions—without the high costs and privacy challenges of Bitcoin's publicly available ledger and proof-of-work consensus mechanism. Nodes in traditional blockchains are all peers with the same privileges and functions. However, permissioned platforms often specify, or allow, a structure with certain privileged nodes for performing sensitive tasks, such as verifying identity, validating transactions, and maintaining network consensus.

(i) Hyperledger

In 2016, a consortium of thirty businesses launched Hyperledger, a project headed by the nonprofit Linux Foundation.[14] Hyperledger's goal is to create and promote open-source software for the development and implementation of blockchain technology in multiple industries.[15] Hyperledger is effectively an umbrella project: it includes several different blockchain software platforms as well as software tools for blockchain-technology projects. IBM and Digital Asset Holdings initially contributed the Fabric project, the first Hyperledger blockchain-technology platform;[16] later

---

14   *Linux Foundation's Hyperledger Project Announces 30 Founding Members*, THE LINUX FOUNDATION,   https://www.hyperledger.org/announcements/2016/02/09/linux-foundations-hyperledger-project-announces-30-founding-members-and-code-proposals-to-advance-blockchain-technology (Feb. 9, 2016).

15   *About Hyperledger*, THE LINUX FOUNDATION, https://www.hyperledger.org/about.

16   *Hyperledger Announces Production-Ready Hyperledger Fabric 1.0*, THE LINUX FOUNDATION, https://www.hyperledger.org/announcements/2017/07/11/hyperledger-announces-production-ready-hyperledger-fabric-1-0 (July 11, 2017).

contributions have come from other consortium members, including Intel, which contributed its Sawtooth project.[17]

(ii) Corda

Corda is a software platform developed by R3, a technology company founded in 2014 and leading a consortium of some of the largest companies in the financial services industry. Corda provides a blockchain-technology derived platform to record and manage financial agreements among financial-services companies and those who do business with them.[18] Strikingly—and to some observers, controversially—Corda does not use an actual blockchain as that term is used in Nakamoto's Bitcoin white paper. Instead, it can be said to record transactions and other information in a data graph, a structure with more complex relationships between nodes than the one-dimensional links between blocks in the Bitcoin blockchain. Moreover, unlike in Bitcoin, transactions are typically transmitted to, and validated by, only the nodes either participating in the transactions or necessary to the validation of the transaction, rather than to the entire network. Also, unlike in Ethereum, smart-contract code is typically executed only by the nodes participating in transactions affected by the code.

(iii) Ethereum

In addition to the public Ethereum blockchain and the Ether cryptocurrency described above, the Ethereum software platform also includes built-in support for private blockchains in which network connections are limited to nodes that the network creator specifically allows.[19] These private Ethereum networks possess all of the power and functionality of the public network, including the EVM's ability to execute complex smart-contract code. A consortium of large companies interested in using the Ethereum platform for business processing, including through private Ethereum-based blockchains, is the Enterprise Ethereum Alliance.[20]

---

17 *Sawtooth v1.0.2*, https://sawtooth.hyperledger.org/docs/core/releases/latest/contents .html.

18 *Introducing R3 Corda: A Distributed Ledger Designed for Financial Services*, https:// gendal.me/2016/04/05/introducing-r3-corda-a-distributed-ledger-designed-for-financial-services (Apr. 5, 2016).

19 *Ethereum Wiki on GitHub*, https://github.com/ethereum/go-ethereum/wiki/ Private-network (Mar. 27, 2017).

20 *See* ENTERPRISE ETHEREUM ALLIANCE, *About*, https://entethalliance.org/about/.

(f) Hybrid Chains

Bitcoin's demonstrated success, longevity, and security has led people to consider whether its public operations can be leveraged to add security and confidence to additional and typically privately implemented functionality.

- *Sidechains.* Using Bitcoin's scripting ability or other mechanisms, Bitcoin monetary transactions could be linked to those on other public or private blockchains. By sending Bitcoins to a special address where he would remain locked on the Bitcoin blockchain, a user would automatically create funds on another system or blockchain with different rules or functions.
- *Tagged Transactions.* Bitcoins are not fungible; a spending transaction on the Bitcoin blockchain must identify specific Bitcoins that were previously received and unspent. This fact, combined with the ability to add a small amount of customized metadata to a Bitcoin transaction, allows use of the Bitcoin system to represent assets or other real-world things that are described more fully in another system or blockchain.

Other platforms with on-chain processing capability, such as the Ethereum platform, make it even easier to implement an interface between the public blockchain and additional private blockchains or other functionality.

3. BLOCKCHAIN FOR BUSINESS: ADVANTAGES AND DISADVANTAGES

(a) Advantages

(i) Disintermediation

Many businesses processes involve complex interactions among multiple individual or institutional intermediaries that are intended to serve as a check on one another. In a blockchain network, careful planning can allow cryptography and consensus mechanisms to take the place of human judgments about trust, just as they do in the Bitcoin network.

In some cases, Nakamoto's full objective—the complete elimination of the trusted third party altogether—may not be possible or desirable. But blockchain developers need not go that far to obtain benefits from the decentralizing of trust. Some permissioned blockchains may include nodes with different levels of privileges and specifically crafted for limited purposes. For example, on the Ethereum platform, all nodes perform all the computations in every processed transaction; a permissioned blockchain, by contrast, could identify a smaller subset of highly capable nodes with more storage and processing power to perform this function. Similarly, instead of all nodes participating in the establishment of a network-wide consensus, a permissioned blockchain could identify a limited set of highly trusted nodes charged with doing so, while still implementing some of the ideas that make public blockchains so robust.

(ii) Transparency and Immutability

The basic operation of a blockchain system is the creation and addition of validated blocks to a chain of prior blocks. These blocks provide a complete record of all transactions and operations processed by the system. Cryptography ensures that blockchain records, once recorded, cannot be forged or altered.

(iii) Resiliency

Blockchains distribute the responsibility for storing and processing information across multiple nodes in a networked system. In doing so, they reduce the number of possible points of failure, or points of attack from malicious third parties.

(iv) Automatic Rule Enforcement

The nature of blockchain systems disallows certain kinds of errors and malfeasance that, in other systems, might require specialized code or human intervention. In the Bitcoin system, for example, there is no need for precautions against counterfeiting or overdrawing an account; these things are simply incompatible with the operation of the system. Similarly, smart-contract code on a platform like Ethereum executes as written even if the author of the code or the originator of the relevant transaction no longer wishes or intends it to do so.

(v) User Autonomy

Blockchain systems can allow users great autonomy in the control over their own transactions. In the Bitcoin network, for example, as long as the network continues to operate, there is no way to prevent a user from transferring Bitcoins or to force an unwanted transfer without the user's private keys. Similarly, beyond Bitcoin, in any blockchain using digital signatures to validate authorized transactions, the initiation of transactions will be entirely under the control of the party with possession of the appropriate keys.

(b) Disadvantages

(i) Performance and Resources

The features that provide blockchain technology its advantages come with performance and resource costs. The most obvious cost in the Bitcoin system is the proof-of-work consensus mechanism, which requires enormous and growing dedicated computational resources, using large amounts of energy. Other blockchains might adopt less computationally intensive consensus mechanisms, such as proof of stake, but even they can impose large costs in storage, computing power, and network bandwidth. The most basic characteristic of a blockchain system—the maintenance of multiple copies of the chain at every node—makes the system resilient, but imposes significant storage costs. Even digital signatures, which provide the assurances of identity and authority we need for every transaction in a blockchain system, can be computationally costly to calculate.

For these reasons, and as a general matter, blockchain-based systems perform much more slowly, and use far more energy and computing resources, than systems based on centralized ledgers. Perhaps more important, blockchain systems that perform adequately under moderate loads—the Bitcoin system is an example—are notoriously difficult to scale up to handle much higher volumes of transactions.

(ii) Complexity, Errors, and Vulnerabilities

Blockchain systems are highly complex and difficult to develop. Moreover, the design and programming of smart-contract systems utilizing blockchain systems is a separate source of complexity. Large programming projects, of course, are almost certain to produce significant bugs and vulnerabilities that can lead to execution flaws or exploitation by malicious actors. The successful public blockchain systems, such as Bitcoin and Ethereum, have benefitted from long periods of design, review, and testing, and now from an extended period of live use, and therefore are freer from such issues in comparison to less tested smart-contract code executed on such systems as well as private blockchain systems themselves.

(iii) Privacy

The operation of blockchain systems creates inherent privacy risks. The blockchain itself contains a full and detailed record of every transaction processed using the system, and the consensus mechanism of the system ensures the replication of that full record across multiple nodes of the system. These risks do not necessarily prevent the use of blockchain technology for sensitive information, but they do need to be accounted for, and they add complication to the design of the system.

4. CONCLUSION

In the chapters that follow, we will explore some of these challenges in depth.

- Chapter 2 explores the currently active market for ICOs and includes as well a detailed discussion of securities and other kinds of regulations as applied to ICOs, to cryptocurrencies, and to blockchain technology more generally.
- Chapter 3 discusses the issues arising, and likely to arise, from the ability of blockchains and other kinds of blockchain-inspired distributed ledger technologies to execute "smart contracts" and "smart code."
- Chapter 4 addresses the serious security and privacy issues implicated by blockchain technology.
- Chapter 5 focuses on antitrust issues raised by the technology.
- Chapter 6 discusses the federal and state regulation of money transmission and how those laws and regulations apply, and are likely to apply, to cryptocurrencies and to blockchain technology more generally.
- Chapter 7 surveys the many state legislative innovations in the field of blockchain technology.
- Finally, Chapter 8 addresses issues of liability, jurisdiction, and similar topics in an era of blockchain processing when the identity and location of the platform and its users may be indeterminate.

Blockchain systems offer great promise in bringing significant, if not revolutionary, improvement to many business processes. These changes will create difficult challenges for the lawyers advising these businesses, as well as for the legislatures, courts, and government agencies regulating their conduct. This book is a start, but only a start, in the ongoing task to provide the necessary tools for confronting those challenges.

CHAPTER 2

Cryptocurrencies, Initial Coin Offerings, and Financial Regulations

Mark W. Rasmussen
Emily O. Harris
Locke R. McMurray
Nicholas Dimitriou

One of the most popular applications of blockchain technology to date has been to create and distribute new types of virtual currency in initial coin offerings ("ICOs"). In recent years, ICOs have undergone explosive growth. In 2017, ICOs reportedly generated cumulative sales of roughly US$5.6 billion, compared to a reported US$240 million in 2016[1] and US$14 million in 2015.[2] Helping to fuel this staggering increase in virtual currency sales, celebrities and sports figures have used their public platforms to advertise ICOs to their social media followers. Musicians such as DJ Khaled and The Game, athletes such as Floyd Mayweather and Dennis Rodman, and actors such as Jamie Foxx and Paris Hilton have all thrown their weight behind an ICO. With all this star power, the ICO marketplace has generated a lot of media headlines and interest among the public. Regulators—and, in some cases, disgruntled investors—have likewise taken notice. Federal and state authorities have cracked down on those

---

1 *The State of the Token Market: A Year in Review & an Outlook for 2018*, Fabric Ventures & Token Data, https://static1.squarespace.com/static/5a19eca6c027d8615635f801/t/5a73697bc8302551711523ca/1517513088503/The+State+of+the+Token+Market+Final2.pdf.

2 *2014-2017 ICO Category Breakdown and Funding*, Autonomous Next (July 11, 2017), https://next.autonomous.com/insights/2017/8/2/2014-2017-ico-category-breakdown-and-funding.

ICOs that they perceive to be illegal securities offerings, and some early contributors to ICOs have likewise filed their own litigation.

At the same time, other blockchain applications have received much less fanfare, even though they may ultimately be as influential, or even more so, in comparison to ICOs. Indeed, blockchain applications are being developed that could revolutionize the securities, commodities, and financial services industries. Major corporations are developing blockchain and other DLT applications to help them increase liquidity, reduce errors, and improve transparency in many types of financial transactions. As exciting as the possibilities are, companies that are evaluating and adopting blockchain technologies must of course be aware of relevant laws and regulations to ensure they stay in compliance. This chapter assesses the legal landscape for ICOs, cryptocurrencies, and other financial blockchain applications.

1. CRYPTOCURRENCIES

The concept of creating a virtual currency using cryptography was introduced by David Chaum in a 1983 paper titled "Blind Signatures for Untraceable Payments."[3] Chaum's idea of electronic cash was then realized in practice through his corporation ("Digicash") and was actually trialed in a micropayment system in the 1990s by a bank in the United States.

More than twenty years later, in 2008, when Satoshi Nakamoto published the Bitcoin whitepaper[4] and (a few months later) mined Bitcoin's genesis block, Bitcoin was the only cryptocurrency in circulation. It took until April 2011 to create Namecoin, the first alternative cryptocurrency, and for an even longer period, all the cryptocurrencies in circulation were considered as a medium of exchange and (more or less) a substitute for government currency. Consequently, from an economic, legal, and regulatory standpoint, cryptocurrencies largely were treated the same.

In time, more cryptocurrencies emerged, and the functions of these cryptocurrencies have become more diverse. Thus, it has become increasingly important to distinguish between various types of cryptocurrency. Although a common nomenclature is still developing, we attempt in this section to provide a clear description of the different cryptocurrencies that exist in the blockchain ecosystem.

---

3 David Chaum, *Blind Signatures for Untraceable Payments*, (1983), https://www.chaum .com/publications/Chaum-blind-signatures.PDF.

4 Satoshi Nakamoto, *Bitcoin: A Peer-to-Peer Electronic Cash System*, (2008), https://bitcoin .org/bitcoin.pdf.

(a) How Do We Define Virtual Currency?

Before we define cryptocurrency, we start with what we believe to be a broader category—virtual currency. At one level, a virtual currency can be any kind of digital asset that can be redeemed by a user for value. For example, frequent-flier miles, customer loyalty points, or video game currency can all be considered virtual currencies. These are examples of centralized virtual currencies because a single administrator issues them, maintains a ledger, validates transactions, and has authority to redeem them. There are also decentralized virtual currencies. This type of virtual currency has no central administrator; instead, the ledger showing transactions is distributed across and maintained by a peer-to-peer network of users.

Government agencies in the United States have attempted to define virtual currencies. For example, in 2013, the Financial Crimes Enforcement Network ("FinCEN"), a bureau of the United States Department of the Treasury, issued interpretive guidance regarding the application of FinCEN's regulations to virtual currencies. Under FinCEN regulations, "real" currency is legal tender issued by the United States or another country that is used and accepted as a medium of exchange in the country of issuance. FinCEN compared real currency to virtual currency, which it classified as a "medium of exchange that operates like a currency in some environments but does not have all the attributes of real currency. In particular, virtual currency does not have legal tender status in any jurisdiction."[5]

The Internal Revenue Service ("IRS") similarly defined virtual currency in a 2014 notice as "a medium of exchange, a unit of account, and/or store of value."[6] Like FinCEN, the IRS said that a virtual currency sometimes acts like "real" currency but does not have legal tender status in any jurisdiction. Virtual currency often can be converted into or act as a substitute for real currency. In such cases, it is referred to as "convertible virtual currency," according to FinCEN and the IRS.

Other regulators have likewise weighed in with their own definitions of virtual currencies. The Securities and Exchange Commission ("SEC") has defined a virtual currency as a "digital representation of value that can be

---

5 *Application of FinCEN's Regulations to Persons Administering, Exchanging, or Using Virtual Currencies*, FinCEN Guidance FIN-2013-G001, U.S. Dep't of the Treasury, FinCEN (Mar. 18, 2013), https://www.fincen.gov/resources/statutes-regulations/guidance/application-fincens-regulations-persons-administering.

6 *See id.*; *IRS Virtual Currency Guidance*, Notice 2014-21, IRS, https://www.irs.gov/pub/irs-drop/n-14-21.pdf.

digitally traded and functions as a medium of exchange, unit of account, or store of value."[7] The Commodity Futures Trading Commission (CFTC), in a proposed rule interpretation related to retail commodity transactions involving virtual currency, stated that virtual currency encompasses:

> any digital representation of value (a "digital asset") that functions as a medium of exchange, and any other digital unit of account that is used as a form of a currency (i.e., transferred from one party to another as a medium of exchange); may be manifested through units, tokens, or coins, among other things; and may be distributed by way of digital "smart contracts," among other structures.[8]

The CFTC noted, however, that it does not intend to create a bright-line definition of virtual currency at this time, given the "evolving nature of the commodity" and the underlying blockchain technology.

Based on these definitions, we adopt the view that a virtual currency acts as a store of value, unit of account, or medium of exchange and is generally accepted in exchange for goods and services but does not have legal tender status in the United States.

(b) How Do We Define Cryptocurrency?

In the context of blockchain technology, people often refer to virtual currencies generally as cryptocurrencies. By one definition, cryptocurrency refers to a "math-based, decentralized convertible virtual currency that is protected by cryptography."[9] Purists might consider that a cryptocurrency must also be universally accessible and peer-to-peer (or node-to-node), whereas pragmatists might argue that a cryptocurrency simply needs to use distributed ledger technology to allow remote peer-to-peer transfer of electronic value in the absence of trust between contracting parties.[10]

---

7 *Investor Bulletin: Initial Coin Offerings*, SEC (July 25, 2017), https://www.sec.gov/oiea/investor-alerts-and-bulletins/ib_coinofferings.

8 Proposed Interpretation, 82, Fed. Reg. 60335, at 60388.

9 *Virtual Currencies: Key Definitions and Potential AML/CFT Risks*, Financial Action Task Force (June 2014), http://www.fatf-gafi.org/media/fatf/documents/reports/Virtual-currency-key-definitions-and-potential-aml-cft-risks.pdf.

10 Morten Linnemann Bech & Rodney Garratt, *Central Bank Cryptocurrencies*, Bank for International Settlements (Sept. 17, 2017), https://www.bis.org/publ/qtrpdf/r_qt1709f.htm.

From a U.S. legal perspective, courts have defined cryptocurrency in various ways. In *United States v. Ulbricht*,[11] the court ruled that Bitcoin is "an anonymous but traceable digital currency." In *United States v. Brown*,[12] the court described Bitcoin as "a virtual, sovereign-free currency." Bitcoin has also been defined as "a decentralized form of online currency that is maintained in an online 'wallet,'" in *United States v. Lord*.[13]

For our purposes, we define cryptocurrency as a virtual currency that relies on public key cryptography whose transactions are recorded on a blockchain-based ledger that is maintained by and distributed across a peer-to-peer network.

(c) How Do We Define Coins and Tokens?

Given Bitcoin's status as the first decentralized cryptocurrency to gain widespread adoption, it is often regarded as the original cryptographic coin, whereas all other cryptocurrencies that have come after Bitcoin are often collectively referred to as *altcoins*. Although "altcoin" is a useful shorthand for anything that is not Bitcoin, it encompasses far too many cryptocurrencies that have distinguishable characteristics to be useful in most contexts. We therefore further define cryptocurrencies and altcoins according to the attributes they possess and the utility that they provide.

Some cryptocurrencies could be described as *protocol coins* in the sense that they facilitate transactions on a blockchain protocol and act as a financial incentive for those who maintain the protocol and ledger of transactions. The term *protocol*, in the context of blockchain technology, typically refers to the common rules that the nodes in a blockchain network follow. More specifically, a blockchain's protocol defines how nodes communicate with each other, which usually entails sharing a database or ledger of transactions using a native coin. In addition, these native coins act as incentives for people who are responsible for maintaining the network by acting as a reward for their investment of resources. Each blockchain protocol generally has its own native coin. We refer to this type of cryptocurrency as a protocol coin. For the Bitcoin blockchain, the native coin is called Bitcoin. For the Ethereum blockchain, the coin is called Ether. Other examples of protocol coins are Tezzies for the Tezos blockchain, Decred for the Decred blockchain, and Waves for the Waves blockchain.

---

11 858 F.3d 71, 82–83 (2d Cir. 2017).
12 857 F.3d 334, 337 (6th Cir. 2017).
13 No. CR 15-00240-01/02, 2017 WL 1424806, at *1 (W.D. La. Apr. 20, 2017).

Protocol coins are generally not linked to any centralized entity or any traditional real-world assets.

Other cryptocurrencies could be described as *decentralized application tokens*, or *dApp tokens* for short. Such tokens are associated with specific decentralized applications that run on top of an existing blockchain protocol, rather than being directly associated with the underlying protocols themselves. Many distributed applications that have been developed over the past few years run on the Ethereum blockchain. Their dApp tokens are commonly described as being ERC-20 compliant because they incorporate a specific set of rules established by the developers of Ethereum for the operation of smart contract tokens on the Ethereum blockchain. The Ethereum whitepaper outlines three types of decentralized applications that can be built on top of Ethereum.

> Financial dApps: Financial dApps provide users with ways of managing and entering into contracts using their funds or tokens such as financial derivatives, hedging contracts, savings wallets, and wills.

> Semi-Financial dApps: Semi-financial dApps include both a monetary (i.e., native token based) and a nonmonetary (i.e., based on sets of information obtained from outside the blockchain network) element. An example of this kind of dApp is an insurance-based product that would pay out in the token if a certain external "off-chain" event occurred.

> Non-Financial dApps: These are dApps that have no financial element or reward, such as dApps that facilitate decentralized governance.[14]

Developers of dApps often distribute their tokens in ICOs to raise capital and retain some amount for themselves so that if the distributed application proves popular, the dApp token will increase in value. As we discuss in more detail below, dApp tokens have been subdivided by some market participants into "security" tokens and "utility" tokens, depending on their specific attributes. dApp tokens are generally not linked to any "traditional" real-world assets.

---

14   *A Next-Generation Smart Contract and Decentralized Application Platform*, GitHub, https://github.com/ethereum/wiki/wiki/White-Paper.

Another type of cryptocurrency can be described as *asset-backed tokens* because they represent all or a portion of some underlying asset—essentially acting as a cryptographically secured "IOU" for that underlying asset. Some asset-backed tokens are designed to be permanently pegged to, and are one-to-one backed by, a traditional currency, while others are backed by an underlying asset (e.g., gold, real estate, collectibles) and are sometimes designed with the intention of increasing in value over time. Some asset-backed tokens are referred to as stablecoins, which are simply cryptocurrencies designed to have stable value over time. Another type of asset-backed token that is largely still in the conceptual stage is cryptocurrency issued by a central bank. A central bank would issue the cryptocurrency and would have a one-for-one convertibility with cash and reserves.[15] Central-bank issued cryptocurrency in theory could be used in wholesale or retail transactions.[16] Some jurisdictions are testing the use of cryptocurrencies on a wholesale basis. For example, the Bank of Canada and the Monetary Authority of Singapore have experimented with real-time gross settlement systems on a distributed ledger platform.[17] Venezuela, a country experiencing severe economic and monetary dislocations in its fiat currency, has launched a cryptocurrency called the petro, which is backed by state-owned oil assets.[18] Purists might say that these currencies cannot be considered as true cryptocurrencies due to their centralized nature. Pragmatists, on the other hand, might argue that the characteristic of a token or digital currency operating independently of a central bank or central entity is not fundamental to that token's classification as a cryptocurrency.

2. INITIAL COIN OFFERINGS

(a) What Is an ICO?

At its core, an ICO is a mechanism for an entity to issue a new virtual currency to buyers in exchange for value of some kind. In a typical ICO, buyers receive coins or tokens that are related to a specific company, project, dApp, or protocol, in exchange for consideration in the form of either fiat currency or some virtual currency (most often Bitcoin or Ether).

---

15 Morten Linnemann Bech & Rodney Garratt, *Central Bank Cryptocurrencies*, Bank for International Settlements (Sept. 17, 2017), https://www.bis.org/publ/qtrpdf/r_qt1709f.htm.

16 *Id.*

17 *Id.*

18 Petro White Paper, Financial and Technology Proposal (Mar. 15, 2018), http://www.elpetro.gob.ve/pdf/en/Whitepaper_Petro_en.pdf.

These coins or tokens can be customized to carry a variety of different rights or utilities that are determined by the issuing entity. For example, they could act like a license or could be exchanged for products or services that the offering entity provides currently or will provide in the future. Alternatively, they could be structured more like investments and carry the right to receive profits, dividends, or interest. Some entities issuing the tokens use the money raised through the ICO as capital to develop their business or the ecosystem on which the token will exist and operate.

Entities issuing tokens typically announce their offering and then issue a white paper or some other disclosure document that provides information regarding the entity, the rights associated with the token, how the token sale will proceed, and the ecosystem that the entity or project team is developing. White papers for ICOs vary in quality. Some are short, provide scant information about the offering, and are riddled with typographic and formatting errors; others have a more professional feel to them, with detailed information about how the ICO proceeds will be used, roadmaps for ecosystem development, disclosures about the risks associated with the offering, and biographies for the founders, key officers, and advisers of the entity. ICOs are often done by early stage start-up companies with no operating history, so these white papers often do not provide any meaningful financial information about the company. However, in light of recent regulatory activity suggesting that many tokens issued in ICOs may be securities, some entities have pursued ICOs structured to comply with exemptions from the registration requirements of the U.S. securities laws. In these cases, the white papers have increasingly conformed to more traditional private placement memorandums.

ICOs can be structured in a variety of ways, but the current trend is to divide the ICO into phases and market the ICO on websites and blogs dedicated to virtual currency and blockchain technology. The first phase of an ICO is often designated as a "presale period" when the tokens are offered only to individuals or institutions personally known to the project team. These presale buyers can include angel investors, venture capital funds, or entity insiders. During the presale, the issuer typically sets the price of the tokens at a significant discount compared to the pricing in later phases, although sometimes the price will rise over a set period of time or as certain sales thresholds are met. This structure encourages people to buy the tokens early. The early favorable pricing is especially attractive because the sales may come with no resale restrictions, which allows buyers to sell their tokens on secondary markets at higher prices after the ICO launches to the general public.

After the presale, the main sale to the public begins. In some cases, tokens are distributed to the buyers immediately after the main sale concludes. Other times, the issuing entity will wait a period of time to audit the transactions. At some point after the sale, the tokens often are traded on the secondary market (through exchanges or in direct peer-to-peer transactions), and once the protocol platform or dApp has been developed, the tokens can be used on that protocol or dApp.

Some ICOs can be legitimate opportunities for some buyers and experienced investors, but others carry a potential for fraud, as the value of the tokens being offered can depend on the entity actually creating the products, services, or value that it promises. In addition, some ICOs are structured in such a way that they represent offerings of securities, which must be registered with the SEC (or offered under a recognized exemption), must be accompanied by important disclosures, and must comply with various restrictions (e.g., limitations on the universe of potential purchasers, resales, and secondary trading markets) that traditional ICOs sought to avoid. This topic is addressed in more detail later in the chapter.

(b) What Are Some Significant ICOs?

The ICO era began with the launch of Mastercoin in July 2013. The idea behind the Mastercoin ICO was announced in January 2012, when a software engineer named J.R. Willett published a white paper titled "The Second Bitcoin White Paper," detailing how people could use the existing Bitcoin network as "a protocol layer, on top of which new currency layers with new rules [could] be built." The white paper also theorized that the new protocol layers could provide funds and reward early adopters of the new protocol.[19] Mastercoin put this theory into practice and raised US$5 million in Bitcoin through what is generally recognized as the first ICO.

Not long after Mastercoin's ICO, a programmer named Vitalik Buterin proposed a new blockchain protocol called Ethereum, which would allow far more powerful blockchain-executed scripts than was permitted in Bitcoin. Although Ethereum would have its own protocol currency, Ether, Buterin also envisioned that the Ethereum protocol would move

---

19 J. R. Willett, *The Second Bitcoin Whitepaper*, version 0.5, (Jan. 2012), https://blog.omni .foundation/tag/jr-willett/.

"far beyond just currency." "Protocols around decentralized file storage, decentralized computation and decentralized prediction markets, among dozens of other such concepts," he theorized, "have the potential to substantially increase the efficiency of the computational industry, and provide a massive boost to other peer-to peer protocols."[20] In other words, Ethereum would act as a world supercomputer and allow decentralized applications of all stripes to run on it. In order to fund the development of the Ethereum protocol, in July 2014, Buterin and his team began selling Ether and ultimately raised US$18 million in Bitcoin.[21]

A few ICOs were launched in 2015 and 2016, but the market exploded in 2017, with more than US$5 billion reportedly raised that year alone.[22] One of the more prominent ICOs that launched in 2017 was by Tezos. Through the sale, Tezos raised US$232 million, which was the highest amount publicly raised through the sale of digital currencies up to that point.[23] Shortly after the Tezos ICO ended, another company called Filecoin surpassed Tezos's fundraising record. Filecoin, which offers decentralized file storage, conducted its ICO in an innovative way. Rather than selling the tokens directly to the public as Tezos and other ICO promoters had done, Filecoin entered into an investment contract known as a Simple Agreement for Future Tokens ("SAFT"), under which investors contributed funds to Filecoin in exchange for the future right to receive tokens from Filecoin once the Filecoin network became functional. Because Filecoin conceded that its offering was a "security" under U.S. securities laws, it limited its sale of tokens only to accredited investors, pursuant to Rule 506 of the Securities Act of 1933. (We will discuss SAFTs and the securities law implications of ICOs later in the chapter.) Through the ICO, Filecoin raised almost US$257 million.[24]

---

20   *A Next-Generation Smart Contract and Decentralized Application Platform*, GitHub, https://github.com/ethereum/wiki/wiki/White-Paper.

21   Bart Chilton, *Bitcoin's $6,400 Price Tag Explained by Initial Coin Offering Craze*, FORBES (Nov. 1, 2017), https://www.forbes.com/sites/insideasia/2017/11/01/bitcoins-6400-price-tag-explained-by-initial-coin-offering-craze/#2986cb3c37d6.

22   *The State of the Token Market: A Year in Review & An Outlook for 2018*, *supra* note 1.

23   Stan Higgins, *$232 Million: Tezos Blockchain Project Finishes Record-Setting Token Sale*, Coindesk.com (July 13, 2017), https://www.coindesk.com/232-million-tezos-blockchain-record-setting-token-sale/.

24   Stan Higgins, *$257 Million: Filecoin Breaks All-Time Record for ICO Funding*, Coindesk.com (Sept. 7, 2017), https://www.coindesk.com/257-million-filecoin-breaks-time-record-ico-funding/.

3. OTHER FINANCIAL BLOCKCHAIN APPLICATIONS

Cryptocurrencies and ICOs have garnered most of the blockchain press in recent history, but there is a wide range of uses for blockchain technology in related industries, including the securities, commodities, and financial services industries. We highlight several developments in these industries below.

(a) Securities
(i) Delaware Corporate Law Amendment and Implications

Delaware has been an early leader in the adoption of blockchain technology. As the home jurisdiction for over 60 percent of the companies on the Fortune 500 list, this has significant implications for the securities industry. On August 1, 2017, Delaware became the first state to allow corporations to use blockchain technology to maintain corporate records. This development came almost a year after Vice Chancellor J. Travis Laster of the Delaware Court of Chancery asked corporations, investors, and financial intermediaries to use the technology to "fix the plumbing" of the voting and stockholding infrastructure of the U.S. securities markets.[25]

In his speech to the Council of Institutional Investors in September 2016, Vice Chancellor Laster lamented the complexities created by the nominee system for registering ownership of stock. Under the current system, depositories such as the Depository Trust Company hold stock certificates as owners of record and track transfers using an electronic book-entry system. He noted the problems the nominee system can create for voting, including the many opportunities for errors arising from the multiple parties and transactions required for beneficial owners to vote on matters submitted to stockholders.

Vice Chancellor Laster urged industry participants to explore the use of blockchain-based distributed ledger technology to address these problems and reduce overall transaction costs. The new Delaware law addresses the problems identified by Vice Chancellor Laster by amending Title 8 of the Delaware General Corporation Law to allow corporations to use electronic databases such as blockchain-based distributed ledgers to create and maintain corporate records, including a corporation's stock ledger.[26] Under the new law, stock ownership can be registered, transfers can be recorded, and proxy votes can be tracked and verified using a blockchain. Delaware's new

---

25 Vice Chancellor J. Travis Laster, *The Block Chain Plunger: Using Technology to Clean Up Proxy Plumbing and Take Back the Vote*, Keynote Speech, Council of Institutional Investors (Sept. 29, 2016), https://www.cii.org/files/09_29_16_laster_remarks.pdf.

26 *See* 8 Del. C. §§ 219, 224.

law allows corporations to leverage the power of blockchain technology to manage corporate records and answer Vice Chancellor Laster's call to unclog the pipes of the voting and stockholding infrastructure of the U.S. securities markets.

(ii) Securities Issuance

In late 2016, a major online retailer became the first publicly traded company to offer digital securities using blockchain technology. These securities trade independently from the company's traditional stock, which is listed on a national securities exchange. The company began the process of registering this offering in 2015, with the filing of a shelf registration statement for the issuance of stock to the company's existing shareholders. The company's registration statement was declared effective by the SEC in late 2015, and the rights offering began on November 15, 2016 and concluded on December 15, 2016.[27]

The mechanics of the offering are similar to other rights offerings, except that no physical stock certificates were issued and all transactions were recorded on a blockchain. As described in the company's registration statement and prospectus, an interested investor first had to open a brokerage account with a single broker that was authorized to access the alternative trading system ("ATS") on which the company's digital securities trade. The investor would then initiate the purchase of the company's digital securities through this broker-dealer on the ATS. Private and public keys were then generated to make the purchase. Although every transaction was recorded on a permanent private blockchain ledger, the company also reported the transactions to a clearing broker so that it could independently match and settle the transactions and a transfer agent so that it could keep the official log of stock ownership. When applied to securities issuance and trading, blockchain technology displayed the potential to speed up clearing and settlement times and decrease errors.

(iii) Exchange Traded Funds

Several entities have filed proposed rules changes to list and trade shares in exchange traded funds ("ETFs") that hold cryptocurrency as the only asset. For example, the Bats BZX Exchange applied to the SEC to list and

---

27   Tom Zanki, *Overstock Issues First-Ever Blockchain Shares in $11M Offer*, Law360 (Dec. 16, 2016), https://www.law360.com/articles/873790/overstock-issues-first-ever-blockchain-shares-in-11m-offer.

trade shares of the Winklevoss Bitcoin Trust, which would hold only Bit-coins as an asset. In March 2017, the SEC rejected the application, explaining that it was concerned that the market for Bitcoins was not mature enough to protect against manipulation of the underlying asset.[28] The SEC expressed concerns that much of the Bitcoin trading occurs in non-U.S. markets where there is little to no regulation and, therefore, no meaningful government oversight to detect and deter fraudulent activity. The SEC also stated that there are no significant, well-established, and regulated futures markets associated with Bitcoin that would allow for meaningful monitoring of the underlying asset. As described below, such futures markets have since emerged.

Other entities have filed registration statements for ETFs tied to Bitcoin, including ProShares[29] and VanEck Vectors ETF Trust,[30] but as of June 2018, the SEC had still not approved trading of Bitcoin ETFs. In January 2018, the SEC elaborated on its reasons for refusing the ETF applications, indicating that it would not be open to approving cryptocurrency ETFs until a number of concerns are addressed.[31] Two of the main issues related to the volatility of the cryptocurrency marketplace and the liquidity of cryptocurrencies in general. Thus, at least for the time being, Bitcoin ETFs are not available for investors. But if there is sufficient interest in Bitcoin ETFs, it stands to reason that the market will figure out how to address the SEC's concerns.

(b) Derivatives
(i) *Bitcoin Futures on CME and Cboe*

On December 1, 2017, two financial institutions—the Chicago Mercantile Exchange ("CME") and the CBOE Futures Exchange ("Cboe")—announced that they had self-certified contracts for Bitcoin futures trading.[32] Under

---

28 *Self-Regulatory Organizations; Bats BZX Exchange, Inc.; Order Disapproving a Proposed Rule Change, as Modified by Amendments No. 1 and 2, to BZX Rule 14.11(e)(4), Commodity-Based Trust Shares, to List and Trade Shares Issued by the Winklevoss Bitcoin Trust,* Release No. 34-80206, SEC (Mar. 10, 2017), https://www.sec.gov/rules/sro/batsbzx/2017/34-80206.pdf.

29 Form S-1 Registration Statement, Proshares Trust II, SEC (Sept. 27, 2017), https://www.sec.gov/Archives/edgar/data/1415311/000119312517296263/d464351ds1.htm.

30 Form N-1A Registration Statement, VanEck Vectors ETF Trust, SEC (Dec. 8, 2017), https://www.sec.gov/Archives/edgar/data/1137360/000093041317004010/c89704_485apos.htm.

31 Dalia Blass, *Staff Letter: Engaging on Fund Innovation and Cryptocurrency-Related Holdings,* SEC (Jan. 18, 2018), https://www.sec.gov/divisions/investment/noaction/2018/cryptocurrency-011818.htm.

32 *CFTC Statement on Self-Certification of Bitcoin Products by CME, CFE and Cantor Exchange,* Press Release No. 7654-17, CFTC (Dec. 1, 2017), https://www.cftc.gov/PressRoom/PressReleases/pr7654-17.

the Commodity Exchange Act, certain market participants can either self-certify that their contracts comply with the CEA and related regulations or voluntarily submit to review by the CFTC. Following their self-certification, the CFTC engaged in a "heightened review" of the terms and conditions of the Bitcoin futures contracts and established certain standards that are meant to police the market for fraud. The CFTC provided details of these standards in a paper published in January 2018.[33]

On December 10, Cboe began offering Bitcoin futures contracts to investors, and CME followed suit on December 17. This development has enabled investors (including institutional investors, which had largely stayed away from trading in cryptocurrencies) to establish positions for or against the price of Bitcoin, without holding Bitcoin. Bitcoin futures contracts provide investors with price transparency, centralized clearing, risk management tools, and the ability to hedge exposure to the underlying Bitcoin marketplace.

(ii) Equity Swap Smart Contracts

In October 2016, several firms announced that they had completed a successful test of over-the-counter equity swaps using blockchain technology and smart contracts.[34] The project tested automated lifecycle management and the synchronization of swaps involving individual stocks, index funds, and stock portfolios. As part of the tests, smart contracts were generated that had computational logic written into them to calculate payments based on market events. In addition, the group of firms conducted more than fifty tests of the underlying blockchain infrastructure, including assessments of access and permission controls, updates to the blockchain protocol, message processing speeds, and resilience to various network events. The test reportedly had a 100 percent success rate.

(iii) DTCC Credit Default Swap Platform

The Depository Trust and Clearing Corporation ("DTCC") provides posttrade clearing and settlement services for fixed income, equities, and derivatives. Across all platforms, the DTCC's daily volume averages over

---

33 *CFTC Backgrounder on Oversight of and Approach to Virtual Currency Markets*, CFTC (Jan. 4, 2018), https://www.cftc.gov/sites/default/files/idc/groups/public/@newsroom/documents/file/backgrounder_virtualcurrency01.pdf.

34 *Firms Complete Successful Blockchain Equity Swap Smart Contract*, Practical Law Finance (Nov. 3, 2016), https://uk.practicallaw.thomsonreuters.com/w-004-3726?transitionType=Default&contextData=(sc.Default)&firstPage=true&bhcp=1.

100 million individual trades and its systems can handle over 800 million. The DTCC began a project in early 2017 to use blockchain technology to build a platform to process $11 trillion worth of credit default swaps.[35] The platform can simplify the process of clearing, tracking, and settling derivatives trades and make the information visible to all participants on a shared record. This derivatives clearing platform is expected to go live in 2018. One important question that will have to be addressed is whether distributed ledger technology can be scaled sufficiently to process large volumes of transactions.

(iv) Bitcoin Options

In July 2017, the CFTC approved the registration filing of a cryptocurrency trading platform operator to clear derivatives contracts that settle in cryptocurrencies.[36] This enabled markets participants to hedge cryptocurrencies using option contracts. The platform reportedly processed over US$1 million in transactions in the first week of operation.

(c) Financial Services

Over the past year, companies in the financial services industry have tested permissioned and permission-less blockchain applications to their businesses. Below are several examples of such applications that are at various stages of development.

(i) Cross-Border Payments Processing

One promising application of blockchain technology is to streamline cross-border payment processes. The transfer of value across borders can in some cases be complicated and slow. But a number of companies are developing blockchain-based solutions to streamline the process and reduce transaction costs. A major international bank, for example, has invested billions of dollars to develop an in-house global payment technology that is a permissioned implementation of the Ethereum blockchain.[37] In addition,

---

35 *DTCC Selects IBM, AXONI and R3 to Develop DTCC's Distributed Ledger Solution for Derivatives Processing*, Press Release, Depository Trust & Clearing Corporation (Jan. 9, 2017), http://www.dtcc.com/news/2017/january/09/dtcc-selects-ibm-axoni-and-r3-to-develop-dtccs-distributed-ledger-solution.

36 *CFTC Grants DCO Registration to LedgerX LLC*, Press Release No. 7592-17, CFTC (July 24, 2017), https://www.cftc.gov/PressRoom/PressReleases/pr7592-17.

37 Robert Hackett, *Big Business Giants from Microsoft to J.P. Morgan Are Getting Behind Ethereum*, FORTUNE (Feb. 28, 2017), http://fortune.com/2017/02/28/ethereum-jpmorgan-microsoft-alliance/.

a large money transfer services provider has announced plans to work with Ripple to use XRP, Ripple's cryptocurrency, to facilitate transfers of value between people around the globe.[38] These applications of blockchain technology for cross-border payments have the potential to speed up the process to nearly instantaneous, while creating an immutable, tamper-proof ledger of the transactions.

(ii) Trade Finance

Blockchain technology also has the potential to transform trade finance, the monetary activities related to domestic and international commerce. Trade finance helps to facilitate transactions between importers and exporters. In a typical transaction, letters of credit are used to guarantee payment to the exporter upon receipt of evidence that goods have shipped. This reduces the risk that the exporter will ship goods and never receive payment. The issuance of letters of credit can be cumbersome and slow, however.

Several international banks are experimenting with a blockchain solution to address these problems. Working collaboratively with R3 and its Corda platform, they are piloting a solution that will track assets and make it easier to export goods and receive payment confirmation through smart contracts.[39] The project involves the digitization of letters of credit and bills of lading to cut down the time it takes for companies to complete and share documentation that is necessary for trade finance. Two banks (one from Australia and one from the United States) successfully tested this technology to facilitate the sale and export of cotton from a U.S.-based seller to an Australia-based buyer.

Trade finance is just one of many use cases to which Corda technology has been applied. Others include supply chain management, syndicated loan management and processing, and insurance contract automation. Corda is an open source blockchain project that is specifically designed for businesses and financial institutions. It has no cryptocurrency built into it and does not require resource-intensive proof-of-work mining operations. Nor does it require parties to share transactions with the entire network.

---

38 Jeff John Roberts, *Western Union Is Testing Ripple and XRP for Money Transfers*, Fortune (Feb. 14, 2018), http://fortune.com/2018/02/14/ripple-xrp-western-union-money-transfers/.
39 For more information on Corda, *see* https://www.corda.net/.

(iii) Retail Banking and Credit

Relative to other financial services, the application of blockchain technology to the retail banking and credit sector has been slower to take off. One can imagine a number of different areas where blockchain could improve the retail banking experience, including more efficiently managing account set-up documentation, contracts, and notifications. But it is the application of blockchain technology to retail payment transactions that holds the most appeal. A major credit card company announced in late 2017 the launch of its own payment-processing network using a private blockchain.[40] The company is not using a cryptocurrency to facilitate transactions but rather is tracking on its blockchain the details of transactions, with the goal of allowing retailers to receive payment faster. The company also touts the added feature of allowing people to track the provenance of pharmaceuticals, art, and luxury goods on its blockchain.

(iv) Private Funds

An increasing number of private funds are focusing on blockchain technology and related assets as investments. New hedge funds that trade exclusively in cryptocurrencies have been established, and existing hedge funds have added cryptocurrencies as an asset class. The research firm Autonomous Next has collected data showing that as of February 2018, over 220 funds were focused on investing in cryptocurrencies.[41] In addition, certain private funds are using blockchain technology to facilitate and automate operations. For example, private funds are testing the use of smart contracts to automate fund administration and support.

4. SECURITIES LAWS AND REGULATIONS

One of the most frequently discussed legal issues related to blockchain technology is whether federal securities laws and state "blue sky laws" apply to cryptocurrencies and ICOs. Before addressing legal precedent relevant to that issue, we provide an overview of the federal securities law framework in the United States. This is not intended to capture all of the federal securities laws and regulations that might be implicated but rather to note some of the more significant laws that a practitioner should be

---

40 Jen Wieczner, *Mastercard Will Now Let You Pay with Blockchain—But Not Bitcoin*, Fortune (Oct. 20, 2017), http://fortune.com/2017/10/20/mastercard-blockchain-bitcoin/.

41 *See generally Crypto Fund List Segmentation*, Autonomous Next, https://next.autonomous .com/cryptofundlist/.

aware of. In light of the serious consequences of any violation of securities laws, an ICO transaction would require a comprehensive analysis of U.S. (federal and state) and foreign securities laws.

(a) Federal Securities Laws

We will discuss four federal statutes that relate to "securities": the U.S. Securities Act of 1933 as amended (the "Securities Act"),[42] the U.S. Securities Exchange Act of 1934 as amended (the "Exchange Act"),[43] the U.S. Investment Advisers Act of 1940 as amended (the "Advisers Act"),[44] and the U.S. Investment Company Act of 1940 as amended (the "Investment Company Act").[45] Although each of these four statutes addresses different types of activities, they share the following characteristics: (1) the involvement of a "security" and (2) the presence of U.S. jurisdiction.

Although the definition of a "security" in the four statutes varies, the term has generally been interpreted similarly under each. Further, the analysis of whether an instrument is a "security" under those statutes is technical and does not always lead to an intuitive result. The statutory definition of "security" includes both specific terms (e.g., any "stock," "bond," "note," "debenture") and general terms (e.g., any "investment contract"). Many of those terms have been the subject of interpretation in U.S. court decisions, which has led to a significant number of varying outcomes that are highly dependent on the specific facts and circumstances.

(i) U.S. Securities Act of 1933[46]

Under the Securities Act, the offering and selling of securities in the United States or to U.S. persons generally requires the prior registration of such securities with the SEC or the reliance on an exemption from registration. Registration of securities under the Securities Act requires, among other things, the filing of extensive disclosure documents with the SEC and permits an issuer to sell a large amount of securities to an unlimited number of purchasers, including retail investors. Issuers that do not want to incur the time and expense of the registration process (and that can operate within certain limitations on offering amounts or investor qualifications) typically seek an exemption from the registration requirements

---

42 15 U.S.C. § 77a *et seq.*
43 15 U.S.C. § 78a *et seq.*
44 15 U.S.C. §§ 80b-1–80b-21.
45 15 U.S.C. §§ 80a-1–80a-64.
46 15 U.S.C. § 77a *et seq.*

of the Securities Act. Most commonly, issuers seeking to offer securities in a transaction exempt from the Securities Act's registration requirements rely on private placement exemptions provided by Section 4(a)(2) and Regulation D under the Securities Act. These provisions are discussed in detail later in the chapter.

(ii) U.S. Securities Exchange Act of 1934

Under the Exchange Act, subject to certain exemptions, "brokers" and "dealers" must register as such with the SEC. Section 15(a)(1) of the Exchange Act generally provides that it is unlawful for a broker or dealer "to effect any transactions in, or to induce or attempt to induce the purchase or sale of, any security . . . unless such broker or dealer is registered" with the SEC. Section 3(a)(4)(A) of the Exchange Act defines the term *broker* to mean "any person engaged in the business of effecting transactions in securities for the account of others." As a general matter, under Exchange Act Section 3(a)(5), a "dealer" is defined as "any person engaged in the business of buying and selling securities . . . for such person's own account, through a broker or otherwise."

The phrases "engaged in the business" and "effecting transactions in securities" are both interpreted broadly. For example, a person may be deemed to be "engaged in the business" by receiving transaction-based compensation and "effecting transactions in securities" by participating in the "chain of distribution" (e.g., screening potential purchasers, structuring transactions, performing due diligence, and providing valuations).

In the United States, the broker-dealer registration process requires both the filing of applications (Form BD with the SEC and Form NMA and Form U4 with the Financial Industry Regulatory Authority) and the successful completion of the qualification examinations required of principals and registered representatives of broker-dealers. Among other requirements, registered broker-dealers must (1) establish, maintain, and enforce written supervisory procedures; (2) maintain specified books and records and prepare and submit certain monthly and quarterly reports; (3) periodically inspect branch offices; (4) remain in compliance with the SEC Net Capital Rule; (5) maintain an anti-money laundering compliance program; and (6) register in every state in which they intend to maintain offices and may have to register as broker-dealers in certain other states in which they conduct business. All registered representatives and principals must participate in ongoing internal training and training conducted by the Financial Industry Regulatory Authority, more commonly known as FINRA.

Some of the more commonly used exemptions from broker-dealer registration include (1) the "issuer exemption" (which generally exempts an associated person (or employee) of an issuer who participates in the sale of the issuer's securities)[47] and (2) Rule 15a-6 under the Exchange Act (which permits a non-U.S. broker-dealer to facilitate limited contacts with persons physically located in the United States).

The Exchange Act also contains provisions related to reporting and registration of securities. For example, Section 12(g)(1) of the Exchange Act requires an issuer to register a class of equity securities (other than exempt securities) within 120 days after its fiscal year-end if, on the last day of its fiscal year, the issuer has total assets of more than $10 million and a class of equity securities "held of record" by either (1) 2,000 or more persons or (2) 500 or more persons who are not "accredited investors."[48]

In addition, the Exchange Act prohibits fraudulent misstatements or omissions of material fact in connection with the purchase or sale of any security, registered or not. The relevant rule is Rule 10b-5, which makes it "unlawful for or any person, directly or indirectly, by the use of any means or instrumentality of interstate commerce, or of the mails or of any facility of any national securities exchange, (a) to employ any device, scheme, or artifice to defraud, (b) to make any untrue statement of a material fact or to omit to state a material fact necessary in order to make the statements made, in the light of the circumstances under which they were made, not misleading, or (c) to engage in any act, practice, or course of business which operates or would operate as a fraud or deceit upon any person, in connection with the purchase or sale of any security."

---

47   Rule 3a4-1 under the Exchange Act is a "non-exclusive safe-harbor" under which an "associated person" of an issuer that performs limited securities sales for the issuer as prescribed by the rule would be deemed not to be a "broker" under Section 3(a)(4) of the Exchange Act and, thus, not required to register in accordance with Section 15 of the Exchange Act.

48   "Accredited investors" include, among other persons, (1) any organization described in section 501(c)(3) of the Internal Revenue Code, corporation, Massachusetts or similar business trust, or partnership, not formed for the specific purpose of acquiring the securities offered, with total assets in excess of $5,000,000; (2) any natural person whose individual net worth, or joint net worth with that person's spouse, exceeds $1,000,000; (3) any natural person who had an individual income in excess of $200,000 in each of the two most recent years or joint income with that person's spouse in excess of $300,000 in each of those years and has a reasonable expectation of reaching the same income level in the current year; and (4) any entity in which all of the equity owners are accredited investors. (*See* Rule 501 under Regulation D for a complete definition of an "accredited investor.")

(iii) U.S. Investment Advisers Act of 1940

The Advisers Act generally requires an "investment adviser" to register (or be exempt from registration) under the Advisers Act with the SEC and subjects the adviser to the Advisers Act's restrictions and requirements. Further, any person who meets the definition of an "investment adviser" under the Advisers Act (whether or not registered with the SEC under the Advisers Act) is deemed to be a fiduciary to his clients. As a fiduciary, an investment adviser has the obligation to act with an "eye single to the benefit of the client" and an affirmative obligation to provide full and adequate disclosure to clients regarding matters that may have an impact on the investment adviser's independence and judgment (for example, any material conflicts of interest).[49]

An "investment adviser," for purposes of the Advisers Act, means any person who (1) for compensation; (2) engages in the business of; (3) advising others or issuing reports or analyses; (4) regarding securities.[50] It should be noted that the terms of the definition of an "investment adviser" are read broadly by the SEC; thus, the terms in the definition have to be analyzed in order to determine the applicability of the Advisers Act. Additionally, the SEC looks at substance over form in determining whether the Advisers Act applies as it would be unlawful for any person to participate indirectly in any activities that would be unlawful for such person to do directly under the Advisers Act.

The following summarizes the framework for analyzing the elements of the definition of an "investment adviser" under the Advisers Act[51]:

> (a) The term "compensation" has been broadly construed by the SEC and U.S. courts. Generally, the receipt of any economic benefit, whether in the form of an advisory fee, some other fee relating to the total services rendered, a commission, reimbursement of expenses, indemnification or some combination thereof, satisfies this element;[52]

---

49 SEC v. Capital Gains Research Bureau, Inc., 375 U.S. 180, 184 (1963).

50 *See* Advisers Act Section 202(a)(11).

51 Absent a very specific set of facts (e.g., a wholly owned subsidiary advising its parent, or an internally managed company), advisers are generally assumed to advise "others." Therefore, the summary below does not provide additional details related to part (3) of the definition of an "investment adviser."

52 *See Applicability of the Investment Advisers Act of 1940 to Financial Planners, Pension Consultants, and Other Persons Who Provide Others with Investment Advice as a Component*

(b) Whether a person is "engaged in the business" or in "regular business" of providing investment advice depends upon all of the relevant facts and circumstances, not just the frequency with which a person provides advice.[53] This does not have to be the sole or even primary activity of the person; and

(c) To satisfy the "investment adviser" definition, the advice given must be with respect to a "security."

The Advisers Act status of a person who is deemed to be an "investment adviser" depends on a variety of factors, including the location of the person's principal office and place of business, the person's regulatory assets under management and the types of clients that the person advises.

A person who is required to register as an "investment adviser" with the SEC (1) is required to file a Form ADV (and potentially a Form PF) with the SEC; (2) must adopt and implement written policies and procedures reasonably designed to prevent violations of the Advisers Act and hire or designate a chief compliance officer; (3) is subject to examination by the SEC; and (4) is generally subject to restrictions and requirements related to trading practices; advertising materials (including social media); books and records; custody of client assets; best execution of client transactions; advisory agreements; solicitation arrangements; performance-based fees; proxy voting; valuation; personal trading of certain employees; supervision of employees and service providers; privacy; gifts and entertainment; cybersecurity monitoring; business continuity; pay to play; and anti-money laundering.

---

of Other Financial Services, Release No. 1092, SEC (Oct. 8, 1987), https://www.sec.gov/rules/interp/1987/ia-1092.pdf; *see also Kenisa Oil Company*, SEC Letter, SEC (May 6, 1982); *SEC v. Fife*, 311 F. 3d 1 (1st Cir. 2002) (a person provides advice "for compensation" if it understands that successful investment will yield it a *commission*); *In the Matter of Alexander v. Stein*, Release No. 1497, SEC (June 8, 1995) (a person receives *"compensation"* if it fraudulently converts client funds to its own use).

53 *See Applicability of the Investment Advisers Act of 1940 to Financial Planners, Pension Consultants, and Other Persons Who Provide Others with Investment Advice as a Component of Other Financial Services*, Release No. 1092, SEC (Oct. 8, 1987), https://www.sec.gov/rules/interp/1987/ia-1092.pdf (SEC Staff noted that even though the elements "engaged in the business" and "regular business" in the definition of "investment adviser" are phrased somewhat differently, it is the SEC Staff's opinion that such elements should be interpreted in the same manner and that in both cases, the determination to be made is whether the degree of the person's advisory activities constitutes being "in the business" of an investment adviser).

Common exemptions under the Advisers Act from registration include (1) the foreign private adviser exemption; (2) the venture capital fund adviser exemption; and (3) the exemption for private fund advisers with less than $150 million under management. Further, the amount of an adviser's regulatory assets under management will determine whether the person may be subject to federal or state adviser regulation. For example, advisers with less than $25 million in regulatory assets under management are generally prohibited from registering with the SEC and must comply with applicable state investment adviser regulations.[54]

(iv) U.S. Investment Company Act of 1940

The Investment Company Act generally requires "investment companies" to register with the SEC and subjects them to certain operational restrictions and requirements. There are two principal types of investment companies: those falling under Section 3(a)(1)(A) of the Investment Company Act, which are companies commonly considered to be investment companies (e.g., mutual funds),[55] and those falling under Section 3(a)(1)(C) of the Investment Company Act, which are holding companies or operating companies that may be deemed to be investment companies because a substantial portion of their assets is invested in investment securities.[56] A third type of investment company, described in Section 3(a)(1)(B) of the Investment Company Act, is one that is in the business of issuing face-amount certificates of the installment type. These types of investment companies are quite rare.

If an issuer (such as a fund or operating company) is deemed to be an "investment company," it must either register with the SEC under the Investment Company Act or qualify for an exclusion or exemption. Registration under the Investment Company Act does not impose any restrictions or requirements related to the sophistication or wealth of

---

54 *See* Section 203A(a)(1) of the Advisers Act. The prohibition does not apply if the investment adviser is an adviser to an investment company registered under the Investment Company Act or if the adviser is eligible for one of six exemptions the SEC has adopted.

55 Under Section 3(a)(1)(A), an "investment company" means any issuer which "is or holds itself out as being engaged primarily, or proposes to engage primarily, in the business of investing, reinvesting, or trading in securities."

56 Under Section 3(a)(1)(C), an "investment company" means any issuer which "is engaged or proposes to engage in the business of investing, reinvesting, owning, holding, or trading in securities, and owns or proposes to acquire investment securities having a value exceeding 40 per centum of the value of such issuer's total assets (exclusive of Government securities and cash items) on an unconsolidated basis."

investors but requires the filing of registration materials with the SEC and imposes restrictions and requirements related to the issuer's operations— for example: (1) the safekeeping of investment company assets (Section 17(f)); (2) prohibiting or limiting self-dealing and other transactions between investment companies and their affiliates (Section 17); (3) the capital structure of investment companies (including the imposition of significant asset coverage requirements as a precondition to borrowings or other issuances of senior securities and limitations on warrant issuances) (Section 18); and (4) requirements for the issuer's board of directors to have a percentage of disinterested directors and to have certain arrangements approved by such directors (Section 10(a)).

Alternatively, an issuer that is deemed to be an "investment company" may seek to rely on one of the exclusions or exemptions from registration under the Investment Company Act. Two of the most common exclusions are (i) Section 3(c)(1), which excludes from the definition of an "investment company" any issuer whose outstanding securities (other than short-term paper) are beneficially owned by not more than 100 persons and that is not making or proposing to make a public offering of their securities; and (ii) Section 3(c)(7), which excludes from the definition of an "investment company" any issuer whose outstanding securities are only owned by persons that at the time of acquisition of those securities were "qualified purchasers"[57] and that does not make or propose to make a public offering of its securities. Other commonly used exemptions such as Section 3(c)(5)(C) (for issuers primarily engaged in acquiring mortgages and other liens on and interests in real estate) and Rule 3a-7 (for issuers of asset-backed securities) restrict the types of an issuer's investments (and not the types of an issuer's investors). Unlike a registered investment company, issuers that are exempt from the Investment Company Act or excluded from the definition of an "investment company" under the Investment Company Act are not required to comply with substantially all of the provisions of the Investment Company Act.

(b) The Definition of "Security" and the Howey Test
The mission of the SEC is to protect investors; maintain fair, orderly, and efficient markets; and facilitate capital formation by regulating

---

57   A "qualified purchaser" (as defined in Section 2(a)(51) of the Investment Company Act) includes, among other persons, a natural person who owns not less than $5,000,000 in investments, and any person, acting for its own account or the accounts of other qualified purchasers, who in the aggregate owns and invests on a discretionary basis, not less than $25,000,000 in investments.

securities transactions and certain individuals and entities that oper-ate in the securities industry. It does not regulate transactions involving currencies or commodities. Thus, for the SEC to have jurisdiction over a cryptocurrency, it must fit the definition of a security under federal securities laws.

Some cryptocurrencies that exist do not fit the definition of a secur-ity and will likely never be regarded as such. For example, a senior SEC official has said that Bitcoin and Ether are not securities. But as SEC chairman Jay Clayton has noted, "simply calling something a 'currency' or a currency-based product does not mean that it is not a security."[58] It is necessary, instead, to look beyond mere labels and analyze the essen-tial characteristics of the cryptocurrency in question. The SEC has stated that one must assess the "facts and circumstances" of the offer and sale of the cryptocurrency to assess whether it is a security. Federal courts have likewise concluded that when evaluating whether something is a security, "form should be disregarded for substance."[59]

The definition of "security" in Section 2(a)(1) of the Securities Act includes the following types of instruments:

> any note, stock, treasury stock, security future, security-based swap, bond, debenture, evidence of indebtedness, certificate of interest or participation in any profit-sharing agreement, collateral-trust certificate, preorganization certificate or subscription, transferable share, investment contract, voting-trust certificate, certificate of deposit for a security, fractional undivided interest in oil, gas, or other mineral rights, any put, call, straddle, option, or privilege on any security, certificate of deposit, or group or index of securities (including any interest therein or based on the value thereof), or any put, call, straddle, option, or privilege entered into on a national securities exchange relating to foreign currency, or, in general, any interest or instrument commonly known as a "secur-ity," or any certificate of interest or participation in, temporary or interim certificate for, receipt for, guarantee of, or warrant or right to subscribe to or purchase, any of the foregoing.

---

58   Chairman Jay Clayton, *Chairman's Testimony on Virtual Currencies: The Roles of the SEC and CFTC*, SEC (Feb. 6, 2018), https://www.sec.gov/news/testimony/testimony-virtual-currencies-oversight-role-us-securities-and-exchange-commission.

59   Tcherepnin v. Knight, 389 U.S. 332, 336 (1967).

In the world of cryptocurrencies and ICOs, the SEC has focused on the term *investment contract* from the list above. That term was defined in the seminal case *SEC v. W.J. Howey Co.* as an investment of money in a common enterprise with a reasonable expectation of profits to be derived solely from the entrepreneurial or managerial efforts of others.[60]

In *Howey*, the U.S. Supreme Court analyzed whether an offering of units in a citrus grove, together with a contract for the maintenance and marketing of the grove, constituted an investment contract under the Securities Act. The court noted that the term *investment contract* was undefined in the Securities Act or in the relevant legislative history. But it was commonly used in many state blue sky laws that existed before the Securities Act was enacted and had a long history of being interpreted by state courts.

Through those judicial decisions, the definition of investment contract came to include "situations where individuals were led to invest money in a common enterprise with the expectation that they would earn a profit solely through the efforts of the promoter or of someone other than themselves."[61] Further, *Howey* noted, "[f]orm was disregarded for substance and emphasis was placed upon economic reality."[62] *Howey* went on to rule that Congress, when it approved the Securities Act, would have been fully aware of these interpretations by state courts, and it was reasonable to attach that meaning to the term as used in the Securities Act.[63] In the seven decades since *Howey*, numerous court decisions have applied this test in deciding whether a product is an investment contract under the federal securities laws.[64]

Before the rise of the ICO, the definition of an investment contract was a matter of interest mostly for securities lawyers. Now, however, the entire blockchain community, it seems, can recite the *Howey* test. In July 2017, the SEC issued a report pursuant to Section 21(a) of the Exchange Act regarding an ICO involving "the DAO," a decentralized virtual organization that was offering DAO tokens. The SEC's DAO Report is significant on many levels, including the fact that it is the first time the SEC formally

---

60 328 U.S. 293, 301 (1946).

61 *Id.*

62 *Id.*

63 *Id.*

64 *See, e.g.,* SEC v. Edwards, 540 U.S. 389, 393 (2004); SEC v. Tropikgadget FZE, 146 F. Supp. 3d 270, 279 (D. Mass. 2015); Louros v. Cyr, 175 F. Supp. 2d 497, 508-09 (S.D.N.Y. 2001); Steinhardt Grp. Inc. v. Citicorp, 126 F.3d 144, 145 (3d Cir. 1997).

applied the *Howey* test to the new world of cryptocurrencies. [65] Notably, the DAO Report was not an administrative or court decision but rather an investigative report that the SEC issued to provide clarity and guidance regarding the application of securities laws to cryptocurrencies. The SEC believed that it was in the public interest to clearly state the principles of federal securities laws and describe how the SEC believes those laws apply to blockchain technology and cryptocurrency.

As the DAO Report explains, from April 30, 2016, until May 28, 2016, the DAO offered and sold roughly 1.15 billion DAO tokens for approximately 12 million Ether, which was equivalent to approximately US$150 million at the time. Contributors who purchased DAO tokens would be entitled to vote on and reap rewards from various projects that were intended to be autonomous with little to no central administration. Unfortunately, just before the end of the ICO, there were concerns about the security of the computer code associated with the DAO. On June 17, 2016, a hack occurred, resulting in a third of the total Ether that was raised to be diverted to accounts held by the hackers. Ultimately, the stolen Ether was returned to the contributors, but it had to be done through a hard fork, which is a change in the underlying Ethereum protocol.

The SEC conducted an investigation and issued the DAO Report to "stress that the U.S. federal securities law may apply to various activities, including distributed ledger technology, depending on the particular facts and circumstances." In the report, the SEC analyzed the *Howey* factors and concluded that the DAO tokens were, in the SEC's view, investment contracts subject to the registration requirements of the federal securities laws. Below we summarize each element of the *Howey* test.

Investment of Money: The first factor of the *Howey* test is that there must be an investment of capital in some form. It is well established in case law that the investment need not be in the form of cash to satisfy the *Howey* test. Multiple decisions by federal courts have concluded that contributions in other forms also qualify.[66]

In a Common Enterprise: The second factor of the *Howey* test is that the investment be made in a common enterprise. Courts have reached different conclusions about what a common enterprise is, with some requiring

---

65 *Report of Investigation Pursuant to Section 21(a) of the Securities Exchange Act of 1934: The DAO*, Release No. 81207, SEC (July 25, 2017), https://www.sec.gov/litigation/investreport/34-81207.pdf.

66 Uselton v. Comm. Lovelace Motor Freight, Inc., 940 F.2d 564, 574 (10th Cir. 1991); SEC v. Shavers, 2014 WL 4652121, at *1 (E.D. Tex. Sept. 18, 2014).

so-called horizontal commonality and others requiring vertical commonality. Courts of appeal from different circuits have reached differing conclusions about what is required, so it is important to know what circuit's law would apply to a given token offering.

For there to be horizontal commonality, assets from multiple investors must be pooled together so that all investors share in the profits and risks.[67] Whereas the emphasis for horizontal commonality is on the aggregation of resources, the focus for vertical commonality is on the skills and expertise of the promoters. Vertical commonality has been subdivided into (i) broad vertical commonality and (ii) narrow vertical commonality. Broad vertical commonality requires a showing that the success of the investor depends on the seller's expertise.[68] Narrow vertical commonality examines whether the profits of an investor are interwoven with those of the seller.[69]

With a Reasonable Expectation of Profits: The third factor of the *Howey* test is that the investor must make the contribution with the expectation that she will receive profits from the venture. Profits can include any manner of returns, including periodic payments, appreciation in value, dividends, and more.[70]

Solely from the Entrepreneurial or Managerial Efforts of Others: The fourth factor of the *Howey* test is that the profits reaped by the investors are derived solely from the efforts of others. Courts have not strictly adhered to the requirement that the profits be "solely" from the efforts of others; instead, they have applied a flexible approach that focuses on "whether the efforts made by those other than the investor are the undeniably significant ones, those essential managerial efforts which affect the failure or success of the enterprise."[71]

In the end, whether something is deemed an investment contract (and therefore a security) depends more on the facts and circumstances of the offering than on the labels that people attach to it. It is important for ICO promoters not to lose sight of the fact that the substance of the offering, not the labels the promoter applies to it, will determine whether it is regarded as a security. For example, some promoters have taken to calling their token a "utility token" to distinguish it from a security token. However, as SEC chairman Clayton has observed, "[m]erely calling a token a

---

67 SEC v. Infinity Grp. Co., 212 F.3d 180, 187–88 (3d Cir. 2000).
68 SEC v. ETS Payphones, Inc., 300 F.3d 1281, 1284 (11th Cir. 2002).
69 SEC v. Glenn W. Turner Enters., 474 F.3d 476, 482 n.7 (9th Cir. 1973).
70 SEC v. Edwards, 540 U.S. 389, 390 (2004).
71 SEC v. Glenn W. Turner Enters., Inc., 474 F.2d 476, 482 (9th Cir. 1973).

'utility' token or structuring it to provide some utility does not prevent the token from being a security."[72] When promoters emphasize the potential for profits or the secondary market potential for tokens, they run the risk that their token will be regarded as a security and must mind the requirements of federal and state securities laws.

With this framework behind us, we next turn to discuss some of the enforcement actions that the SEC has brought involving cryptocurrencies and ICOs.

(c) SEC Enforcement Actions

(i) SEC v. Shavers[73]

One of the first actions brought by the SEC involving Bitcoin was against Trendon T. Shavers, an investment manager who bought and sold Bitcoin through his fund, Bitcoin Savings and Trust ("BTCST"), beginning in 2011. Shavers raised more than US$4.5 million worth of Bitcoin by offering 7 percent interest weekly (or 1 percent interest daily) that would continue until the investors withdrew their funds. Shavers allegedly facilitated offerings by posting and soliciting investors in an online forum where people shared Bitcoin-centric investment opportunities.

Shavers allegedly offered BTCST investments for approximately one year, during which time Shavers gave fraudulent assurances to bring in more investments and to deter investors from questioning the validity of BTCST's strategy and business dealings. Shavers represented online that BTCST's profits were high, risk was very low, and orders were steady and in high demand. To counter allegations of fraud, Shavers repeatedly assured both current and potential investors that he conducted his business in a manner that ensured that "risk is almost 0" and that when he sells his clients' Bitcoins, "[a]nything not covered is hedged or I take the risk personally."[74]

The SEC brought claims against Shavers and BTCST under Section 17(a) of the Securities Act, Section 10(b) and Rule 10b-5 of the Exchange Act, and Sections 5(a) and 5(c) of the Securities Act. The basis of the claims under Section 17(a) and Section 10(b) was that Shavers defrauded investors by

---

72 Chairman Jay Clayton, *Statement on Cryptocurrencies and Initial Coin Offerings*, SEC (Dec. 11, 2017), https://www.sec.gov/news/public-statement/statement-clayton-2017-12-11.

73 SEC v. Shavers, No. 4:13CV00416, 2013 WL 3810441 (E.D. Tex. July 23, 2013).

74 Complaint, SEC v. Shavers, SEC, https://www.sec.gov/litigation/complaints/2013/comp-pr2013-132.pdf.

making untrue statements of material fact. The SEC sued under Section 5 on the basis that an investment in a fund that holds Bitcoin is a security and that the security was unregistered and not sold pursuant to an exemption from registration. It is important to note that it was the interests in Shavers's fund that the SEC regarded as a security, not the Bitcoin that the fund was purportedly investing in. The court ruled in favor of the SEC on all of its claims, concluding that Shavers and BTCST had violated various securities laws and enjoining them from further violating Section 17(a), Section 10(b), Rule 10b-5, and Sections 5(a) and 5(c). Additionally, the court ruled that Shavers and BTCST were jointly and severally liable for a total of US$40,404,667, representing the illicit profits from the fraudulent offering. Shavers and BTCST were also each fined US$150,000.

(ii) SEC v. Garza[75]

In 2015, the SEC brought another enforcement action against a company offering investment interests in Bitcoin. This case involved investments in cryptocurrency mining operations. According to the SEC's complaint, in March 2014, Homero "Josh" Garza started a company called GAW Miners, LLC to acquire cryptocurrency mining equipment and resell it to customers, who took ownership and possession of the equipment. Garza then began to offer customers hosted mining services. Instead of shipping customers the equipment, Garza and GAW Miners offered to host the hardware at a datacenter. People could access the hardware remotely through the internet, and GAW Miners would be responsible for storing and maintaining the hardware in exchange for a fee. Customers maintained complete control over their equipment and how it was used.

Only a few weeks after GAW Miners began offering this new service, there was another shift in the business's focus. According to the SEC's complaint, Garza decided to create an alternate company, ZenMiner, LLC that offered cloud-based hosted mining services. Users of this service were more limited in how they could use their equipment compared to those who used the hosted mining service. With the cloud-hosting services, customers could only direct their equipment to mine through a handful of mining pools established by ZenMiner.

Garza then changed the services again. This time, he offered customers the chance to buy "Hashlets." A "Hashlet" represented an amount of computing power but did not represent an interest in any piece of computer

---

75 Complaint, SEC v. Garza, No. 15-CV-01760 (D. Conn. Dec. 1, 2015), https://www.sec.gov/litigation/complaints/2015/comp23415.pdf.

hardware. Customers who bought Hashlets were entitled to a share of the profits that Garza and his companies earned through their own mining operations. The SEC claimed that Garza misrepresented that Hashlets were always profitable and that Hashlets were supported by ZenMiner's actual mining operations. In fact, the SEC alleged, mining activity through ZenMiner was virtually nonexistent. The SEC also claimed that Garza oversold the Hashlets and did not have the mining power to support the amount of Hashlets that were sold.

The SEC claimed that the Hashlets constituted investment contracts and thus securities under the federal securities laws and that Garza and his companies had made fraudulent statements in connection with the offer and sale of such securities in violation of Section 10(b) and Rule 10b-5 of the Exchange Act and Section 17(a) of the Securities Act. In addition, the SEC claimed that Garza and his companies violated Sections 5(a) and 5(c) of the Securities Act because they did not register the Hashlets as securities. As part of a settlement that was reached in October 2017, the court enjoined Garza from further violating Section 17(a), Rule 10b-5, Section 10(b), and Sections 5(a) and 5(c) and ordered him to disgorge US$9,182,000, plus interest of US$742,774.

(iii) SEC v. REcoin Group Foundation[76]

The first enforcement action the SEC took against the promoter of an ICO came in late September 2017, roughly two months after the SEC released the DAO Report. In that case, the SEC sued Maksim Zaslavskiy and two companies he controlled, REcoin Group Foundation, LLC ("REcoin") and Diamond Reserve Club ("Diamond"). The SEC alleged that the companies (i) misrepresented that the offerings were backed by various assets. (ii) exaggerated the amount of funds already raised. and (iii) lied about being advised by a professional advisory team.

According to the SEC's complaint, to encourage investors to purchase REcoin tokens, Zaslavskiy and REcoin made several false or misleading representations and omissions to REcoin ICO investors, including investment in REcoin is far more stable and safer than other token investments because REcoin is backed by secure real estate investments in strong economies, which lends itself to potentially high returns; 2.8 million tokens have been sold; REcoin is led and advised by a group of skilled brokers, lawyers, and developers, who advised REcoin in which real estate it should

---

76   Complaint, SEC v. REcoin Grp. Found., LLC, No. 1:17-cv-05725 (E.D.N.Y. Sept. 29, 2017), https://www.sec.gov/litigation/complaints/2017/comp-pr2017-185.pdf.

invest and developed sound strategies for REcoin; and the company is complying with the law.

In addition to the REcoin ICO, Zaslavskiy issued another ICO through Diamond, according to the SEC's allegations. To promote the security and stability of the Diamond ICO, Zaslavskiy allegedly marketed the tokens by falsely stating that they were backed by physical diamonds (similar to the claim that the REcoin tokens were backed by real estate). Zaslavskiy also allegedly marketed the investment in Diamond as an "Initial Membership Offering" rather than an Initial Coin Offering.

The SEC brought claims against REcoin and Diamond under Section 10(b) and Rule 10b-5 of the Exchange Act, Section 17(a) of the Securities Act, and Sections 5(a) and 5(c) of the Securities Act and brought claims against Zaslavskiy for aiding and abetting the companies. The SEC claimed that the "membership" interests were actually securities subject to regulation. The court approved the SEC's request for emergency relief, froze all the defendants' assets, and ordered the defendants to repatriate all funds, assets, and other property. The litigation has been stayed pending the outcome of a parallel criminal proceeding.

REcoin has emphasized several important lessons for potential issuers and market participants interested in token offerings. First, merely labeling a token as something other than a security is not enough to avoid SEC scrutiny; whether something is a security depends on the facts and circumstances of the offering. Second, the SEC likely will treat ICOs that are marketed as investment opportunities that have potential for financial growth and return as securities offerings. Finally, ICO promoters must be very careful about the accuracy of public statements concerning their offering.

(iv) SEC v. PlexCorps[77]

In late September 2017, the SEC created a "Cyber Unit" to target a range of cyber misconduct, including hacking for nonpublic information, disrupting trading platforms, spreading false information through social media, and abusing blockchain technology and ICOs. The Cyber Unit wasted no time in addressing the latter issue, bringing two enforcement actions related to ICOs in less than a two-week span in December 2017.

The first enforcement action the Cyber Unit brought was against PlexCorps, Dominic Lacroix, and Sabrina Paradis-Royer for allegedly

---

77 Complaint, SEC v. PlexCorps, No. 1:17-cv-07007 (E.D.N.Y. Dec. 1, 2017), https://www .sec.gov/litigation/complaints/2017/comp-pr2017-219.pdf.

swindling investor funds through a fraudulent token offering of PlexCoin tokens. In July 2017, PlexCorps announced its ICO, which was to begin on August 7, 2017. According to the SEC's complaint, PlexCorps made many false and misleading statements and omissions while conducting the PlexCoin ICO. For example, in response to a question of what the potential return on investment would be for PlexCoin, the PlexCorps website allegedly said that the return on investment could range from 200 percent to 1,354 percent in less than a month, depending on the stage in which an investor purchases her PlexCoin.

The SEC filed a lawsuit against Lacroix and PlexCorps under Section 10(b) and Rule 10b-5 of the Exchange Act, Section 17(a) of the Securities Act, and Sections 5(a) and 5(c) of the Securities Act and brought claims against Paradis-Royer for aiding and abetting Lacroix and PlexCorps. The SEC alleged that the PlexCoin tokens were securities and were not offered or sold pursuant to a registration statement or any exemptions from registration. In support of this, the SEC alleged that PlexCorps analogized its offering to an IPO and said that the PlexCoin would appreciate in value based on the work of the PlexCorps team. In December 2017, the court granted the SEC's motion for a preliminary injunction against the defendants and froze their assets, pending the outcome of the litigation.

(v) In the Matter of Munchee Inc.[78]

Until December 2017, the SEC had focused its enforcement work in the ICO space on cases where there were allegations of fraud. On December 11, 2017, following a brief investigation by the Cyber Unit, the SEC announced that it had accepted an offer of settlement from Munchee Inc. in regard to Munchee's offering of so-called MUN tokens where there was no allegation of fraud. Munchee was a California start-up business that created an iPhone application for users to review restaurants and post photos of meals. Under the settlement, Munchee agreed to cease and desist from violating Sections 5(a) and 5(c) of the Securities Act.

According to the SEC's findings, which Munchee did not admit or deny, the MUN tokens were part of an overall ecosystem in which Munchee would pay users for food reviews with the tokens and sell advertisements to restaurants in exchange for the tokens. Eventually,

---

78 Order Instituting Cease-and-Desist Proceedings Pursuant to Section 8a of the Securities Act of 1933, Making Findings, and Imposing a Cease-and-Desist Order, In the Matter of Munchee Inc., SEC Administrative Proceeding No. 3-18304 (Dec. 11, 2017), https://www.sec.gov/litigation/admin/2017/33-10445.pdf.

Munchee said, the MUN tokens could even be used to buy food. The SEC concluded that the MUN tokens were investment contracts for various reasons. The MUN tokens did not have immediate functionality because no one could use them to buy goods or services at the time of the offering. Rather, people discussing the tokens online commented on their future utility, and Munchee itself said that it would use the ICO proceeds to further develop the Munchee iPhone application and the token ecosystem. Significantly, the SEC concluded that even if the MUN tokens had practical use at the time of the offering, it would not preclude them from being a security. Also, Munchee promoted the tokens by touting how they could appreciate in value over time as a result of more people joining the ecosystem and discussed the potential for trading the tokens on the secondary market. Yet another indicator that the MUN tokens were securities, according to the SEC's findings, was that Munchee focused its promotional efforts on people interested in investing in Bitcoin and other digital assets, rather than on restaurant owners or current users of the Munchee application.

Munchee started the ICO on October 31, 2017, but shut it down the next day, when it was contacted by the SEC. In total, Munchee raised about 200 Ether (equal to roughly $60,000 at the time of the offering). Munchee did not issue the MUN token to purchasers and instead unilaterally terminated the contracts for sale and returned the money to the buyers. The SEC did not impose a civil penalty, due to Munchee's prompt remedial action and cooperation with the SEC. In the end, this action reinforces that the SEC views how a token is offered and promoted as very important in determining whether it is a security.

(d) Other SEC Guidance

In addition to enforcement actions, the SEC has provided guidance to the marketplace regarding ICOs and cryptocurrencies through a series of investor alerts. The investor alerts include, among other things, guidance on (i) Bitcoin-related investments,[79] (ii) pump-and-dump schemes by companies that associated with blockchain

---

79 *Investor Alert: Bitcoin and Other Virtual Currency-Related Investments,* SEC (May 7, 2014), https://www.investor.gov/additional-resources/news-alerts/alerts-bulletins/investor-alert-bitcoin-other-virtual-currency.

technology and cryptocurrencies,[80] and (iii) celebrity endorsements of ICOs.[81]

(e) Private Securities Litigation Related to ICOs

In recent months, private plaintiffs have brought lawsuits against the promoters of ICOs for alleged violations of securities laws. The risk of private litigation further emphasizes the importance of conducting an ICO in a compliant manner. Below we summarize a few such private litigations.

(i) Tezos

As noted above, in 2017, Tezos became one of the most successful ICOs to date, raising US$232 million from the sale of Tezos tokens, or "Tezzies." Unfortunately, the afterglow faded as reports of delays and conflict among the company leaders began to emerge. The Tezos tokens and the Tezos blockchain had been developed by a company called Dynamic Ledger Solutions Inc. (DLS), which was founded by a couple named Arthur and Kathleen Breitman. The Breitmans had hired Johann Gevers to oversee the Tezos Foundation, a Swiss nonprofit entity that was created to foster the development of the Tezos blockchain. Disputes among the Breitmans and Gevers have given some investors in the Tezzies cause for concern. The Breitmans, along with DLS, are facing multiple lawsuits stemming from the July 2017 ICO. The Tezos Foundation is also a named defendant in the lawsuits. The main allegation in the lawsuits is that the Tezos ICO constituted an unregistered offer and sale of securities in violation of either the federal securities laws or state law.

The first proposed class action, *Baker v. Dynamic Ledger Solutions Inc.,*[82] was initially filed in California state court on October 25, 2017. DLS subsequently removed the case to the U.S. District Court for the Northern District of California. In addition to alleging that the Tezos ICO was an illegal unregistered offering, the plaintiff also asserted federal securities fraud claims as well as claims of false advertising and unfair competition under California state law. Specifically, the plaintiff accused the Breitmans

---

80 *Investor Alert: Public Companies Making ICO-Related Claims*, SEC (Aug. 28, 2017), https://www.investor.gov/additional-resources/news-alerts/alerts-bulletins/investor-alert-public-companies-making-ico-related; *Investor Alert: Investment Newsletters Used as Tools for Fraud*, SEC (June 2, 2014), https://www.investor.gov/additional-resources/news-alerts/alerts-bulletins/investor-alert-investment-newsletters-used-tools.

81 *Investor Alert: Celebrity Endorsements*, SEC (Nov. 1, 2017), https://www.sec.gov/oiea/investor-alerts-and-bulletins/ia_celebrity.

82 Baker v. Dynamic Ledger Solutions Inc., 17-cv-06850 (N.D. Cal. Nov. 29, 2017).

of lying to buyers about the timing of the Tezos project and how the money raised would be used, calling the representations made by the Breitmans leading up to the ICO "either exaggerations or outright lies." A second proposed class action[83] was filed on November 13, 2017 in federal district court in Florida. However, on January 24, 2018, the plaintiff voluntarily dismissed that case without prejudice.

In late November 2017, two additional lawsuits were filed, both in federal court in Northern California. The first, *GGCC, LLC v. Dynamic Ledger Solutions, Inc.*,[84] alleged federal securities law violations. In the second, *Okusko v. Dynamic Ledger Solutions, Inc.*,[85] the plaintiff also sued Tim Draper, a venture capitalist who held an ownership interest in DLS through his firm. The plaintiff alleged that Draper influenced or controlled the decision-making relating to the Tezos ICO, including the decision to engage in the sale of unregistered securities.

Another case, *MacDonald v. Dynamic Ledger Solutions, Inc.*,[86] was filed on December 13, 2017. In it, the plaintiff accused the Breitmans, DLS, Tezos Foundation, Draper, and others of violating California state law that prohibits the offer and sale of unregistered securities, as well as unfair business practices. The plaintiff moved for a fourteen-day temporary restraining order on December 14, 2017, to freeze the bank accounts of the Tezos Foundation to protect investors from Johann Gevers, but that motion was denied. The judge was unconvinced that plaintiff could seek a temporary restraining order on behalf of other Tezos investors without class certification, particularly since some of them had sided with the defendants, and because Tezos still had the funds to reimburse plaintiff.

The plaintiffs from all four of the Northern District of California cases (*Baker, GGCC, LLC, Okusko,* and *MacDonald*) moved to consolidate their cases on December 26, 2017, but subsequently withdrew their motion to allow them to meet and confer further concerning the form of coordination or consolidation. On January 25, 2018, four parties filed motions in *GGCC* to consolidate the Tezos cases and sought appointment as lead plaintiff. Two movants (Trigon Trading Pty Ltd. and GGCC Group) sought to consolidate *Baker, GGCC,* and *Okusko* but not *MacDonald;* two

---

83   Gaviria v. Dynamic Ledger Solutions, Inc., 17-cv-01959-ORL-40-KRS (M.D. Fla. Nov. 13, 2017).

84   GGCC, LLC v. Dynamic Ledger Solutions, Inc., 17-cv-06779 (N.D. Cal. Nov. 26, 2017).

85   Okusko v. Dynamic Ledger Solutions, Inc., 17-cv-06829 (N.D. Cal. Nov. 28, 2017).

86   MacDonald v. Dynamic Ledger Solutions, Inc., 17-cv-07095 (RS) (N.D. Cal. Dec. 13, 2017).

other movants (Silver Miller Group and the Tezos Investor Group) sought to consolidate *MacDonald* and the other three cases (*Baker, GGCC,* and *Okusko*).

In the end, three of the four cases (*GGCC, Okusko,* and *MacDonald*) were consolidated under the caption *In re Tezos Securities Litigation,* 17-cv-06770-RS. The court was not persuaded by the argument that *Mac-Donald* should not be consolidated with *GGCC* and *Okusko* because it only asserted state law claims. The standard for consolidation under Rule 42, the court noted, was whether the cases had common questions of law or fact. Here, the cases all arose from the same facts (the Tezos ICO), rely on the same legal theory, seek the same relief, and were brought on behalf of the same putative class of California contributors to the ICO that is "entirely subsumed by classes in the other three actions." The *Baker* action will be coordinated with the consolidated case for case management purposes. In the consolidation order, the judge also noted that it is "quite possible" that Baker would be consolidated with the three other cases in the future, depending on the outcome of a case before the U.S. Supreme Court. All cases are being overseen by Judge Richard Seeborg.

(ii) Centra Tech

Another high-profile ICO has similarly led to an investor suit that alleges securities law violations. This one involved Centra Tech, a cryptocurrency start-up that used endorsements from Floyd Mayweather, Jr. and DJ Khaled to raise US$32 million in an ICO in September 2017. In December 2017, a proposed class action was filed in the U.S. District Court for the Southern District of Florida that alleges that Centra Tech and four of its senior members violated federal securities laws by selling unregistered securities.[87] The case did not include allegations of fraud.

The complaint claims that defendants sold Centra tokens during the ICO that it portrayed as "utility tokens" but were in fact securities. Investors in the ICO point to the defendants' assertions that the Centra tokens would be worth more than Ether, Bitcoin, Litecoin, and other digital currencies as evidence that the Centra tokens are in fact securities. Further, the defendants' marketing referred to the ICO participants as "investors" and commented on the "growth potential" of the Centra tokens. In combination, the plaintiffs claimed, these facts demonstrate that the ICO was an offer and sale of securities. Additionally, the senior members allegedly violated

---

87   Rensel v. Centra Tech, Inc., 17-cv-24500 (JLK) (S.D. Fla. Dec. 13, 2017).

the Securities Act when they influenced or controlled the decision to sell unregistered securities via the ICO. Defendants moved to compel arbitration and to stay the complaint or, in the alternative, to dismiss the case for failure to state a claim and for lack of subject-matter jurisdiction.

On April 2, 2018, the SEC filed a lawsuit against two principals of Centra Tech in the Southern District of New York.[88] The complaint alleged that the defendants violated the antifraud provisions of the Exchange Act and the Securities Act and engaged in an illegal unregistered securities offering in connection with the Centra ICO. The SEC claimed that the defendants fraudulently promoted the ICO by claiming that Centra had partnered with Visa, MasterCard, and The Bancorp. Also, the defendants allegedly distributed marketing materials that included fake biographies of people who purportedly were associated with Centra Tech. The two defendants were arrested by criminal authorities the day before the SEC filed its complaint and are facing criminal charges for securities fraud, wire fraud, and conspiracy.[89]

✳✳✳

At the time this book went to publication, no court had ruled on the key question at the heart of these disputes: whether and in what circumstances cryptoassets are securities. However, that precise issue has been raised by Maksim Zaslavskiy, the founder of REcoin and Diamond, as a basis for dismissing the criminal indictment currently pending against him, and a hearing was held in May 2018.[90] As private lawsuits, SEC enforcement actions, and criminal cases proceed, we anticipate that a number of courts will address that issue. Any rulings on this issue will be welcome to legal practitioners and markets participants alike, because they will start the development of an important body of law that will either affirm or supplant interpretations made by the SEC and securities lawyers who have to date been grappling to understand the applicability of 20th-century laws to 21st-century technology.

(f) Capital Raising Implications

As the discussion above suggests, the SEC has put significant resources toward charging promoters of ICOs with fraudulent and illegal unregistered offerings. In addition, there is a risk that private investors will bring their own

---

88 SEC v. Sharma, 18-cv-02909, (S.D.N.Y. Apr. 2, 2018).
89 U.S. v. Sharma, et al., 18-cr-00340 (S.D.N.Y.).
90 U.S. v. Zaslavskiy, 17-cr-0647 (E.D.N.Y.).

securities lawsuits based on similar allegations in connection with an ICO. For those contemplating an ICO, this reinforces the importance of understanding the securities laws and ensuring that the ICO complies with relevant laws and regulations. To meet this challenge, potential ICO promoters might consider several different capital raising approaches.

Registered Offerings: An ICO promoter could take the view that the token is a security and register it with the SEC under Section 5 of the Securities Act. As discussed above, this requires the filing of a registration statement with the SEC and addressing any concerns by the SEC staff before the registration statement is declared effective and the issuer is permitted to sell to investors. It also requires the issuer to file with the registration statement a prospectus that includes risks associated with the offering, details about the issuer's leadership, and audited financial disclosures, among other things.

An offering under Section 5 enables the ICO promoter to raise large amounts of funds from all investor types and allows nonaffiliate purchasers maximum freedom to resell their tokens on the secondary market. While these advantages are appealing, an offering under Section 5 comes with significant costs, which are often prohibitive for ICO promoters who tend to be in the early stages of development. It can require anywhere from six months to a year or longer to complete the registration process and therefore has not been a popular avenue for many ICO promoters to date. Also, the issuer may be required or elect to register under the Exchange Act, which requires the company to file annual reports, quarterly reports, and current reports. Further, the characterization of a token as a "security" may require additional registrations (and costs) under the Advisers Act and the Investment Company Act.

Exempt Offerings: Rather than doing a registered offering, some ICO promoters are selling their tokens in offerings that are exempt from the registration requirements of the Securities Act. Some of the advantages of an exempt offering may include: (i) quicker time to market; (ii) more efficient process; and (iii) greater flexibility regarding disclosures. Depending on the type of offering, some drawbacks may include: (i) limited liquidity of the security; (ii) publicity and marketing constraints; (iii) limited pool of investors; and (iv) burdensome compliance with state blue sky laws.

One available exemption to the registration requirements of the Securities Act is under amended Regulation A. Offerings made under this regulation are sometimes referred to as mini-IPOs, and the offering statements must be qualified by the SEC. Regulation A, as amended in June 2015 by Title IV of the Jumpstart Our Business Startups ("JOBS") Act, is intended to facilitate the ability of smaller companies to access capital.[91] The amended rules, which are often referred to as Regulation A+, permit two different tiers of public offerings, without the more demanding IPO process.

Some of the requirements of an offering under Regulation A+ are outside the scope of this chapter but a few warrant discussion here. Under tier 1, an issuer can raise up to US$20 million in a twelve-month period, with no more than US$6 million in sales by selling security-holders that are affiliates of the issuer. Under tier 2, an issuer can raise up to US$50 million in a twelve-month period, with no more than US$15 million in sales by selling security-holders that are affiliates of the issuer. Under both tiers, anyone is permitted to invest, but for tier 2 offerings, nonaccredited investors are capped at 10 percent of their annual income or net worth, whichever is greater (unless the securities are listed on a national exchange upon qualification). Tier 1 offerings do not have ongoing reporting obligations (unless required by Section 12(g) of the Exchange Act), but remain subject to state blue sky law regulations, whereas tier 2 offerings have ongoing reporting obligations and must provide audited financial statements, but are not subject to blue sky law regulations.

Another type of exemption from the registration requirements of the Securities Act permits the sale of securities in what are called "private placements." One such popular exemption is under Section 4(a)(2), which applies to transactions by issuers not involving a public offering. As explained above, Regulation D provides companies a "safe harbor" assurance and exemptions when certain conditions are satisfied.

Under Rule 506(b) of Regulation D, a company can raise an unlimited amount of money from an unlimited number of accredited investors, but may raise funds from no more than thirty-five unaccredited investors. And if such unaccredited investors purchase securities in the offering, (i) these investors must have financial and business knowledge to be able to evaluate the merits and risks of the investment and (ii) documents that are similar to those used in Regulation A or registered offerings, including financial statements, must be provided to them. In addition, Rule 506(b) of Regulation D does not allow general solicitation or advertising to market the securities, and if a company provides information to accredited investors, it must make that same information available to unaccredited investors. Under Rule 506(c), a company may raise an unlimited amount

---

91 *See generally Investor Bulletin: Regulation A*, SEC (July 8, 2015), https://www.sec.gov/oiea/investor-alerts-bulletins/ib_regulationa.html.

of money so long as the investors in the offering are all accredited investors and the company takes reasonable steps to verify that all are accredited investors. Rule 506(c) allows companies to broadly solicit and generally advertise the offering.

Under Rule 504 of Regulation D, a company can raise up to US$5 million in a twelve-month period, with no limitation on the number of investors, provided that the issuer complies with state securities laws. In certain circumstances, Rule 504 allows companies to engage in general solicitation and advertising but only if certain conditions are met, including limiting sales to accredited investors. Generally, securities issued under Rules 504 and 506 are restricted securities and may not be sold for six months to a year without first being registered. Companies that offer securities under Regulation D must file a Form D electronically with the SEC after selling their securities.

One method of conducting a Regulation D offering that has been discussed extensively in the ICO community is the so-called Simple Agreement for Future Tokens. SAFTs, as these agreements are known, are designed to be investment contracts that are derived from Simple Agreements for Future Equity, which are used to generate capital from early stage investors. SAFTs were developed to help mitigate some of the risk associated with selling tokens to the public in an ICO. With SAFTs, the investors immediately fund projects promoted by developers through ICOs. The developers use the funds to create "a functional network, with genuinely functional utility tokens, and then deliver those tokens to the investors once functional."[92] The idea behind the SAFT is that while the SAFT is admittedly a security, the functional tokens that are later delivered to the SAFT investors are consumptive in nature and therefore need not be registered under the securities laws. Certain ICOs have been launched using SAFTs, including the Filecoin offering discussed above. Some commentators have raised concerns about the SAFT framework, questioning whether it could raise greater risk under the federal securities laws.[93]

---

92 Juan Batiz-Benet, Marco Santori, & Jesse Clayburg, *The SAFT Project: Toward a Compliant Token Sale Framework*, Protocol Labs & Cooley LLP (Oct. 2, 2017), https://saftproject.com/static/SAFT-Project-Whitepaper.pdf.

93 *Not So Fast—Risks Related to the Use of a "SAFT" for Token Sales*, Research Report #1, Cardozo Blockchain Project (Nov. 21, 2017), https://cardozo.yu.edu/sites/default/files/Cardozo%20Blockchain%20Project%20-%20Not%20So%20Fast%20-%20SAFT%20Response_final.pdf.

At the time of publication, no single consensus has emerged on the best approach to an ICO. Given the variety of tokens being created in the marketplace, there is no one-size-fits-all solution. Promoters must evaluate carefully what rights their tokens are meant to offer, understand the restrictions imposed by the securities laws, and with the guidance of skilled securities lawyers determine the best way to proceed. In some cases, that will mean that the token should not be offered before it is compatible with a functional and well-developed network. Even then, there is no guarantee that the token will not be regarded as a security by the SEC, a litigious private plaintiff, or a court called on to decide the issue. As SEC chairman Clayton has observed, most ICOs he has seen contain at least some hallmarks of a security. Accordingly, a conservative approach to ICOs is advisable until clearer guidance is provided.

(g) State Enforcement and Blue Sky Laws

To this point, we have addressed federal securities laws. But it is important for businesses developing blockchain applications focused on the financial industry to also keep in mind state blue sky laws. Each state has adopted its own set of regulations to protect investors against securities fraud. The laws vary by state but typically require sellers to register their offerings, provide financial disclosures, and ensure that there are no material misstatements or omissions in connection with their offerings. Many states follow the *Howey* test when it comes to defining an investment contract, although state courts have varied in their interpretation and application of the *Howey* test. But some follow the risk capital test, which looks at several factors including how the funds are being used, to whom the offering is being made, the ability of the investors to influence the success of the enterprise, and whether the investor's money is substantially at risk because it is inadequately secured.[94]

State regulators have followed the lead of the SEC in policing the cryptocurrency market recently. For example, the Texas Securities Commissioner issued a cease-and-desist order to a Dubai-based company and two residents of the United States related to their offer of interests in Bitcoin mining contracts in Texas.[95] On the heels of that action, the Texas Securities Commissioner issued another emergency cease-and-desist order

---

94   Silver Hills Country Club v. Sobieski, 55 Cal. 2d 811 (Cal. 1961).

95   Emergency Cease and Desist Order, *In the Matter of USI-Tech Limited*, No. ENF-17-CDO-1753, Texas State Securities Board (Dec. 20, 2017), https://www.ssb.texas.gov/sites/default/files/USI-Tech%20ENF-17-CDO-1753.pdf.

to halt multiple investment programs tied to a cryptographic token issued by BitConnect, a British company.[96] Both orders arose out of an enforcement sweep into cryptocurrency offerings that the Texas State Securities Board initiated starting in late 2017. Those investigations led to at least ten cease-and-desist orders. These orders are predicated on the notion that the offerings are securities under the Texas Securities Act but were not registered as required by law.

Other state securities regulators have taken similar measures. For instance, New Jersey's Bureau of Securities issued a cease-and-desist order against Bitstrade for offering investors the opportunity to contribute Bitcoin to an investment pool.[97] New Jersey took the position that the offering was an unregistered security under state law and claimed that it was done fraudulently.[98] Likewise, the Massachusetts securities regulator filed an administrative complaint against an ICO promoter for failure to register its token.[99] And the North American Securities Administrators Association ("NASAA")—whose members include sixty-seven state, provincial, and territorial securities administrators—has cautioned investors about cryptocurrencies and identified ICOs as an emerging investor threat for 2018.[100] NASAA also has stated that more regulation is needed for cryptocurrency to provide greater investor protection.

In contrast with those states that have pursued enforcement actions, Wyoming has pursued a more welcoming approach in an effort to become what some have described as a haven for cryptocurrency companies. In March 2018, the governor of Wyoming signed into law several statutes regarding cryptocurrencies. In one such statute, Wyoming lawmakers

---

96 Emergency Cease and Desist Order, *In the Matter of BitConnect*, No. ENF-18-CDO-1754, Texas State Securities Board (Jan. 4, 2018), https://www.ssb.texas.gov/sites/default/files/BitConnect_ENF-18-CDO-1754.pdf.

97 Summary Cease and Desist Order, *In the Matter of Bitstrade*, State of New Jersey Bureau of Securities (Feb. 9, 2018), http://www.njconsumeraffairs.gov/News/PressAttachments/02092018-press-attachment.pdf.

98 *Id.*

99 Administrative Complaint, *In the Matter of Caviar*, No. E-2017-0120, Commonwealth of Massachusetts Office of the Secretary of the Commonwealth, Securities Division (Jan. 17, 2018), http://www.sec.state.ma.us/sct/current/sctbensonoff/Administrative-Complaint-E-2017-0120.pdf.

100 *NASAA Reminds Investors to Approach Cryptocurrencies, Initial Coin Offerings and Other Cryptocurrency-Related Investment Products with Caution*, North American Securities Administrators Association (Jan. 4, 2018), http://www.nasaa.org/44073/nasaa-reminds-investors-approach-cryptocurrencies-initial-coin-offerings-cryptocurrency-related-investment-products-caution/.

amended the Wyoming Securities Act (W.S. 17-4-101 through 17-4-701) to provide an exemption for certain cryptographic tokens.[101] The law states that developers or sellers of "an open blockchain token shall not be deemed the issuer of a security" if certain conditions are met. One of these conditions is that the token being offered must have a consumptive purpose. Another is that the developer or seller may not sell the token as a financial investment. For this second condition, Wyoming law will look at how the token was marketed. The statutory definition of an "open block-chain token" is a digital unit that is:

(i) Created:

(A) In response to the verification or collection of a specified number of transactions relating to a digital ledger or database;

(B) By deploying computer code to a blockchain network that allows for the creation of digital tokens or other units; or

(C) Using any combination of the methods specified in sub-paragraphs (A) and (B) of this paragraph.

(ii) Recorded in a digital ledger or database which is chronological, consensus-based, decentralized and mathematically verified in nature, especially relating to the supply of units and their dis-tribution; and

(iii) Capable of being traded or transferred between persons without an intermediary or custodian of value.[102]

5. COMMODITIES LAWS AND REGULATIONS

(a) The Commodity Exchange Act

The Commodity Exchange Act (the "CEA"),[103] which is administered by the CFTC, regulates exchange-traded commodity futures and options and, as one of the primary consequences of the Dodd-Frank Act, over-the-counter ("OTC") swaps[104] (other than security-based swaps, which

---

101 W.S. 17-4-206.

102 W.S. 17-4-206(e).

103 Codified as amended at 7 U.S.C. §§ 1 *et seq.* References herein to "Section ___" of the CEA will be to the codification in Title 7 of the United States Code.

104 CEA, Section 2(a)(1)(A). For the sake of precision, the CEA does not regulate so-called security-based swaps (e.g., total return swaps and credit default swaps on a single security or

are regulated under the securities laws). "Commodity" is defined broadly under the CEA to include a lengthy series of "enumerated" agricultural items ("except onions . . . and motion picture box office receipts") as well as "all services, rights, and interests . . . in which contracts for future delivery are presently or in the future dealt in."[105] Energy, metals, foreign currencies and even interest rates, credit risk, and climactic variances from the norm are recognized as nonenumerated "commodities" for which futures contracts are traded on exchanges in the United States and internationally.

Exchange-traded futures, options, and swaps are characterized by their standardization in terms of quantity, grade, delivery date, and location. Their fungibility makes them amenable to hedging parties with dynamic needs and to speculators who can trade in and out of positions without the desire or ability to undertake the actual physical delivery mechanics at contract maturity. Another feature of the markets for futures and sufficiently liquid swaps is that all contracts are "cleared," which means that a central counterparty ultimately backed by the creditworthiness of all market participants stands between all counterparties and renders the creditworthiness of any particular market participant irrelevant. However, for swaps that are insufficiently liquid or that for policy reasons are not required to be cleared, counterparties to the original transaction bear the credit risk.

The CEA also includes restrictions on where and with whom futures and swaps may be transacted. Futures and certain particularly liquid swaps may only lawfully be transacted on boards of trade, designated contract markets, or "swap execution facilities."[106] Moreover, only "eligible contract participants" (markets participants deemed sophisticated by virtue of their regulated status or merely by virtue of their assets) may lawfully enter into OTC swaps.[107]

Taken to its logical extreme, the CEA would prohibit the commercial ("off-exchange") sale of this season's wheat crop in advance to one's next-door neighbor. The CFTC has accordingly for decades recognized a "forward contract" exemption from the CEA, which requires the intent on the part of buyer and seller to make or take actual physical delivery of the

---

loan or on a "narrow-based index" of such securities or loans), which are regulated under the securities laws.

105 CEA, Section 1a(9).

106 CEA, Sections 2(h)(8) (swaps) and 6(a) (contracts for the purchase or sale of a commodity for future delivery).

107 CEA, Section 2(e).

underlying commodity.[108] Another pertinent carve-out from coverage of the CEA is for off-exchange foreign exchange forwards and swaps, which similarly contemplate actual, physical delivery.

Although the CEA for the most part addresses derivatives having an element of "futurity" such as futures and swaps, the Dodd-Frank Act also extended the CEA's reach to fraud and market manipulation in connection with spot transactions involving a "contract for the sale of a commodity in interstate commerce"[109] and to purchases or sales of commodities on margin with noneligible contract participants that are not settled by way of physical delivery within twenty-eight days.[110]

(b) CFTC Enforcement Actions

(i) In the Matter of Coinflip, Inc. [111]

Like the SEC, the CFTC has brought a number of enforcement actions against businesses involved in cryptocurrencies and ICOs. The earliest such action occurred in September 2015, when the CFTC announced that that it had accepted an offer of settlement from Coinflip, Inc. d/b/a Derivabit and Francisco Riordan. In that matter, the CFTC found that Coinflip had advertised Derivabit as a "risk management platform ... that connects buyers and sellers of standardized Bitcoin options and futures contract." Coinflip permitted trading of numerous put and call options contracts on the Derivabit platform and designated Bitcoin as the asset underlying the option.

The CFTC charged Coinflip with violating Section 4c(b) of the CEA, because it offered commodity option transactions and confirmed the existence of commodity option transactions without complying with necessary regulations. It also charged Coinflip with violating Section 5h(a)(1) of the CEA, because it operated a facility for the trading of swaps without proper registration. The most significant part of the settled action, however, was the fact that the CFTC declared that "Bitcoin and other virtual currencies

---

108   *See, e.g., Statutory Interpretation Concerning Forward Transactions*, 55 Fed. Reg. 39188 (Sept. 25, 1990).

109   CEA, Section 6b(a)(1).

110   CEA, Section 2(c)(2)(D).

111   Order Instituting Proceedings Pursuant to Sections 6(c) and 6(d) of the Commodity Exchange Act, Making Findings and Imposing Remedial Sanctions, *In the Matter of Coinflip, Inc. d/b/a Derivabit*, No. 15-29, CFTC (Sept. 17, 2015), https://www.cftc.gov/sites/default/files/idc/ groups/public/%40lrenforcementactions/documents/legalpleading/enfcoinfliprorder09172015 .pdf.

are encompassed in the definition and properly defined as commodities" under Section 1a(9) of the CEA.[112] Based on this conclusion, the CFTC has claimed jurisdiction to pursue multiple enforcement actions involving cryptocurrencies and ICOs since the Coinflip matter.

(ii) CFTC v. Gelfman[113]

The CFTC brought its first enforcement action for alleged fraud in the offer or sale of cryptocurrencies in the spot market in September 2017, in *CFTC v. Gelman Blueprint, Inc., et al.* In *Gelfman*, the CFTC alleged that the defendants operated a Bitcoin Ponzi scheme in which they solicited investors to a pooled investment fund that purportedly used high-frequency trading strategies to trade Bitcoin.

The CFTC claimed that the defendants solicited roughly US$600,000 from at least eighty investors through fraudulent solicitations and misleading representations in violation of Section 6(c)(1) and Regulation 180.1(a) of the CEA. These provisions, which were enacted as part of the Dodd-Frank Act, prohibit fraud in connection with the sale of any commodity in interstate commerce.

Among other allegations, the CFTC claimed that the defendants made false statements about investor returns, assets under management, and information accessible to investors on the customer dashboard. In addition, the CFTC alleged that the defendants provided false account statements and misappropriated customer funds. The CFTC is seeking a permanent injunction, civil penalties, restitution, and disgorgement, among other relief. With this case, the CFTC announced that it sees itself as having an important role to play in stamping out fraud in connection with the cryptocurrency marketplace.

(iii) CFTC v. My Big Coin Pay[114]

The CFTC followed the *Gelfman* case with a raft of lawsuits in early 2018. The first enforcement action alleged that defendants My Big Coin Pay, Randall Carter, and Mark Gillespie fraudulently offered a virtual currency called My Big Coin for sale, raising roughly US$6 million from at least twenty-eight customers. According to the complaint, the defendants misrepresented that the coin was being traded on several currency exchanges, falsely reported the daily trading price, and fraudulently claimed that the

112 *Id.*
113 CFTC v. Gelfman Blueprint, Inc, No. 17-7181 (S.D.N.Y. Sept. 21, 2017).
114 CFTC v. My Big Coin Pay, Inc. et al, No. 1:2018cv10077 (Mass Dist. Ct. Jan. 16, 2018).

coin was backed by gold. In reality, the CFTC alleged, any payouts made to customers were derived from funds fraudulently obtained from other customers in a Ponzi scheme.

The CFTC claimed that the defendants misappropriated nearly all of the money contributed to purchase a home, antiques, fine art, jewelry, and other luxury goods. The CFTC claimed that these fraudulent practices violated Section 6(c)(1) and Regulation 180.1(a) of the CEA and is seeking a permanent injunction, civil penalties, restitution, and disgorgement, among other penalties.

(iv) CFTC v. Dillon Michael Dean[115]

The second in the CFTC's series of suits was filed against Dillon Michael Dean and his company The Entrepreneurs Headquarters, Ltd. for allegedly soliciting fraudulently US$1.1 million worth of Bitcoin from more than 600 people to participate in a pooled investment vehicle for trading commodity interests. The CFTC also claimed that the defendants failed to register as a commodity pool operator and an associated person in violation of the CEA.

The CFTC asserted that the defendants made false statements and material omissions regarding Dean's experience and track record and that they falsely claimed that 40 percent of the funds would be traded in binary options and the remainder held in reserve in Bitcoins to fund customer withdrawals. The defendants also allegedly misappropriated customer funds and lied to customers about their account balances. The CFTC claimed that the defendants violated Sections 4c(b), 4k(2), 4m(1), and 4o(1)(A)–(B) of the CEA and Regulations 3.12(a) and 32.4 and seeks a permanent injunction, civil penalties, restitution, and disgorgement, among other penalties.

(v) CFTC v. McDonnell and CabbageTech[116]

The third in the series of lawsuits by the CFTC in early 2018 alleged that Patrick McDonnell and his company CabbageTech, Inc. fraudulently induced customers to send virtual currencies to them in exchange for virtual currency trading advice and for virtual currency purchases. Upon receipt of the funds, the defendants allegedly stopped communicating with the customers and misappropriated the funds.

---

115 CFTC v. Dean, No. 18-CV-0345 (E.D.N.Y. Jan. 18, 2018).
116 CFTC v. McDonnell, No. 18-CV-0361 (E.D.N.Y. Jan. 18, 2018).

The CFTC claimed that these fraudulent practices violated Section 6(c)(1) and Regulation 180.1(a) of the CEA and is seeking a permanent injunction, civil penalties, restitution, and disgorgement, among other penalties. On March 6, 2018, the court issued an order regarding the threshold jurisdictional question—namely, whether the CFTC has authority to bring the action.

Specifically, the court addressed (1) whether virtual currency may be regulated by the CFTC as a commodity and (2) whether the amendments to the CEA under the Dodd-Frank Act permit the CFTC to exercise its jurisdiction over fraud that does not directly involve the sale of futures or derivative contracts. The court held that virtual currency is a commodity that can be regulated by the CFTC and that the CFTC has broad authority that extends to fraud and manipulation both in derivatives markets and underlying spot markets.

(c) Other CFTC Guidance

Like the SEC, the CFTC has provided guidance to participants in the cryptocurrency and ICO marketplace. As early as 2014, then CFTC Chairman Timothy Massad discussed virtual currencies and potential CFTC oversight under the CEA, noting that the "CFTC's jurisdiction with respect to virtual currencies will depend on the facts and circumstances pertaining to any particular activity in question." He further stated that "[d]erivative contracts based on a virtual currency represent one area within our responsibility."[117]

It was not until 2015, however, in the *Gelfman* case discussed above, that the CFTC formally stated its view that virtual currencies are commodities. On October 17, 2017, the CFTC issued a primer on virtual currencies, in which it explained its view of virtual currencies and related technologies, the role of the CFTC in overseeing virtual currency transactions, and the risks associated with virtual currencies.[118] In addition, in January 2018, CFTC Enforcement Director James McDonald issued a joint statement with the SEC Enforcement Co-Directors Stephanie Avakian and Steven Peikin, announcing that:

---

117 *Testimony of Chairman Timothy Massad Before the U.S. Senate Committee on Agriculture, Nutrition & Forestry*, CFTC (Dec. 10, 2014), http://www.cftc.gov/PressRoom/SpeechesTestimony/opamassad-6.

118 *A CFTC Primer on Virtual Currencies*, CFTC (Oct. 17, 2017), http://www.cftc.gov/idc/groups/public/documents/file/labcftc_primercurrencies100417.pdf.

When market participants engage in fraud under the guise of offering digital instruments—whether characterized as virtual currencies, coins, tokens, or the like—the SEC and the CFTC will look beyond form, examine the substance of the activity and prosecute violations of the federal securities and commodities laws.

The Divisions of Enforcement for the SEC and CFTC will continue to address violations and to bring actions to stop and prevent fraud in the offer and sale of digital instruments.[119]

CFTC chairman Christopher Giancarlo testified before the Senate Banking Committee on February 6, 2018, regarding the CFTC's authority and oversight over virtual currencies. He noted that the CFTC does not have jurisdiction under the CEA to conduct regulatory oversight over spot transactions in virtual currencies, but the CFTC does have enforcement jurisdiction to investigate and bring civil enforcement actions against fraud and manipulation in virtual currency derivatives markets and spot markets.

In addition to this guidance, the CFTC has set up an initiative called LabCFTC "to promote responsible FinTech innovation and fair competition" for the public. It has a twofold mission:

- To promote responsible FinTech innovation to improve the quality, resiliency, and competitiveness of our markets; and
- To accelerate CFTC engagement with FinTech and RegTech solutions that may enable the CFTC to carry out its mission responsibilities more effectively and efficiently.[120]

Market participants are able to speak directly with CFTC staff about their FinTech innovations and collaborate regarding potential issues under the CEA. Through this program, the CFTC staff is attempting to proactively engage with the blockchain and cryptocurrency community.

6. TAX LAWS AND REGULATIONS

On March 25, 2014, the IRS provided guidance regarding the federal tax implications of transactions involving virtual currencies. It said that virtual currency operates like "real" currency and thus concluded that

---

119   *Joint Statement from CFTC and SEC Enforcement Directors Regarding Virtual Currency Enforcement Actions*, CFTC (Jan. 19, 2018), http://www.cftc.gov/PressRoom/SpeechesTestimony/mcdonaldstatement011918.

120   *LabCFTC Overview*, CFTC, http://www.cftc.gov/LabCFTC/Overview/index.htm.

"virtual currency is treated as property for U.S. federal tax purposes."[121] Accordingly, the IRS said that:

- Wages paid to employees using virtual currency are taxable to the employee, must be reported by an employer on a Form W-2, and are subject to federal income tax withholding and payroll taxes.
- Payments using virtual currency made to independent contractors and other service providers are taxable and self-employment tax rules generally apply. Normally, payers must issue Form 1099.
- The character of gain or loss from the sale or exchange of virtual currency depends on whether the virtual currency is a capital asset in the hands of the taxpayer.
- A payment made using virtual currency is subject to information reporting to the same extent as any other payment made in property.[122]

Although the IRS made this announcement in 2014, investors in cryptocurrencies were not quick to report their trading gains. In 2014, only 893 individuals reported a transaction related to Bitcoin, and in 2015, only 802 individuals reported such a transaction, according to an affidavit filed by an IRS agent in a court case.[123] Given the low level of reporting of taxable transactions, the IRS in November 2016 issued a broad summons to a large U.S.-based cryptocurrency exchange to obtain trading records. The exchange challenged the summons and ultimately reduced the scope of records that had to be turned over. In the end, the exchange was required to turn over information about those customers who had the Bitcoin equivalent of $20,000 or more in their accounts in any one year between 2013 and 2015, which included approximately 14,000 customers.

7. APPENDIX

The focus of this chapter has been on U.S. federal and state laws related to cryptocurrencies, ICOs, and other financial blockchain applications. Many ICOs are international in nature, however, so legal practitioners and market participants should have familiarity with relevant laws from other jurisdictions. Below we provide a summary of the laws related to ICOs from a selection of jurisdictions.

---

121 Notice 2014-21, IRS (Apr. 14, 2014), https://www.irs.gov/pub/irs-drop/n-14-21.pdf.
122 *Id.*
123 Rebecca Campbell, *Coinbase-IRS Lawsuit: Less Than 1,000 People Declare Bitcoin Earnings Each Year*, CCN.com (Mar. 20, 2017), https://www.irs.gov/pub/irs-drop/n-14-21.pdf; Affidavit of Utzke, U.S. v. Coinbase, Inc., No. 17-cv-01431-JSC (N.D. Cal. Nov. 28, 2017).

Jurisdiction	Summary
Australia	Although there is no specific legislation or regulation in Australia that expressly references ICOs, formal guidance (the Guidance) on the application of regulatory compliance policies to ICOs (INFO 225) was published in September 2017 by the Australian and Securities Investment Commission (ASIC).
	The Guidance essentially states that the legal status of an ICO is dependent on how the ICO is structured and operated and the rights attached to the digital token being offered.
	Some ICOs (or digital token offerings) may be classified under Australia's general consumer law, while other ICOs that offer digital tokens that would otherwise be considered as "financial products" will likely be regulated under the Corporations Act, which in turn requires a range of disclosure, registration, and licensing obligations.
	More specifically, the Corporations Act may apply:
	(i) where the value of, or rights attached to, a digital token offered in a particular ICO is related to the management of an arrangement that resembles a managed investment scheme (as defined within the Corporations Act);
	(ii) when the intention of an ICO is to fund a company (or an undertaking that resembles a company) and the rights attached to a digital token resemble rights commonly attached to a share and the issuer would need to prepare a prospectus as would be the case for an initial public offering; and/or

Jurisdiction	Summary
	(iii) where the digital token being issued derives its value from another underlying instrument or reference asset and a payment is required as part of the rights or obligations attached to the digital token (and the digital token is therefore considered to be a derivative).

Additionally, where any platform enables investors to buy (or be issued) or sell digital tokens that are found to be a financial product, such platform may be deemed to involve the operation of a financial market and the platform operator may therefore need to hold an Australian market license (unless covered by an exemption).

| France | The French Financial Market Authority (AMF) defines an ICO as a fundraising transaction realized through a DLT resulting in the issuance of digital tokens. |

In a consultation paper issued in November 2017 warning investors about the risks associated with ICOs (the "Consultation Paper"), the AMF did not qualify ICOs or digital tokens under French law but did analyze how the characteristics of the digital tokens issued, and in particular the likelihood that digital tokens could be characterized as financial instruments (capital securities, debt securities, Collective Investments in Transferable Securities (UCITS) or Financial Alternative Funds (FIA), may result in such ICO falling within the scope of the French regulatory framework.

Generally speaking, under French law, digital tokens offered by way of ICO are not, by default, considered as capital securities, nor are they considered debt securities. However, digital tokens may still be characterized as capital securities where they carry corporate governance and financial rights similar to those usually granted by ownership of traditional shares.

(*continued*)

Jurisdiction	Summary
	Unless (i) a digital token generally has attached to it rights and undertakings with the sole object of managing collective investment in transferable securities or in other liquid financial assets of capital raised from the public and (ii) that digital token functions on the principle of risk-spreading, it is also unlikely that such digital token could be characterized as a UCITS or FIA.
	The current position taken by the AMF is to conduct a case-by-case analysis of each ICO to determine whether that ICO or the digital tokens being issued are regulated. Until the adoption of a new legislation, the AMF has launched, in parallel with the consultation paper, a program named UNICORN (Universal Node to ICO's Research & Network) in order to support initiators of ICOs and deepen its expertise about ICOs.
	Once participant responses to the consultation paper are analyzed by the AMF, regulations for ICOs will likely then be drawn up and implemented.
Germany	The German Federal Financial Supervisory Authority ("BaFin") has stated in its warning on ICOs dated November 15, 2017 (the "2017 BaFin ICO Warning"), relating to ICOs and its advisory letter dated February 20, 2018, on the classification of tokens, coins, and cryptocurrencies generally (the "2018 BaFin Circular") that it will decide on a case-by-case basis whether the offering and/or trading of a particular cryptographic token as well as other services related thereto require the obtaining of any authorizations pursuant to:

Jurisdiction	Summary

(a) the German Banking Act (Kreditwesengesetz [KWG]) for conducting banking business and providing financial services (including, inter alia, marketing and trading activities including the processing of an ICO or the operation of secondary marketing trading facilities) if the tokens qualify as a financial instrument (including in particular a security or unit of account);

(b) InvestmentCode(Kapitalanlagegesetzbuch[KAGB]) as an investment fund manager if the tokens qualify as units in investment funds; or

(c) Payment Services Supervision Act (Zahlungsdiensteaufsichtsgesetz [ZAG]) for providing payment services or issuing electronic money (e.g., in connection with the transfer (by third parties) of fiat currency between parties on cryptocurrency exchanges).

Similarly, according to the BaFin, the classification of the tokens will also determine whether the offeror of a particular ICO must fulfill prospectus requirements pursuant to:

(a) the Securities Prospectus Act (Wertpapierprospektgesetz [WpHG]) if the tokens qualify as securities;

(b) the Assets Investment Act (Vermögensanlagengesetz [VermAnlG]) if the tokens qualify as asset investments; or

(c) the KAGB if the tokens qualify as units in investment funds triggering further filing and approval requirements.

(continued)

Jurisdiction	Summary
	In the 2017 BaFin ICO Warning, the BaFin generally considered virtual currencies (such as Bitcoin) to be units of account (as defined in KWG) and therefore financial instruments. As a result, authorization from BaFin is generally required prior to any undertakings or persons being able to, inter alia, (i) arrange the acquisition of or sell or purchase such digital tokens on a commercial basis or (ii) operate secondary market platforms on which such digital tokens are traded. In the 2018 BaFin Circular, the BaFin takes a broader approach and considers not only virtual currencies but also tokens, coins, and cryptocurrencies generally. The BaFin clarifies that tokens not only may in particular constitute units of accounts but also may qualify as (i) securities, (ii) asset investments, (iii) units in investment funds, or (iv) underlyings of derivatives contracts. In line with BaFin's supervisory practice so far, the 2018 BaFin Circular makes clear that ICOs are generally feasible in Germany provided that they comply with existing regulatory requirements. However, the exact classification of a particular token design remains subject to some uncertainties as the requirements for the classification leave room for interpretation. Therefore, careful structuring of the ICO is imperative to avoid undesired regulatory implications.
Hong Kong	The Hong Kong Securities and Futures Commission ("SFC") made it clear in September 2017 that any digital tokens that are offered or sold by way of ICO may be subject to the securities laws of Hong Kong where such digital tokens fall under the definition of "securities" under the Securities and Futures Ordinance. This determination applies regardless of whether the ICO purports to offer a digital token described or otherwise labeled as a "virtual commodity."

Jurisdiction	Summary
	Where the digital tokens involved in an ICO fall under the definition of "securities," any party dealing in or advising on such digital tokens or managing or marketing a fund investing in them and targeting the Hong Kong public is required to be licensed by or registered with the SFC, irrespective of where the party is located.
	Although Hong Kong is a part of the People's Republic of China, by virtue of its status as a Special Administrative Region, PRC laws and regulations relating to ICOs will not apply in Hong Kong unless they are listed in Annex III of the Basic Law and implemented by the Hong Kong legislature.
Japan	The Financial Services Agency of Japan (FSA) released a statement on 27 October 2017 stating that:

(i) "if digital tokens issued by an ICO meet the relevant criteria and are therefore categorized as virtual currencies,[1] an issuer and promoter of the ICO is required to register as an operator of a Virtual Currency Exchange Business" and may therefore be regulated under Japanese law, including by the Payment Services Act and the Financial Instruments and Exchange Act; and

(ii) ICOs may also be subject to the Financial Instruments and Exchange Act (FIEA) in the event that such ICO is deemed as a collective investments scheme[2] (as defined in the FIEA), the issuer and promoter of such ICO is required to be registered as an operator of a Type II Financial Instruments Exchange Business and/or Investment Management Business, and it will also be subject to various regulations under the FIEA.

The FSA has also emphasized that a person engaging in ICO activities without required registrations may be subject to criminal penalties.

(continued)

Jurisdiction	Summary
People's Republic of China	In the People's Republic of China, the relevant authorities appear to have taken the approach of prohibition rather than regulation when it comes to ICOs. Several government agencies published a notice stating that the issuance of digital tokens by way of an ICO is "an unauthorized and illegal public financing activity, which involves financial crimes such as the illegal distribution of financial digital tokens, the illegal issuance of securities and illegal fundraising, financial fraud and pyramid scheme." The authorities further state that digital tokens that are distributed during the digital token fundraising are "not issued by the monetary authority, which has no legal property as fiat currency and cannot circulate in the monetary market." Additionally, as of the date of the announcement, all kinds of fundraising activities through digital token issuance had to immediately cease and any completed fundraising activities had to be unwound and all virtual currencies used to purchase the issued digital tokens be returned to investors.
Singapore	As with most other jurisdictions, there is no legislation that specifically refers to how ICOs or digital token offerings should be treated, but the Monetary Authority of Singapore (MAS) did issue a statement on ICOs in August 2017 and then released nonbinding Guidelines on Digital token Offerings in November 2017 (the MAS Guidelines) addressing also how current laws will be applied to ICOs and intermediaries in the sector.

Jurisdiction	Summary
	The MAS Guidelines make it clear that an offer of digital tokens that constitute securities or units in a collective investment scheme is subject to the same regulatory regime under the Securities and Futures Act ("SFA) in Singapore as if it were a traditional securities offering. Any such offer must therefore be made in, or accompanied by, a prospectus that is prepared in accordance with the SFA and registered with the MAS.

Exemptions from the application of the SFA as described above (subject to certain conditions) include where an offer of digital tokens is:

(a) a "small offer" (US$5 million or less in a year);

(b) a "private placement" (no more than 50 persons in a year);

(c) made to "institutional investors" (as defined in the SFA) only; or

(d) made to "accredited investors" (as defined in the SFA).

Unless otherwise exempted, intermediaries that carry out the following activities may be deemed to be undertaking a "regulated activity," which would require that such intermediary hold a relevant capital markets services license under the SFA:

(i) operation of a platform on which offerors make primary offers or issues of digital tokens (a "primary platform");

(ii) provision of financial advice in respect of digital tokens (a "financial adviser," who must also be authorized and hold a financial adviser's license [or be exempt]); or

(continued)

Jurisdiction	Summary
	(iii) operation of a platform on which digital tokens can be traded (a "trading platform"; anyone establishing a trading platform in Singapore must also be approved by MAS as an approved exchange or recognized by MAS).
	While there is a lack of relevant case law in Singapore, the MAS Guidelines do set out several indicative and nonconclusive case studies relating to different types of digital token offerings and intermediary activities to help current and potential participants assess whether or not the relevant legislation and regulations apply.
	It should also be noted that as with U.S. regulations, the requirements of the SFA and FFA may apply extraterritorially and intermediaries based outside Singapore may still be subject to such requirements if it is intended, or likely, that they may induce members of the public in Singapore to use their services (being regulated activities).
United Kingdom	The UK Financial Conduct Authority (FCA) released a statement in September 2017 on ICOs focusing on the circumstances in which an ICO might fall within the scope of the FCA's current regulatory boundaries, as well as the potential risks to consumers of participating in ICOs.
	In that statement, the FCA confirmed that many ICOs will fall outside the scope of current UK financial services regulation. However, where the ICO structure has parallels with initial public offerings, private placement of securities, or similar investment structures, the businesses involved may be carrying out regulated activities or may need to be authorized by the FCA.

Jurisdiction	Summary
	The FCA noted in the statement that certain types of ICOs may also fall within the United Kingdom's Prospectus Rules. Broadly, these rules require a formal prospectus to be published for any offer of transferable securities to the public unless an exemption applies. It should also be noted that the ongoing introduction of the new European Prospectus Regulation (due to come fully into force in 2019) may have an impact on this analysis. The FCA has, since the September 2017 statement, launched a discussion paper on Distributed Ledger Technology in which it clarified (on the basis of feedback from that discussion paper) that while its current regulatory boundaries are flexible enough to accommodate applications of various technologies—including the use of DLT by regulated firms and for regulated purposes—the FCA will need to gather further evidence on the ICO market and conduct a deeper examination of recent ICO/cryptocurrency developments connected to the UK.

CHAPTER 3

Smart Code and Smart Contracts

Dickson C. Chin

The concept of "smart contracts" has different meanings to different people. At one end of the spectrum, they represent a revolutionary method for executing transactions between parties using computer code that performs and enforces agreements without the need for human intervention by lawyers or courts. At the other, they represent an untested method for forming and executing agreements utilizing unproven technology that poses commercial and legal risks for businesses, which at the outset are so potentially broad as to raise questions on whether smart contracts can eventually be relied upon on a commercial scale. As is often the case with encounters between existing legal systems and emerging technologies where questions arise on whether one can accommodate the other, the answers usually evolve from the friction of real-life applications that lead the technology and the law to evolve and adapt concurrently until allocations of the benefits and the risks become clearer to market participants. That process of adaption has happened before. For example, executing transactions over the internet is a common occurrence today, but as recently as a decade ago, serious people questioned whether such transactions could ever be trusted.

The starting point for any discussion of smart contracts is a clear understanding of the scope of the emerging technology. At its core, the technology consists of computer code or script, which we shall refer to as "smart code," that can operate on a blockchain or distributed ledger. Here is a basic example of how smart code might function:

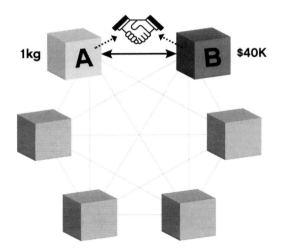

Figure 3.1: Smart Code Example

A and B are users on the same distributed ledger.

They execute a smart contract for the sale of gold based on the spot price of gold.

A agrees to sell 1 kg of gold to B at the prevailing USD spot price at a particular day/time, but only if the spot price is greater than $40,000 at that time.

Smart code would use the following logic—

- On Day/Time, OBTAIN Spot Price
- IF Spot Price >$40,000 then:
  - TRANSFER 1 kg of gold from A to B
  - TRANSFER $x from B to A WHERE x = Spot Price amount for 1 kg of gold in US Dollars at Day/Time

- ELSE
  - Contract terminates

Smart code can have different functionality depending on the structure of the applicable distributed ledger, but its principal feature is the ability for computer programming to automatically execute the transfer of a currency, assets, or data on the satisfaction of certain conditions , which then gets recorded on the distributed ledger.[1] Given the ability of smart code

---

1 Here are high-level examples of the technical functioning of smart code on two distributed ledgers.

In the case of Ethererum, smart code is accessible at a particular address on the distributed ledger. When relevant information is sent as input to that address, every node of the

to implement these transfers on a distributed ledger with mathematical precision and free from human intervention, some commentators have raised the proposition that smart code could eventually replace the law in connection with the execution and enforcement of commercial transactions. However, this proposition falls short because not all of the terms of an agreement between parties can be embodied using smart code. For example, provisions that require discretion and judgment such as requiring a counterparty to perform its obligation using "reasonable efforts" and limiting defaults to "material" breach of an obligation are important features in the conduct of business contractual relationships that require express human intervention. Other sample provisions that are not readily executable by smart code include governing law, jurisdiction, representations and warranties, indemnification, and jury trial waiver. These "nonoperational" clauses will likely remain relevant for businesses even if someday the "operational clauses" of smart code on a distributed ledger could, for example, receive data from sensors at a store that a product needed restocking, which would automatically trigger orders with a vendor and activate deliveries from the vendor's warehouse straight to the shelves using robots and driverless vehicles.[2]

A vital challenge in navigating these developments is to identify, evaluate, and mitigate any risks associated with the potential use of smart code for business transactions. If a division or unit of a company

---

permissionless distributed ledger executes the smart code using the information that was sent, which produces either an output state effecting the transfer of a currency, assets, or data or an interim state of the smart code that is stored on the distributed ledger. Smart code under Ethereum can also be designed to be modular and reference other smart code to perform additional functions and be stored in virtual libraries to be called on when needed. *Contracts,* ETHEREUM, http://solidity.readthedocs.io/en/v0.4.21/contracts.html#inheritance (last visited Mar. 29, 2018).

In the case of R3's Corda platform, smart code constitutes transactions that consume existing states in the form of inputs to create new states in the form of outputs. Transaction may also specify an ordered list of zip file hashes, where each zip file may contain code, data, certificates, or supporting documentation for a transaction. When smart code confirms that all of the required keys have provided their validated signatures, a transaction will execute on the applicable nodes of the permissioned distributed ledger, which produces an output state with information on the resulting status of the relevant currency, assets, or data. Under Corda, the output state will also include a contract reference code pointing to the smart code and legal prose reference pointing to the legal prose for a transaction. Mike Hearn, *Corda: A Distributed Ledger,* CORDA (Nov. 29, 2016), at 13–14, https://docs.corda.net/_static/corda-technical-whitepaper.pdf.

2 Although some smart-contract platforms such as Corda allow nonoperational clauses to be stored as text accompanying smart code, they are not themselves executable in the manner of computer code or script and require human intervention outside of the distributed ledger for performance.

proposes transacting with counterparties using smart code, does the overall facts and circumstance lead to the conclusion that the smart code, in conjunction with any other written documentation and applicable user interface, meets the requirements of an enforceable contact under applicable law and hence constitutes a "smart contract"? If a company seeks to develop a platform, whether alone or in a joint venture or consortium, for using smart code to transact with others, what are the factors it needs to consider in structuring an enforceable "smart contract"? What unique challenges does the technology pose with respect to performance and dispute resolution of smart contracts under applicable laws? This chapter will take a hands-on practical approach by reviewing (1) the potential types of platforms on which smart contracts could be executed and their unique risks, (2) the factors to consider in evaluating the enforceability, performance, and termination of smart contracts, and (3) the disparate means of addressing dispute resolution of smart contracts.

It is important to note that this chapter distinguishes between "smart code," which is computer programming on a distributed ledger that can perform various functions such as transfer currencies, assets, and data upon the satisfaction of certain conditions, and "smart contracts," which are agreements that include "smart code" in any manner that meets the requirements of an enforceable contact under applicable law.[3] Outside this context, market participants sometimes refer to the term *smart contract* interchangeably to mean either the programming code or enforceable contracts without distinction. The differences and the dynamics between these two concepts will be one of the central themes of this chapter.

1. SMART-CONTRACT PLATFORMS

Unlike agreements documented on paper, smart contracts require a platform on which to operate. Such platforms come in a variety of formats, and the following descriptions outline different types of potential platforms a

---

3   Although market participants may refer to "smart code" as "smart contract code," the "smart contract code" may or may not actually form the basis for an enforceable contract under applicable law. For example, a business could utilize programming code to automate posting and transfer of supply chain information on a distributed ledger (or hire a third party to help it do so) without the legal consequences of using the programming code to form contracts with third parties. In either case, "smart code" or "smart contract code" simply provides a means of performing functions on a distributed ledger using programming code.

business may encounter. Most of these platforms are in the development stage and not yet fully operational on a commercial scale.

(a) Third-Party Platform

A third-party platform is a permissioned distributed ledger established and overseen by a third-party owner/operator that permits market participants to transact and execute smart contracts with one another. The third-party owner/operator might consist of a joint venture or consortium of market participants who themselves also transact on the platform or a nonmarket participant third-party owner/operator. Unlike a permissionless distributed ledger, where all information is visible to everyone accessing the distributed ledger, market participants on a third-party platform only see the information on the distributed ledger that relates to themselves and their transactions with counterparties. A third-party platform could be specific to an industry and, even further, specific to certain types of transactions within an industry, such as swaps or commodities. Market participants would primarily use templates of smart code designed by the third-party owner/operator, with the potential option to use smart code designed by the market participants themselves. Depending on the classes of transactions executed on a third-party platform, regulators may have access to portions or all of the information on the distributed ledger. A prospective market participant may need to meet certain requirements to join the third-party platform.

(b) Counterparty Platform

A counterparty platform is a permissioned distributed ledger established and overseen by a counterparty that permits market participants to transact and execute smart contracts with this single counterparty. These transactions relate to the business of the counterparty. Market participants would primarily use templates of smart code designed by the counterparty. Market participants on a counterparty platform see the information on the distributed ledger that relates only to themselves and their transactions with the counterparty. A "business counterparty platform" is intended to facilitate transactions between a counterparty and other businesses, while a "retail counterparty platform" is intended to facilitate transactions with consumers.

(c) Peer-to-Peer Platform

A peer-to-peer platform is a permissioned distributed ledger established and overseen by a group of market participants that is restricted to members of the group transacting and executing smart contracts with each other.

These transactions are specific to the purposes of the group. Market participants would primarily use templates of smart code designed by the group (or a lead member of the group or a third-party developer). Market participants on a peer-to-peer platform only see the information on the distributed ledger that relates to themselves and their transactions within the group. A "business peer-to-peer platform" is intended to facilitate transactions among a group of businesses, whereas a "retail peer-to-peer platform" is intended to facilitate transactions among consumers.

(d) Counterparty-to-Counterparty Platforms

A counterparty-to-counterparty platform is a permissioned platform developed by a third-party owner/operator that enables market participants to join and transact with each other across a wide range of business transactions that are not industry specific. Market participants would primarily use templates of smart code designed by the third-party owner/operator that pertain to common transactions between businesses generally, with potential for select customization by market participants. Market participants on a counterparty-to-counterparty platform only see the information on the distributed ledger that relates to themselves and their transactions with counterparties.

(e) Permissionless Platforms

Existing permissionless platforms such as Ethereum provide smart-contract features that enable any participant to write and deploy smart code on its distributed ledger, which could form the basis for smart contracts. However, the very aspects of permissionless distributed ledgers that make it appealing for certain segments of users, such as the transparency of all transactions coupled with the pseudonymity of individual accounts, also make it a challenge for businesses to transact using smart contracts. However, it may be possible to implement modifications to a permissionless platform so that it functions in a manner similar to the other permissioned platforms described above.

(f) Other Platforms

Certain existing securities and commodities exchanges, which clear transactions by taking positions between seller and buyers, could potentially transition from existing technology to distributed ledger technology and deploy smart contracts to implement transactions under the oversight of applicable regulators. Potential applications include using distributed ledger technology to reduce the time it takes to clear transactions from weeks to nearly instantaneously and enable real-time monitoring of collateral and technology-agnostic instant clearing transaction acknowledgment.[4]

Businesses may also encounter other platforms that utilize smart code with distributed ledgers, but without the execution of smart contracts as one of its features. In addition to the transfer of currencies and assets, smart code can also automate the transfer of data based on specified preconditions. For example, autonomous platforms could utilize smart code to facilitate the pairing of buyers with sellers based on price, quantity, and creditworthiness, which results in the unmasking of the matched prospective counterparties and the execution of contracts outside the platform through traditional means. Supply chain platforms could also use smart code to automate the tracking of manufacture, transportation, export, import, and delivery of products along the supply chain to increase efficiencies, reduce credit exposure, and facilitate the identification of defects. If a business intends to utilize these types of platforms, it may need to execute a services agreement with third-party providers to incorporate the terms of use for these services. Also, just as companies developed intranets from internet technology for internal purposes, so might companies develop intracompany distributed ledgers to use smart code to better track and manage its internal resources that do not involve entering into smart contracts with third parties.

2. RAMIFICATIONS OF SMART-CONTRACT PLATFORMS

(a) Role of Platform as Intermediary

Given Satoshi Nakamoto's original objective for the complete elimination of the intermediary in the creation of the Bitcoin blockchain, an ironic consequence arising from the emergence of smart contracts as an important

---

4   Michael del Castillo, *DTCC Milestone: $11 Trillion in Derivatives Gets Closer to the Blockchain*, CoinDesk (Oct. 23, 2017), https://www.coindesk.com/dtcc-milestone-11-trillion-derivatives-gets-closer-blockchain/; Alex Lielacher, *DTCC to Launch Blockchain Credit Default Swaps Reporting in Early 2018*, NASDAQ (May 25, 2017), http://www.nasdaq.com/article/dtcc-to-launch-blockchain-credit-default-swaps-reporting-in-early-2018-cm794771; Jeremy Nation, *Citi and CME Group Leverage Blockchain Technology for Operations*, EthNews (Dec. 15, 2017), https://www.ethnews.com/citi-and-cme-group-leverage-blockchain-technology-for-operations; Helen Bartholomew, *Derivatives-DTCC on Track for Q1 2018 Blockchain CDS Reporting*, Reuters (May 19, 2017), https://www.reuters.com/article/derivatives-dtcc-on-track-for-q1-2018-bl/derivatives-dtcc-on-track-for-q1-2018-blockchain-cds-reporting-idUSL8N1IJ5BF.

feature of distributed ledger technology is the requirement for a platform that introduces the role of an intermediary in the formation and performance of smart contracts. Contracts can be executed by parties on the back of a napkin, in a 500-page document, or over the telephone without the involvement of a third party, but smart contracts cannot, as a practical matter, be executed without a platform as intermediary. Platform operators are central to the formation and performance of smart contacts. They create, operate, and maintain the distributed ledger on which the smart code is deployed, generate the smart code or facilitate the generation of smart code by others, and establish the terms by which smart code is executed. The presence of a platform as intermediary raises various risks that are generally unique to smart contracts, which businesses must address.

(b) Risk of Platform Security Breaches

The storage of currency, assets, or data on a platform raises risks of security breaches. Although the distributed ledger itself might be immutable, the various interfaces with the distributed ledger might themselves be vulnerable.[5]

High-profile examples include the theft of around $30 million worth of Ether through a security vulnerability in the multi-signature wallets of Parity, a company that makes software for wallets that are designed to be opened only with the permission of two or more individuals.[6] In another instance, hackers siphoned away $53 million worth of Ether by taking advantage of a bug in the code of the DAO, a specific decentralized autonomous organization formed by German startup Slock.it. This resulted in countermeasures that included the dramatic move by certain Ethereum developers to use the same bug to "hack" the remaining Ether in The DAO and siphon those funds into a secure account to prevent a further breach.[7] Parity suffered yet another high-profile hack when an individual

---

5   In the case of Ethereum, the smart code itself exists in various states over time in the performance of its functions, which makes it vulnerable to security breaches with respect to execution. *State Machine*, SOLIDITY, http://solidity.readthedocs.io/en/develop/common-patterns .html?highlight=state#state-machine (last visited Mar. 29, 2018).

6   Wolfe Zhao, $30 Million: Ether Reported Stolen Due to Parity Wallet Breach, ConDesk (July 19, 2017), https://www.coindesk.com/30-million-ether-reported-stolen-parity-wallet-breach/.

7   David Siegel, Understanding The DAO Attack, CoinDesk (Updated June 27, 2016), https://www.coindesk.com/understanding-dao-hack-journalists/; Elaine Ou, *Smart Contracts Are Still Way Too Dumb*, BLOOMBERG VIEW (Nov. 16, 2017), https://www.bloomberg.com/view/ articles/2017-11-16/smart-contracts-are-still-way-too-dumb. The Ethereum Foundation also subsequently elected to implement a fork to the Ethereum code to reverse the DAO theft. Because

accidentally froze up to $300 million of Ether by deleting the function of the smart code that allowed the owners of wallets to transfer their Ether. Although the Ether still exists, the lack of access to the amounts in the wallet essentially renders the Ether useless.[8]

If a business is seeking to transact on a smart-contract platform on a commercial scale or a business is seeking to create a smart-contract platform, it will need to address the potential for security breaches, as set forth in Chapter 4.

(c) Risk of Mistake in Smart Code

Risk of mistake in smart code can result in severe adverse consequences to a business. A platform can mistakenly transfer funds and assets or inadvertently disclose data due to flawed smart code. Similar to the "Conditions of Use" for a typical website, will platform operators require market participants to agree that the services of a smart-contract platform are provided "on an 'asiis' and 'as-available' basis"? Will market participants and platform operators allocate liability as between them under negotiated services agreements?

Or will other potential approaches fill these gaps? A number of companies now offer smart-contract security audits, which analyze smart contracts for security vulnerabilities, deploy and run tests, and issue and provide reports of their findings.[9] Or will businesses use their own internal programmers to conduct diligence of the source code? Or will the source code be made publicly available for all market participants to evaluate and report any bugs to the platform operator?

In addition to the risk of mistakes as between a platform operator and market participants, the counterparties to smart contracts on a platform will also need to address the impact of potential mistakes on their

---

some users did not adopt the new version, this fork effectively split Ethereum into two versions (Ethereum and Ethereum Classic). Jordan Pearson, *How Coders Hacked Back to "Rescue" $208 Million in Ethereum*, MOTHERBOARD (July 23, 2017), https://motherboard.vice.com/en_us/article/qvp5b3/how-Ethereum-coders-hacked-back-to-rescue-dollar208-million-in-Ethereum.

8   Becky Peterson, Someone Deleted Some Code in a Popular Cryptocurrency Wallet—and As Much As $280 Million in Ether is Locked Up, BUSINESS INSIDER (Nov. 7, 2017), http://www.businessinsider.com/ethereum-parity-wallet-hack-freeze-missing-code-2017-11; Thijs Maas, *Yes, This Kid Really Just Deleted $300 MILLION by Messing Around with Ethereum's Smart Contracts*, HACKERNOON (Nov. 8, 2017), https://hackernoon.com/yes-this-kid-really-just-deleted-150-million-dollar-by-messing-around-with-ethereums-smart-2d6bb6750bb9.

9   Alexander Seleznev, *Narrative Smart Contracts Security Audit*, SMARTDEC (Nov. 9, 2017), https://blog.smartdec.net/narrative-smart-contracts-security-audit-284cd8ef3a9f.

contractual relationship with each other. The potential legal consequences for mistake in smart code as between the counterparties to a smart contract will be discussed later in this chapter.

(d) Cost of Executing Smart Contracts

In addition to the cost of establishing, operating, and maintaining a distributed ledger, the development and execution of smart code for transactions also result in expenses. A permissionless platform such as Ethereum allocates these expenses by requiring the payment of "gas."[10] When submitting a transaction, a market participant specifies the gas limit and gas price (in Ether) it is willing to pay to complete the transaction. The Ethereum miner that incorporates the transaction in a successfully validated block is entitled to collect the gas, along with the transaction fee and mining reward. The network also lets miners set the minimum gas price they are willing to accept, which could eventually lead to pricing some smaller players out of the market if they are not willing to pay a high enough gas price to attract the interest of miners in executing their transactions. Through the charging of "gas," the Ethereum platform rewards efficient source code.

Under a permissioned platform where the platform operator created the source code, a different compensation mechanism may apply as between the platform operator and the market participant. Other fees may apply if market participants create and load their own source code. In any case, the payment of a fee to execute smart code is a consideration for a business seeking to utilize a smart-contract platform or a business seeking to establish a smart-contract platform.

(e) Risk of Platform Insolvency (and Lack of Portability)

In seeking to use a platform to execute smart contracts, a business also needs to address the potential risk of insolvency of the third-party owner/operator of a platform. If a third-party owner/operator is unable to restructure under a bankruptcy or similar proceeding and the only option remaining is liquidation, what happens to the smart contracts with remaining terms of performance? As a practical matter, will smart contracts be portable to other smart-contract platforms? Or if a business and its counterparty wish to continue contracting with each other using substantially similar arrangements, will the source code need to be rewritten on a new smart-contract platform?

---

10   *Account Types, Gas, and Transactions*, Ethdocs.org, www.ethdocs.org/en/latest/ contracts-and-transactions/account-types-gas-and-transactions.html (last visited Mar. 29, 2018).

Even in the absence of insolvency, will the smart contracts on a platform be "portable" to enable parties to transfer their smart contracts to another platform? Or what happens if a counterparty wishes to assign a smart contract to another third party? And what if that third party is not a market participant on the existing platform?

(f) Regulatory Risks

It is worth noting that transactions executed on a smart-contract platform remain subject to all laws that are applicable to the execution of transactions generally. For example, if the products of transactions are themselves subject to regulatory oversight such as swaps or certain commodities, then the smart contracts will continue to bear the risks and regulatory requirements associated with those products. In addition, the function of the smart-contract platform as an intermediary may trigger the obligation for the platform to register with a regulator, which may in turn require the platform to impose regulatory requirements on market participants transacting on the platform. Likewise, various laws and other constraints against transacting with prohibited nations, entities, or individuals still apply. Ensuring compliance with all applicable laws should be a fundamental component of transacting on any smart-contract platform.

3. ENFORCEABILITY, PERFORMANCE, AND TERMINATION OF SMART CONTRACTS

If a division or unit of a company proposes transacting with counterparties using smart contracts or if a company seeks to develop a platform, whether alone or in a joint venture or consortium, for using smart contracts to transact with others, there are various factors to consider in evaluating the enforceability, performance, and termination of smart contracts to be transacted under the proposed platform.

(a) General Application of Contract Law

Generally, the principles of contract law regarding formation of an enforceable contract (or lack thereof), performance, and termination apply to agreements memorialized in smart code as they do with agreements memorialized on paper or other means. Within the U.S. legal system, a contract is "an agreement between two or more parties creating obligations that are enforceable or otherwise recognizable at law."[11] Of course,

---

11 Bryan Garner, A Dictionary of Modern Legal Usage 215 (2d ed. 1987).

as with all disputes, parties can elect to resolve their differences without resorting to a process that involves the application of law through a court or alternative dispute resolution. But if a business were to transact on a smart-contract platform, confirming that the requirements for an enforceable contract have been met under applicable law would provide it with additional remedies in the event any of the remedies provided under the terms of the smart-contract platform were insufficient.

(b) Enforceability

For an agreement to be enforceable under applicable U.S. law, there must be (1) an offer or a willingness to enter into a binding agreement by the offeror and an acceptance of the terms of the agreement by the offeree, often expressed as mutual assent or a "meeting of minds" regarding the essential terms of the contract, (2) consideration represented by a mutual exchange of value, (3) an agreement that is sufficiently definite, (4) legal capacity, and (5) legality.[12] Smart contracts, like written contracts, can be challenged if any of these elements are absent.

In addition to evaluating prospective smart-contract platforms to confirm that the basic requirements for forming an enforceable contract have been satisfied, there are various specific points of risk arising from the nature of the distributed ledger technology and smart contracts that should be reviewed and, as needed, mitigated. The following are a few nonexhaustive examples.

(i) Identification of Contract Documents

If a business is presented with the potential to enter into smart contracts on a platform or a business is seeking to establish a smart-contract platform, a principal consideration is to identify all of the components of the "smart contract," including any relevant smart code and other applicable terms and conditions. This exercise is important because it establishes the boundaries of the terms of the smart contract, which will form the basis on which the parties (or a court or other dispute resolution mechanism) will interpret the agreement. By identifying all of the components of the smart contract and incorporating a contract provision that clearly specifies the components, a business can avoid subsequently asking the question "what are the complete terms of the parties' agreement?" and circumvent the distributed-ledger equivalent of searching through a jumble

---

12   John Edward Murray Jr., MURRAY ON CONTRACTS 43 (5th ed. 2011).

of e-mails, telephone conversations, and course of conduct to determine the contract terms.[13]

In the case of distributed ledger technology, the components of a smart contract could consist of smart code provisions or natural language provisions (i.e., written in same manner as existing contracts, which admittedly may seem unnatural to nonlawyers) or a combination thereof. The natural language provisions could exist in paper form separate from the distributed ledger or as a text file in nonexecutable form on the distributed ledger. Smart code could exist in a single location on the distributed ledger, or smart code could exist in various locations organized in a hierarchy with primary programming code for a transaction and a "satellite" or "library" of functions that can be called on by the primary programming code when executing a transaction. The output of the execution of the smart code may result in information that is recorded on the distributed ledger (e.g., calculation of a monthly settlement by smart code could generate data that provides the result of executed code).[14] There might be other relevant components to a smart contract depending on the architecture of the applicable platform.[15]

Depending on the characteristics of a smart-contract platform, an express provision that clearly specifies the components of a smart contract may require new terminology to identify the components (e.g., by hashes

---

13 Courts are often forced to determine whether a contract is integrated, either partially or completely. This will determine whether parol evidence such as telephone conversations and e-mails will be allowed in to determine the contract terms. *See, e.g.*, Middletown Concrete Products, Inc. v. Black Clawson Co., 802 F. Supp. 1135 (D. Del. 1992); LNV Corp. v. Studle, 743 S.E.2d 578, 580 (Ga. App. 2013).

14 Generally, existing written agreements do not consider ordinary course settlements to be part of the contract documents (e.g., invoices showing settlement amounts). Given the logic of distributed ledger technology where the programming language functions and the transaction records are intertwined, will those transaction records also constitute part of the "contract"?

15 Corda and Bitcoin follow the UTXO computer model that consists of inputs, outputs (arising from the application of programming language), and signatures. These platforms are considered "stateless." The application of smart contracts can either succeed, in which case inputs are consumed and new unspent outputs are created, or it will fail without causing any consequences. Kelly Olson et al., *Sawtooth: An Introduction*, HYPERLEDGER (2018), at 4, https://www.hyperledger.org/wp-content/uploads/2018/01/Hyperledger_Sawtooth_WhitePaper.pdf; Hearn, *supra* note 2 at 6, 13. By contrast, Ethereum follows the virtual computer model and is considered "stateful." Olson, *supra* note 15 at 4. Specifically, Etherum utilizes contract accounts that can have multiple stages and maintain internal states that exist independent of generating output. *Account Types, Gas, and Transactions*, ETHDOCS, http://ethdocs.org/en/latest/contracts-and-transactions/account-types-gas-and-transactions.html (last visited Mar. 29, 2018). Would these internal "states" of contract accounts also be considered part of the "contract"?

or other identifiers). Or perhaps one of the functions of the smart code could include a tracker that lists and updates all of the components of a smart contract as it evolves. Identification of the contract components would enable the parties to incorporate a "merger" or "integration" clause to manifest a clear intent to create a completely integrated agreement, with the goal of minimizing potential disputes over what terms are part of the agreement.[16]

(ii) Smart Code Provisions and Natural Language Provisions

In connection with reviewing a smart contract, a principal consideration is to identify the extent to which the agreements between parties are expressed in smart code provisions or natural language provisions or a combination both. If the agreement is represented by a combination of both, a platform may need to further determine (or grant the parties a right to elect) whether the smart code provisions or the natural language provisions control. Or a platform may provide that the smart code provision governs, but include the natural language provision as a component of the smart contract in a manner similar to recitals as an aid to interpretation in the event a court or arbitrator is tasked with interpreting an ambiguous provision, which may include deciphering flawed programming code arising from bugs or mistakes in memorializing the intent of the parties.[17] There are various approaches to incorporating smart code provisions and natural language provisions into smart contracts.

(A) Natural Language Model
Under the natural language model, the contract would be written in the same manner, using legal language, as existing contracts. The smart code is not defined as a contract document and does not legally bind the parties. It is merely a mechanism for implementing

---

16   Murray, *supra* note 12 at 421–22. In Betz Labs. v. Hines, the following merger clause appeared in the writing: "This agreement contains the whole agreements between the Seller and Buyer and there are no other terms, obligations, covenants, representations, statements, or conditions, oral or otherwise, of any kind whatsoever." 647 F.2d 402, 403 (3d Cir. 1981). There is however a split of authority regarding whether a merger clause is conclusive, as some courts are not prepared to ignore collateral evidence even where the writing contains such a merger clause.

17   "The contract recitals create a context through which the operational portion of the contract can be better understood, because they indicate the relevant circumstances to its execution." Fed. Deposit Ins., Corp. v. FBOP Corp., 252 F. Supp. 3d 664, 702 (N.D. Ill. 2017) (quoting Hagene v. Derek Polling Const., 902 N.E. 2d 1269, 1274 (Ill. App. 5th Dist. 2009).

the transaction, which is not significantly different from parties using automatic billing and recurring payment systems as a means of performing under a contract in written form. By its very structure, the natural language provisions control if the smart code were to produce results that are different from what is required under the natural language provisions.

(B) Dual Language Model A dual language model would consist of provisions in both natural language and programming language, with each version intended to be an identical translation of the other. Of course, the reality of a dual language approach has many practical challenges of implementation. The cycle of memorializing an agreement could begin with computer programming and end with natural language translation or begin with natural language and end with computer programming or a hotchpotch of both. In each case, it would carry the full panoply of potential risks associated with mistakes in translation, plus the inherent limits of achieving 100 percent accuracy even absent mistakes. As a practical matter, perhaps best practices on translations could be eventually developed by market participants to partly address these risks, as other industries have with the application of ISO 17100 for translation services, as promulgated by the International Organization of Standardization whose standards are used in various fields worldwide such as health care engineering, information technology, aircraft and space vehicle engineering, and so on.[18]

A primary question to address under a dual language model is which language will control in the event of a conflict? If a business selects natural language as the governing language, then the dual language model is little different from the natural language model. If a business selects programming language as the governing language, then it will assume the risk that the programming language accurately reflects the intent of the parties. It will then bear the additional procedural complexities, costs, and uncertainties in outcome from resolving a dispute over programming language before a court or arbitrator for whom programming language will require translation and explanation. A business could mitigate the

---

18   *ISO 17100 Translation Services Management System*, QSL, https://www.isoqsltd.com/iso-certification/iso-17100-translation-services-management-certification/ (last visited Mar. 29, 2018).

risk of mistake by using its programmers or third-party auditors to scrutinize the smart code or relying on smart code that is publicly available and subject to industry-wide evaluation. A business might also determine that the burdens associated with resolving disputes over programming are manageable in a manner that is similar to managing patent disputes with complex technical concepts or international disputes before foreign language courts.

A secondary question to address under the dual language approach is whether the secondary language will be included or excluded as a contract document. A business could choose to include the natural language provisions in a manner similar to recitals to aid in interpretation in the event there is a dispute over the intended functionality of smart code. Alternatively, a business could choose to exclude the natural language provisions, in which case if there is any dispute over the functionality of the smart code, then it may need to rely on a future determination by a court or arbitrator as to the admissibility of evidence outside the contract documents (i.e., parol evidence of a "prior agreement") under a contract-law doctrine that permits the admission of such evidence, such as the doctrine of mistake.

Overall, the dual language approach can be categorized into smart contacts that consist of (i) programming language with natural language equivalent outside the contract ("Programming Language Exclusive Provisions");[19] (ii) programming language with natural language equivalent within the contract where programming language governs in the event of any inconsistency between the programming language and natural language ("Programming Language Primary Provisions"); and (iii) programming language with natural language equivalent within the contract where natural language governs in the event of any inconsistency between the programming language and natural language ("Programming Language Secondary Provisions").

(C) Potential Issues with Programming Language Exclusive Provisions Are there ramifications to contract formation if the programming language provisions are prepared by programmers but are unread or not understood by the principals representing the parties to an agreement? As a general legal matter, a party may be bound by an instrument that she or he has not read. For example, under *Kai Peng v. Uber Technologies, Inc.*, a court

---

19 As a practical matter, any programming language will likely always have a natural language equivalent outside of the contract, whether embodied in the form of a summary, fragments of electronic communications, handwritten notes, verbal conversations, or otherwise.

held that drivers who spoke little or no English were bound by an agreement to arbitrate as the inability to read or understand the language of the agreement was not a defense to contract formation.[20]

If a business is presented with a smart-contract platform that utilizes Programming Language Exclusive Provisions (i.e., where the programming language is the governing language and natural language is excluded from the contract), the business will assume the risk that the programming language does not accurately reflect the intent of the parties and it will bear the additional risks involved with resolving disputes over programming language. Moreover, without natural language within the "four corners" of the contract to aid in contract interpretation, it may need to rely on the doctrine of mistake to determine the admissibility of evidence outside the contract documents to seek reformation of the disputed programming code.

(iii) Mutual Assent to Contract Terms

Generally, the formation of a contract requires a bargain in which there is a manifestation of mutual assent to the exchange and consideration. One relevant example is click-wrap agreements, where the terms of use appear on an internet webpage and a consumer is required to click on a dialogue box stating "I agree" to proceed with a transaction or gain access to the website services. In applying the requirement for mutual assent with respect to a click-wrap agreement, courts evaluate whether the consumer was put on notice of the terms of the clickwrap agreement and whether he or she assented to those terms.[21] Moreover, courts consider whether the terms were clearly presented to or easily accessible by the consumer, whether the consumer had an opportunity to read the agreement, and whether the consumer manifested an unambiguous acceptance of the terms.[22]

---

20 237 F. Supp. 3d 36 (E.D.N.Y. 2017).

21 In 2003, the American Bar Association (ABA) Joint Working Group on Electronic Contracting Practices laid out recommendations regarding what constitutes adequate notice in the electronic contracting context. The Electronic Contracting Working Group suggested that a user should only be considered to have "validly and reliably" assented to the terms of an electronic agreement if (1) the user is provided with adequate notice of the existence of the proposed terms, (2) the user has a meaningful opportunity to review the terms, (3) the user is provided with adequate notice that taking a specified action manifests assent to the terms, and (4) the user takes the action specified in the latter notice. The Working Group presented its findings at the Spring Meeting of the Business Law Section in Los Angeles on April 4, 2003. Anandashankar Mazumdar, *ABA Group Participants Formulating Guidelines for Browsewrap Contract Terms,* Electronic Com. & L. Rep. (BNA) 387 (Apr. 16, 2003).

22 *See, e.g.,* Schwartz, *Consumer Contract Exchanges and the Problem of Adhesion,* 28 Yale J. on Reg. 313 (2011); B. Waleski, *Enforceability of Online Contracts: Clickwrap v. Browse Wrap,*

A principal consideration for smart-contract platforms is whether the terms of agreement are clearly presented to the parties. The practical point is to identify the means of presentation for both the natural language provisions and the programming language provisions of an agreement. Where natural language provisions are executed outside the platform in the form of a written agreement, the requirement for presentation is more easily satisfied. Natural language provisions can also lend themselves to display on a web portal to a smart-contract platform in a manner similar to click-wrap agreements. But where Programming Language Exclusive Provisions apply, an important inquiry is whether a party has been presented with the opportunity to read the programming language and been provided with the ability to manifest an unambiguous acceptance of the terms.

A natural question in a book for lawyers is whether the display or availability of programming language on the user interface of a smart-contract platform meets the requirement for assent when there is a likelihood that the user may not be able to read programming language. In addition to *Kai Peng v. Uber Technologies, Inc.*, where a court found that the inability to read or understand the language of the agreement was not a defense to contract formation,[23] the Fifth District Court of Appeals held in *Merrill, Lynch, Pierce, Fenner & Smith, Inc. v. Benton*[24] that "[p]ersons not capable

---

19 E-COMMERCE LAW & STRATEGY 7 (2002) at 1; Caspi v. Microsoft Network, 732 A.2d 528 (N.J. Super App. Div. 1999) (reasoning that even though the clause was not set apart by any special typeface from the rest of the document, "[t]o conclude that plaintiffs are not bound by that clause would be equivalent to holding that they were bound by no other clause either, since all provisions were identically presented"); Forrest v. Verizon Communications, Inc., 805 A.2d 1007 (D.C. App. 2002) (holding that the forum selection clause was enforceable because it was reasonably communicated and the enforcement of the clause would not be unreasonable); Bar-Ayal v. Time Warner Cable Inc., 2006 WL 2990032 (S.D.N.Y. 2006); Williams v. America Online, Inc., 2001 WL 135825, at *2 (Mass. Super. 2001) (rejecting America Online's motion to dismiss based on its forum selection clause in a click-wrap agreement because the plaintiffs did not have notice of it before their damages were incurred); Appliance Zone, LLC v. NexTag, Inc., 2009 WL 5200572, *4–5 (S.D. Ind. 2009). "Although the existence of a box labeled "I Agree" in the online contract context does not always indicate assent or signature to an agreement, the procedural fairness of the contract-formation process in this case is clear. NexTag made the Agreement highly visible and easily accessible and required as well an affirmative acceptance of the terms of the Agreement as a prerequisite to completing registration. Justin Allen provided precisely that sort of affirmative agreement to the contract, after which Appliance Zone readily engaged in and paid for NexTag's services. Appliance Zone cannot escape the "fundamental principle of contract law that a person who signs a contract is presumed to know its terms and consents to be bound by them." *Id.* (quoting Paper Exp., Ltd. v. Pfankuch Maschinen GmbH, 972 F.2d 753, 757 (7th Cir. 1992).

23   237 F. Supp. 3d 36 (E.D.N.Y. 2017).

24   467 So. 2d 311, 313 (Fla. 5th Dist. App. 1985).

of reading English, as well as those who are, are free to elect to bind themselves to contract terms they sign without reading. . . . The burden is on the person who cannot read to know that he cannot read and if he desires to have an instrument read and explained to him to select a reliable person to do so before he signs it." Thus, even though the brokerage firm's employee was aware that Ms. Benton could not read English, the fact the employee did not read or explain the contractual documents was insufficient to invalidate the documents or to constitute a defense to them where there was no evidence Ms. Benton was in any way prevented from reading the documents.[25] It is unclear whether courts would reach similar conclusions with respect to programming language.

(iv) Electronic Signatures

Legal frameworks exist for electronic signatures that can be expected to apply to smart contracts. Both the Electronic Signatures in Global and National Commerce Act (ESIGN) and the Uniform Electronic Transactions Act (UETA) provide that a signature may not be denied legal effect or enforceability solely because it is in electronic form, and that if a law requires a signature, an electronic signature satisfies that law.[26]

ESIGN is the federal statutory framework that governs e-signatures in the United States. By contrast, the UETA is a model uniform e-signature law that has been enacted in forty-seven states (Illinois, New York, and Washington have their own e-signature laws). Both were promulgated to bolster the enforceability of contracting electronically by specifically construing electronic records and electronic signatures as "writings" for purposes of satisfying the statute of frauds. In enacting ESIGN, Congress sought to create a uniform, nationwide law while also minimizing preemption of the UETA and other state laws that are consistent with ESIGN. Therefore, a state UETA law, rather than ESIGN, will govern if the state law meets certain requirements. Certain contracts are not covered by ESIGN or UETA, including wills, codicils, or testamentary trusts and certain UCC transactions.[27] Finally, ESIGN prohibits any state or federal statute from requiring a specific technology for electronic transactions.

---

25 *Id.*

26 15 U.S.C.A. § 7001; UETA § 7(a), http://www.uniformlaws.org/shared/docs/electronic%20transactions/ueta_final_99.pdf.

27 The ESIGN Act provides that it does not apply to a contract or other record to the extent it is governed by the UCC, other than §1-107 (waiver of claims after breach), §1-206 (statute of frauds for personal property), Article 2 (sale of goods) and Article 2A (leases of goods). 15

An electronic signature is defined by ESIGN as "an electronic sound, symbol, or process, attached to or logically associated with a contract or other record and executed or adopted by a person with the intent to sign the record."[28] The UETA provides a number of threshold requirements, namely that (i) there should be an agreement between the parties to conduct the transaction electronically, (ii) there should be an ability to retain and reproduce the writing for later reference by all parties entitled to retain the contract or record, and (iii) the electronic signature must be attributable to that person.[29] Whether there was an agreement to conduct the transaction electronically is determined from the context, the surrounding circumstances, and the parties' conduct, though mere use of the electronic option may in some cases be sufficient to show agreement.[30] This is one area in which the UETA differentiates itself from ESIGN. According to the UETA guidelines, the type of agreement that must be made for an e-signature to be legally valid varies depending on the context and the circumstances. With respect to the attribution element, an electronic signature is attributable to a person if it was the act of that person. The burden of proof is on the person seeking to enforce the signature.

Digital signatures seem a natural fit for these elements of ESIGN and UETA. As discussed in Chapter 1, if Alice, using public-key cryptography, digitally signs a message by encrypting it with her private key, which only she possesses, then anyone can read the message and verify that Alice encrypted it by successfully decrypting the message using Alice's public key, which is freely available. The fact that the message can be decrypted using Alice's public key proves that Alice—and only Alice—digitally signed the text with her private key, since only Alice possesses the private key. Subject to the existence of the required facts and circumstances, asymmetric encryption is generally viewed as capable of meeting the requirements of ESIGN and UETA.[31]

U.S.C.A. § 7003, https://www.law.cornell.edu/uscode/text/15/7003. The UETA contains an equivalent provision. UETA, *supra* note 26. Article 3 (Negotiable Instruments), Article 4 (Bank Deposits and Collections), Article 4A (Funds Transfers), Article 5 (Letters of Credit), Article 6 (Bulk Sales), Article 7 (Documents of Title), Article 8 (Investment Securities), and Article 9 (Secured Transactions) remain governed by the UCC.

28   E-Sign § 106(5).

29   UETA § 5(b).

30   UETA § 5.

31   Alex Cohn, Travis West, & Chelsea Parker, *Smart After All: Blockchain, Smart Contracts, Parametric Insurance, and Smart Energy Grids*, 1 GEO. L. TECH. REV. 273 (2017), https://www.georgetownlawtechreview.org/smart-after-all-blockchain-smart-contracts-parametric-insurance-and-smart-energy-grids/GLTR-04-2017/; Reggie O'Shields, *Smart Contracts: Legal Agreements for*

Other risks may arise, however, in the context of a business executing agreements on a smart-contract platform utilizing public key cryptography. When there are individuals with legal authority to sign a contract on behalf of a company using the company's private key, a business will need to address the potential risks associated with the unauthorized utilization of private keys to execute transactions on behalf of the company.

The management of cryptographic keys is an important factor to consider in connection with the execution of smart contracts. Guidelines will cover practices such as key life cycle management (generation, distribution, exchange, replacement, destruction), key storage, key compromise and recovery and audit. In contrast to the secure computational aspects of cryptography that currently exists,[32] successful key management involves elements of social engineering such as systems policy, user training, and organizational coordination.[33]

(c) Performance

Smart contracts are often associated with the concept of automatic performance or self-enforcement, which potentially eliminates the risk of nonperformance by the counterparty.[34] Assuming that a particular

---

the Blockchain, 21 N.C. Banking Inst. 177 (2017), http://scholarship.law.unc.edu/cgi/viewcontent .cgi?article=1435&context=ncbi; Alex Cohn, Travis West, & Chelsea Parker, *The Enforceability of Smart Contracts*, STEPTOE BLOCKCHAIN: BLOG (May 4, 2017), https://www.lexology.com/library/ detail.aspx?g=25a03fad-60f4-4e2d-b25e-8e2185d68cee. In Arizona, the "Signatures; Electronic Transactions; Blockchain Technology" statute was signed into law by Arizona governor Doug Ducey in late March 2017. The statute expressly permits signatures secured through blockchain technology to serve as valid electronic signatures and establishes smart contracts as legal, enforceable contracts under the state's law. Ariz. Rev. Stat. Ann. § 44-7061.

32   "Quantum computers" have been designed and (in prototype) built that theoretically could break certain types of encryption that are considered safe today, but they are unlikely to pose any real threat until the 2030s at the earliest. Paul Teich, *Quantum Computing Will Not Break Your Encryption, Yet*, FORBES (Oct. 23, 2017), https://www.forbes.com/sites/ tiriasresearch/2017/10/23/quantum-will-not-break-encryption-yet/#4f26c3f47319.

33   *Key Management Cheat Sheet*, OWASP.ORG, https://www.owasp.org/index.php/Key_ Management_Cheat_Sheet (last visited Mar. 29, 2018).

34   "Allegedly, smart contracts can streamline the contracting process, reduce transaction costs by eliminating intermediaries and, most importantly, simplify enforcement by obviating the need to seek protection from traditional legal institutions, such as courts. . . . The very idea of smart contracts is thus inextricably tied to the elimination of human judgement, the reduction of dependence on financial intermediaries and, in many instances, a detachment from the legal system. . . . The legal analysis of smart contracts is rendered difficult by the fact that the phenomenon originated in technical writings, which are characterized by an inconsistent and incorrect use of legal terms. Given the complexity of the technologies underlying smart contracts

transaction is capable of being fully performed by smart code (which may not be the case if, for example, physical deliveries are made outside the distributed ledger), there are risks associated with performance of an agreement using programming code. These include risk of mistakes in the code with respect to bugs or the memorialization of the parties' intent and the risk of inflexibility arising from the loss of discretion to deviate from the terms of the agreement.

Such risks are especially heightened in an environment where the code is purportedly "immutable." Even though there can exist programming techniques to "amend" the functionality of smart code in a prescribed manner, there may be no guarantee that the functionality can be fully revised in a wide ranging manner required by a business without terminating the code in its entirety and executing a new smart contract on the distributed ledger.

(i) Risk of Mistake

It is an often repeated tale that in 1945, engineers opened Panel F, Relay #70 of the Harvard Mark II system due to errors from running a test of its multiplier and adder when they discovered a moth trapped inside, which resulted in the journal entry "first actual case of a bug being found."[35] Despite best efforts, programming bugs continue to persist. Another key challenge is ensuring that the programming code provisions match the intent of the counterparties. The risk of mistakes in the code with respect to the memorialization of the counterparties' intent may also be amplified in a situation where the smart contract consists of Programming Language Exclusive Provisions.

If there were no natural language version of the code within the "four corners" of the smart contract—whether as Programming Language Secondary Provisions, in which case the governing natural language would reflect the definitive agreement, or as Programming Language Primary Provisions, in which case the natural language could provide a basis for

---

(distributed networks and asymmetric cryptography, amongst others) it is also difficult to evaluate many claims concerning their actual capabilities and real potential to change (speak: revolutionize) the commercial and legal landscape." Eliza Mik, *Smart Contracts: Terminology, Technical Limitations and Real World Complexity*, RESEARCH COLLECTION SCHOOL OF LAW (2017) at 2, http://ink.library.smu.edu.sg/sol_research/2341.

35 *Moth in the Machine: Debugging Origins of "bug,"* COMPUTERWORLD (Sept. 3, 2011), https://www.computerworld.com/article/2515435/app-development/moth-in-the-machine--debugging-the-origins-of--bug-.html; Simson Garfinkel, *History's Worse Software Bugs*, WIRED (Nov. 8, 2005), https://www.wired.com/2005/11/historys-worst-software-bugs/.

inferring intent in a manner similar to recitals—the programming code provisions with the bug would constitute the sole agreement of the counterparties. In such cases, the counterparties might need to rely on parol evidence of a "prior agreement" to determine intent in the event of a dispute over the intended function of the code without the bug or mistake.[36] An important legal distinction to make is that the parties made no mistake in their actual agreement; in other words, though there was a meeting of minds, there was a mistake in the expression of the agreement.[37] Under these circumstances, a court sitting in equity may reform the writing to express the intention of the parties by considering the prior evidence of the parties intention, which will be admissible.[38]

An example of how this could potentially be adjudicated can be found in *Cerberus International Ltd. v. Apollo Management*,[39] where the plaintiffs proved their entitlement to reformation of erroneously drafted provisions. In its opinion, the Court of Chancery of Delaware explained the basis for its power "to reform a contract to express the 'real agreement' of the parties involved."[40] Two key doctrines allow reformation.[41] The first is the doctrine of mutual mistake. In such a case, the plaintiff must show that both parties were mistaken as to a material portion of the written agreement. The second is the doctrine of unilateral mistake. The party asserting this doctrine must show that it was mistaken and that the other party knew or should have known that the other party was mistaken but remained

---

36 The parol evidence rule states that where the parties embody the provisions of their agreement in a written contract, intending the writing to be a final expression of the agreement, then the terms of the writing may not be contradicted by evidence of a prior agreement. There are a number of categories to which the parol evidence rule does not apply, including (i) determining the preliminary question of whether the contract is a full and complete integration of the parties' intent; (ii) resolving contract interpretation questions, where trade usages, course of dealing, and course of performance evidence is admissible; (iii) determining whether the contract is void, voidable, or unenforceable; (iv) determining that the writing is mistaken, where one of the parties is seeking reformation of the contract based on a mistake in the writing; and (v) determining whether the parties intended that the contract was conditioned on the fulfilment of a condition precedent. 11 WILLISTON ON CONTRACTS § 33 (4th ed.).

37 *See, e.g.*, Olds v. Jamison, 238 N.W.2d 459 (Neb. 1976) (where the word *lessor* was written instead of the word *lessee*).

38 Restatement 2d, § 155.

39 Cerberus Int'l, Ltd. v. Apollo Mgmt., L.P., 794 A.2d 1141, 1151 (Del. 2002).

40 *Id.* (citing Colvocoresses v. W.S. Wasserman Co., 28 A.2d 588, 589 (Del. Ch. 1942)).

41 Reformation will also be available where there is an omission in the writing or a mistake as to the legal effect of the expression of the contract. In Bollinger v. C. Pennsylvania Quarry Stripping & Const. Co., the plaintiffs satisfied the burden of proving mutual mistake by providing evidence that the defendant initially complied with the omitted terms. 229 A.2d 741 (1967).

silent.[42] Reformation will be granted to reflect the true intention of the mistaken party. "Regardless of which doctrine is used, the plaintiff must show by clear and convincing evidence that the parties came to a specific prior understanding that differed materially from the written agreement."[43] The prior understanding "need not constitute a complete contract in and of itself," but could be something as simple as a handwritten note "This looks fine" on a proposed term sheet.[44] The equitable remedy of reformation, if granted, will depend heavily on the facts and circumstances and particularly on the credibility of the evidence presented by the mistaken party.[45]

(ii) Risk of Inflexibility

In commercial relationships, it is common for the counterparties to deviate from the strict requirement of a written contract in a manner that is reasonable from a business perspective. These deviations can run the gamut. A buyer could request that a product be delivered to an alternative location, and a seller could agree to the change without amending the contract. Alternatively, a seller could withhold deliver of a product to buyer upon rumors of financial difficulties, whereupon buyer provides satisfactory assurances and seller resumes performance. Under an inflexible smart contract, those deviations could result in automatic termination of the transaction, which may not serve the goals of either counterparty. Before commencing to execute smart contracts, it may be advisable for a company to examine whether the smart-contract platform is structured with sufficient flexibility to enable the exercise of business judgement on issues that are critical to it.

(d) Terminating or Amending "Immutable" Smart Contacts

What does it mean for a smart contract to be "immutable"? Depending on the platform, it could mean that after the smart-contract code becomes part of the distributed ledger, it cannot be changed. But even if the code is fixed, it is possible that the functionality of the code can be altered. A close examination of the potential mechanics for terminating or "amending" a smart contract should be a part of any review process in determining

---

42   Cerberus, *supra* note 39 at 1151.

43   *Id.* at 1151–52.

44   ASB Allegiance Real Est. Fund v. Scion Breckenridge Managing Member, LLC, CIV.A. 5843-VCL, 2012 WL 1869416, at *13 (Del. Ch. May 16, 2012), judgment entered, (Del. Ch. June 3, 2012), and aff'd, 68 A.3d 665 (Del. 2013).

45   Restatement 2d. § 155 comment (c).

whether to utilize a smart-contract platform or establishing a contract platform.

With respect to Solidity, a programming language for Ethereum, even though the smart code cannot be changed after it has been injected onto the blockchain, the state of the smart code is not immutable. Because the programming code must be adjusted to be executed, the state of the smart code is dynamic.

Although the programming language cannot be altered, there are two methods to undo smart code in its entirety. A self-destruct function can be written into the smart code, which deletes the programming language from the block if it is called from the address with the right to exercise the self-destruct.[46] If the agreement calls for more than one party to approve termination, then conditions can be added to the self-destruct that requires the state of the self-destruct to have logged the consent of the other required party (or parties) whose consent is required. It is important to note that the self-destruct feature can also be programmed to include other conditions, such as a requirement that compensation be paid for any partial performance or a requirement that a termination fee be paid prior to execution of the self-destruct. If the agreement calls for either party to have the right to terminate, the code could require that both parties validate each execution of the smart code, where if either party fails to validate, then the function is effectively terminated.

Certain types of "amendments" to a smart contract are possible even if the programming code cannot be changed. If an agreement references an index price that fluctuates and a circumstance arises where that index price needs to be replaced by another index price, a smart contract can be programmed before it is inserted onto the blockchain to permit the modification of a variable by assigning a new value to the variable. If programmed into the original code, functions can be added, modified, or deleted by creating satellite contracts with functions represented by specific addresses. To make changes to the smart contract, the parties can provide their consent to change the pointer from one address to another in the satellite contracts to activate or deactivate functions. It is also possible to change the pointer to "libraries" of functions that are available to all users of Ethereum.

---

46 Ari Juels and William Marino, Understanding Smart Contract Mechanics, Practical Law Practice Note w-005-3262 (2017) (March 1, 2017); *Ethereum*, Solidity, https://solidity .readthedocs.io/en/v0.4.24/introduction-to-smart-contracts.html (last visited May 29, 2018).

By looking at the examples above, it becomes clear that while a platform may permit a smart contract to be terminated or amended, the ability to exercise those actions requires careful planning to capture a multitude of scenarios prior to execution of the smart contract and injection onto the distributed ledger. The examples also highlight the differences between natural language and programming language with respect contract drafting and the challenges of translating from one to the other given current technology. Currently, there simply cannot be the same flexibility in programming language as in natural language for capturing the wide range of permutations for terminations and amendments of an agreement. At this stage of development, unless a platform was designed to permit broad technical flexibility in amending smart code, a business would need to carefully review the evolving advantages and limitations of smart contract technology to determine the appropriate circumstances in which to execute smart contracts.

4. DISPUTE RESOLUTION OF SMART CONTRACTS

At present, the nature and outcome of potential disputes under smart contracts is potentially unpredictable given the novelty of the technology. To address these uncertainties, dispute resolution mechanisms should be tailored to facilitate the challenges of ensuring efficient and informed decisions. Like any contract, smart contracts should contain a dispute resolution clause, which specifies, among other things, choice of law and choice of jurisdiction.

The role of a smart-contract platform as intermediary also raises an additional wrinkle by introducing the possibility of two dispute resolution provisions, where one would govern disputes between the platform operator and market participants with respect to the user agreement for the platform and the other would govern disputes between market participants under smart contract transactions executed between them. These two dispute resolution provisions may conceivably be different depending on the approach of the applicable smart-contract platform.

(a) Governing Language

With Programming Language Exclusive Provisions and Programming Language Primary Provisions in smart contracts between counterparties on a platform, courts may face difficult interpretation issues because programming languages are typically hard to understand without training in programming. Unless lawyers and judges learn to read, write, and interpret the various programming languages underpinning different smart-contract platforms, courts may need to rely on approaches used in litigation in other areas that involve technical issues such as intellectual property, engineering, and so on. In these situations, expert witnesses may act as translators for the court, breaking down technically complex concepts, and interested parties may file *amicus curiae* briefs to inform the court of legal arguments or practical implications not already brought to its attention by the parties.

Unless smart contracts develop to a point where they can be coded in natural language, best practice from other similarly technical areas dictates that disputes over programming language call for the establishment of translation protocols. Translation and interpretation of smart code can be difficult and complex. There is generally not a "one-to-one relationship between languages" and translation of any kind involves some level of approximation, with the translator choosing how to best convey the original message.[47] Although court interpreters are mandated to give the most accurate translation without "embellishing, omitting, or editing," interpretation inevitably changes the meaning of the speaker's words.[48] The problem may be even more acute when translating computer/machine language because in some instances, the meaning and logical reasoning of coded language are substantially different from the equivalent formulations of natural language. Given the paucity of court rules or case law regarding translation and interpretation and the complexity of the task, parties might aim to establish clear and specific translation protocols. They may require, for example, (i) the number of translators permitted by each party and whether a "check interpreter" should be employed in addition to the interpreter(s) of record, (ii) the procedure for objecting to the translation and resolving translation disputes, or (iii) how fees and costs will be shared by the parties.[49]

(b) Specialist Courts

Someday there might come a time when specialist courts are established to adjudicate smart-contract disputes, in a similar manner to the specialized

---

47 Lisa C. Wood, *Translation Protocols: The Time Has Come*, American Bar Association (2015), http://www.foleyhoag.com/-/media/files/foley%20hoag/publications/articles/2015/wood_antitrust_spring2015.ashx?la=en.

48 *Id.*

49 Pretrial Order No. 63, In Re: Baycol Products Litigation, MDL No. 1431; 15 Minn. Prac., Civil Practice Forms § 26.54 (2d ed.).

jurisdiction of the United States Court of Appeals for the Federal Circuit over patent appeals, appeals from the U.S. Trademark Trial and Appeal Board, and issues arising out of the U.S. International Trade Commission.[50] The establishment of a specialist court to review appeals of patent litigation has improved reliability and predictability and in turn encouraged innovation and investment in research and development.[51] As patent litigation has proliferated, various stakeholders have taken the situation one step further by calling for the establishment of specialist patent trial courts, arguing that "uncertainty at the trial level is inefficient because it stimulates appeals rather than settlements."[52]

If smart contracts were to proliferate, specialized district trial courts and appellate courts for smart contracts, with expert knowledge and understanding of the procedures and technicalities associated with smart contract cases and the interpretation of the code, could make more cost-efficient and predictable decisions in smart contract disputes. Judicial competence and consistency would increase confidence in smart contract litigation and encourage technological development and investment in the United States.

(c) Arbitration

As market participants are generally aware, a well-drafted arbitration agreement could enable smart contracting parties to resolve disputes in the parties' preferred manner. Arbitration is suited to technology disputes since certain procedural aspects of the arbitration can be specifically tailored to smart contract and distributed ledger issues, including where the agreement or a portion of it is written in code. The need for experts and an appropriate arbitration panel is likely to lend itself to establishing specialist groups of arbitrators with appropriate knowledge of the technology. In addition, parties drafting arbitration provisions should consider the law of the seat of arbitration (and the governing law of the arbitration) and select a recognized arbitral forum where the local laws do not render smart contracts illegal or unenforceable.

---

50   Rohazar Wati Zuallcobley et al., Study on Specialized Intellectual Property Courts (2012), http://iipi.org/wp-content/uploads/2012/05/Study-on-Specialized-IPR-Courts.pdf.

51   *Id.*

52   The Federalist Society for Law & Public Policy 2008 National Lawyers Convention, Panel Discussion on Specialized Courts: Lessons From The Federal Circuit, 8 Chi. Kent. J. Int. Prop. 317 (2009) (comments of Prof. Rai).

Under the New York Convention, arbitral awards are enforceable in 158 countries worldwide and enforcement can be challenged only in special circumstances.[53]

(d) Dispute Resolution Services

Models for adjudicating smart contract disputes could also mirror the approaches adopted by the derivatives industry, which is regarded as a sector that generates significant disputes that require extensive knowledge of complex market practices.

The Panel of Recognized International Market Experts in Finance (P.R.I.M.E. Finance) was established in 2012 as a nonprofit organization to provide dispute resolution services on complex financial transactions in both developing and mature financial markets, including arbitration services.[54] The institute was established in response to the growing need for innovative responses to dispute resolution in light of the complexity of financial markets. In 2013, the institute was one of seven international arbitration centers named by the International Swaps and Derivatives Association (ISDA) in its 2013 Arbitration Guide.[55] The P.R.I.M.E. Finance Arbitration Rules have been specially adapted for financial markets disputes concerning cross-border finance documentation.[56] P.R.I.M.E. Finance also provides mediation, expert opinions, determinations, and risk assessment services, as well as education and judicial training, and a library and database of relevant cases.[57] P.R.I.M.E. Finance is increasingly being called on by parties to disputes involving derivatives and financial transactions to provide expert witness panels and advice. The P.R.I.M.E. Finance Experts include sitting and retired judges, central bankers, regulators, academics, representatives from private legal practice, and derivative market participants.[58]

---

53 *Contracting States-List of Contracting States*, NEW YORK ARBITRATION CONVENTION, http://www.newyorkconvention.org/list+of+contracting+states (last visited Mar. 29, 2018).

54 *History*, P.R.I.M.E. FINANCE, https://primefinancedisputes.org/page/history (last visited Mar. 29, 2018).

55 *2013 ISDA Arbitration Guide*, ISDA (2013), https://www.isda.org/a/6JDDE/isda-arbitration-guide-final-09-09-13.pdf.

56 *Supra* note 54.

57 *Id.*

58 *Id.*

5. CONCLUSION

As with many emerging technologies, there are a multitude of questions to be answered in deploying smart contracts on a commercial scale. Approaches to addressing the various risks and maximizing the technological benefits that are unique to smart-contract platforms will likely evolve over time. For a business seeking to establish a smart-contract platform or seeking to execute transactions on a smart-contract platform, one of the key factors to examine will be whether the technology meets the needs of market participants for establishing and managing contractual relationships.

Given the prominence of legal doctrine (as well as potential regulatory requirements) to the core business case of a smart-contract platform, developers will likely be called on to focus on the legal requirements in establishing the scope of work for a project at a much earlier stage than it might for other projects. Likewise, market participants will likely be called on to evaluate whether a smart-contract platform meets a company's legal requirements as well as commercial needs at an earlier stage. But ultimately, as is often the case, it will probably take everyone's collective efforts to develop and advance industry standards for smart contracts to reach their full potential.

CHAPTER 4

Blockchain Technology, Security, and Privacy

Richard J. Johnson
Samir C. Jain
Richard M. Martinez

1. DATA SECURITY AND THE BLOCKCHAIN

Blockchain security threats fall into two categories: existential threats that can destroy whole products or networks and ordinary threats that can hurt individual users but do not necessarily threaten the underlying technology.

(a) Existential Threats

The most obvious existential threat to any public blockchain in which consensus is determined by proof of work (examples include Bitcoin, Ethereum, and most other active cryptocurrencies) is a so-called majority attack, which occurs when one malicious actor controls much of the network's mining (processing) power and thus can enforce a false consensus on the blockchain, validating double-spending transactions that otherwise should be rejected. Such behavior could destroy user confidence in the network. Bitcoin has never suffered a successful majority attack, though smaller blockchains may have fewer "good" participants and thereby require less effort by malicious actors to successfully take over a network in this manner.[1] One response to such an attack may be to institute a "fork"

---

1 *Majority Attack*, Bitcoin Wiki, https://en.bitcoin.it/wiki/Majority_attack (Aug. 10, 2017).

in the blockchain—a software update—that would bar the malicious actor from participating in the network.[2]

A second and potentially far greater existential threat to blockchains, both public and private, would be a hack of the underlying cryptography that protects them. In the Bitcoin blockchain, for example, the developers chose the Elliptic Curve Digital Signature Algorithm, a digital-signature standard accepted by the National Institute of Standards and Technology (NIST), as the cryptographic mechanism for creation of the public-private key pairs.[3] Similarly, the Bitcoin developers chose the SHA-256 hashing standard for ensuring the validity and immutability of blocks once added to the blockchain.[4] Although these algorithms have been closely examined by expert cryptographers for years, it is always possible that a weakness or vulnerability could be found or that revolutionary new computing techno-logies (such as "quantum computers") could be developed, which would jeopardize the security of existing algorithms. In some cases—but not all—developers could again respond to such vulnerabilities by forking the blockchain to use stronger forms of cryptography.

Government intervention may pose a final threat that could rise to the level of existential. Certain blockchain applications may pose obstacles to governmental policies, and their responses may include regulation that has the effect of undermining privacy and security or banning certain applications altogether. For example, cryptocurrencies may threaten the government's ability to control and track the flow of money—a power that many governments rely on, among other things, to prevent and punish crime. Cryptocurrencies also potentially threaten a government's ability to conduct foreign policy. For example, blockchain-based cryptocurren-cies may make it difficult to control cross-border spending and to enforce sanctions regimes.[5] In some cases, governments may choose to respond by imposing greater recordkeeping requirements or measures that undermine the anonymity or pseudonymity of blockchain transactions. For example, various U.S. states are considering registration laws for organizations that

---

2   *Weaknesses*, Bitcoin Wiki, https://en.Bitcoin.it/wiki/Weaknesses (July 4, 2017).

3   *FIPS PUB 186-4, Digital Signature Standard (DSS)*, Nat. Inst. of Standards & Tech, https://nvlpubs.nist.gov/nistpubs/FIPS/NIST.FIPS.186-4.pdf (July 2013).

4   *FIPS PUB 180-4, Secure Hash Standard (SHS)*, Nat. Inst. of Standards & Tech, https://nvlpubs.nist.gov/nistpubs/FIPS/NIST.FIPS.180-4.pdf (Aug. 2015).

5   *See* Nathaniel Popper, Oleg Matsnev, & Ana Vanessa Herrero, *Russia and Venezuela's Plan to Sidestep Sanctions: Virtual Currencies*, New York Times (Jan. 3, 2018), https://www.nytimes.com/2018/01/03/technology/russia-venezuela-virtual-currencies.html.

transfer cryptocurrencies.[6] Under a proposed uniform statute, covered businesses would be required to maintain records of currency transactions for five years.[7] In other cases, governments may seek to control or end certain blockchain practices. In 2013, China restricted financial services companies' use of Bitcoin and in 2017 banned Initial Coin Offerings ("ICOs") altogether.[8] Other countries have taken less dramatic steps: in 2017, the United States shut down certain ICOs, intervening in those it said were shams or were not registered as securities offerings.[9]

Further, some countries are undermining cryptocurrencies as a collateral effect of their foreign policy: North Korea, for instance, is suspected of hacking several South Korean cryptocurrency exchanges.[10] And as mining for public blockchains becomes increasingly concentrated in countries like China where energy—and thus mining—is cheap, it may become easier for certain countries to threaten an international blockchain network.[11]

(b) Ordinary Threats

Ordinary threats may harm individual users without necessarily threatening whole blockchain networks. For example, hackers often compromise cryptocurrency intermediaries, such as exchanges, digital wallets, and commerce sites, in order to misappropriate funds. Because cryptocurrencies like Bitcoin and Ether rely on public ledgers, it is often easy to see where the stolen money goes and thus hard for thieves to use any stolen

---

6 Uniform Law Commission, *Regulation of Virtual-Currency Businesses Act*, http://www.uniformlaws.org/Committee.aspx?title=Regulation%20of%20Virtual%20Currency%20Businesses%20Act.

7 *Uniform Regulation of Virtual-Currency Businesses Act*, NAT. CONFERENCE OF COMM'RS ON UNIF. STATE LAWS, http://www.uniformlaws.org/shared/docs/regulation%20of%20virtual%20currencies/URVCBA_Final_2017oct9.pdf (July 2017).

8 Gerry Mullaney, *China Restricts Banks' Use of Bitcoins*, NEW YORK TIMES (Dec. 5, 2013), http://www.nytimes.com/2013/12/06/business/international/china-bars-banks-from-using-bitcoin.html; BBC, China Bans Initial Coin Offerings Calling Them "Illegal Fundraising" (Sept. 5, 2017), http://www.bbc.com/news/business-41157249.

9 Evelyn Cheng, *SEC Steps Up Scrutiny of Digital Coin Sales with Order to Freeze "PlexCoin" Founders" Assets*, CNBC (Dec. 4, 2017), https://www.cnbc.com/2017/12/04/sec-steps-up-ico-scrutiny-with-order-to-freeze-plexcoin-assets.html; *Company Halts ICO After SEC Raises Registration Concerns*, SECURITIES AND EXCHANGE COMMISSION (Dec. 11, 2017), https://www.sec.gov/news/press-release/2017-227.

10 Sean Gallagher, *North Korea Suspected in Latest Bitcoin Heist, Bankrupting Youbit Exchange*, ARS TECHNICA (Dec. 20, 2017), https://arstechnica.com/tech-policy/2017/12/north-korea-suspected-in-latest-bitcoin-heist-bankrupting-youbit-exchange/.

11 Raghunadha Kotha, *Security Risks with Public and Private Blockchains*, PENTEST (Sept. 13, 2017), https://pentestmag.com/security-risks-public-private-blockchains/.

money received. Nevertheless, hackers are sometimes able to convert at least a portion of the stolen money to fiat currency through unscrupulous exchanges.[12] Companies and developers have responded to these attacks by issuing refunds to customers, by declaring bankruptcy, and in extreme circumstances by forking the underlying technology to reverse the theft.

The most famous compromise of a cryptocurrency intermediary was that of Mt. Gox, the leading currency exchange in the early years of Bitcoin. Mt. Gox achieved tremendous popularity with cryptocurrency users, but it had no version control for its software and only belatedly introduced a test environment, both of which are standard practices for software and web technology companies.[13] Mt. Gox was victimized by several hacking incidents as a result, including one in which the hacker stole an astonishing $460 million from the exchange.[14] In 2017, the FBI arrested a Russian hacker suspected of being involved in that theft,[15] though by then Mt. Gox had long since declared bankruptcy and several of its former customers had initiated lawsuits.

A second notable attack occurred against the Distributed Anonymous Organization (DAO), built from smart-contract code on the Ethereum platform. The purpose of the DAO was to function as a decentralized investment fund: the size of your investment in the project determined the level of control you would have over the investment decisions made.[16] The DAO raised over $150 million (as valued at the time) in Ether.[17] But hackers managed to exploit a vulnerability in the DAO software that allowed them to make unlimited withdrawals of Ether into a shadow-DAO the

---

12   *See, e.g.*, Catalin Cimpanu, *BTC-e Owner Arrested for Laundering Stolen Bitcoin, Ransomware Payments*, BLEEPINGCOMPUTER (July 27, 2017), https://www.bleepingcomputer.com/news/security/btc-e-owner-arrested-for-laundering-stolen-Bitcoin-ransomware-payments/ (describing the laundering activities performed through the cryptocurrency exchange BTC-e).

13   Robert McMillan, *The Inside Story of Mt. Gox, Bitcoin's $460 Million Disaster*, WIRED (Mar. 3, 2014), https://www.wired.com/2014/03/Bitcoin-exchange/.

14   *Id.*; Kim Nilsson, *Breaking Open the MtGox Case, Part 1*, WIZSEC (July 27, 2017), http://blog.wizsec.jp/2017/07/breaking-open-mtgox-1.html; McMillan, *supra* note 13.

15   Andrew Norry, *The History of the Mt Gox Hack: Bitcoin's Biggest Heist*, BLOCKONOMI (Nov. 29, 2017), https://blockonomi.com/mt-gox-hack/; Timothy B. Lee, *Feds Say They Caught a Key Figure in the Massive Mt. Gox Bitcoin Hack*, ARS TECHNICA (July 27, 201), https://arstechnica.com/tech-policy/2017/07/feds-indict-a-leading-Bitcoin-exchange-for-money-laundering/.

16   Klint Finley, *A $50 Million Hack Just Showed That the DAO Was All Too Human*, WIRED (June 18, 2016), https://www.wired.com/2016/06/50-million-hack-just-showed-dao-human/.

17   Matthew Leising, *The Ether Thief*, BLOOMBERG MARKETS (June 13, 2017), https://www.bloomberg.com/features/2017-the-ether-thief/.

hackers set up for that purpose.[18] In all, $55 million was stolen.[19] The DAO attack was particularly notable because of the response from the Ethereum community. Because DAO had controlled so much of the world's Ether—about 15 percent[20]—Ethereum developers chose to push out a new version of the Ethereum software, which forked the Ethereum blockchain to reverse the theft. The developers essentially rebuilt the blockchain as if the hack had never happened. The decision to fork, however, was controversial. Some developers felt that reversing the theft was akin to a financial institution bailout and chose to continue developing what they called "Ethereum Classic," a version of Ethereum in which the DAO attack was not reversed.[21] Both Ethereum and Ethereum Classic continue as viable cryptocurrencies (although Ethereum is far more popular).[22]

Mt. Gox and DAO are far from the only thefts from cryptocurrency intermediaries. In 2016, for example, hackers managed to steal $72 million in Bitcoin from Bitfinex, a cryptocurrency exchange.[23] Bitfinex gave affected customers tokens that could be redeemed on its exchange or converted into an investment in Bitfinex's parent company.[24] And in 2017, hackers stole around $32 million of Ether tokens from the e-commerce platform Swarm City by exploiting a vulnerability in the site's multi-signature wallets.[25] Multi-signature wallets purportedly offer cryptocurrency users

---

18 *Id.*

19 *Id.*

20 David Siegel, *Understanding the DAO Hack for Journalists* (June 19, 2016), https://medium.com/@pullnews/understanding-the-dao-hack-for-journalists-2312dd43e993.

21 *Id.*; Antonio Madeira, *The DAO, The Hack, The Soft Fork and The Hard Fork*, CryptoCompare (Jan. 12, 2018), https://www.cryptocompare.com/coins/guides/the-dao-the-hack-the-soft-fork-and-the-hard-fork/.

22 *Compare Cryptocurrency Market Capitalizations: Ethereum*, CoinMarketCap (Jan. 12, 2018), https://coinmarketcap.com/currencies/Ethereum/, *with Cryptocurrency Market Capitalizations: Ethereum Classic*, CoinMarketCap (Jan. 12, 2018), https://coinmarketcap.com/currencies/Ethereum-classic/.

23 *Features*, Bitfinex, https://www.bitfinex.com/features; *Bitfinex Hack*, Wikipedia (Dec. 23, 2017), https://en.wikipedia.org/wiki/Bitfinex_hack.

24 *Can Bitfinex Really Impose a $72 Million Theft on Its Customers?*, Reuters (Aug. 15, 2016), http://fortune.com/2016/08/15/bitfinex-Bitcoin-hack-hong-kong-customers-law/; Garrett Keirns, *Bitcoin Exchange Bitfinex Buys Back All Remaining "Hack Credit" Tokens*, Coindesk (Apr. 3, 2017), https://www.coindesk.com/bitfinex-pledges-buy-back-remaining-hack-credit-tokens/.

25 Luke Graham, *$32 Million Worth of Digital Currency Ether Stolen by Hackers*, CNBC (July 20, 2017), https://www.cnbc.com/2017/07/20/32-million-worth-of-digital-currency-ether-stolen-by-hackers.html.

greater security by requiring several people to consent before a transaction is made.[26]

In addition to the vulnerabilities with cryptocurrency intermediaries like exchanges, wallets, and commerce platforms, ICOs pose a unique set of risks. As discussed in more detail in Chapter 2 in this book, ICOs are frequently used by blockchain-technology companies to raise money. Unlike an initial public offering (IPO), however, investors generally do not receive equity in the company or a dividend. They instead get a unique ability to use the service the company promises to build. Some ICOs have proven to be shams. Others are poorly conceived and organized and vulnerable to hackers.[27] Most prominently, in 2017, a company called Coin-Dash organized an ICO to build a product for managing cryptocurrency investments; unfortunately, malicious actors changed the address on the CoinDash website to which people were supposed to send their investments.[28] Within minutes, over $6 million in cryptocurrencies were sent to the wrong address.[29]

The discussion thus far has focused largely on security concerns posed by public blockchains; there is at least one unique security concern posed by private blockchains. Because private blockchains are, by definition, invitation-only, they tend to have fewer nodes participating. It thus may be comparatively easier for malicious actors to disable the network by launching "Denial of Service" attacks—the transmission of an overwhelming number of requests for information—against the network's nodes.

2. DATA PRIVACY AND THE BLOCKCHAIN

Blockchains raise important data privacy concerns and obligations. Although blockchains are often characterized as anonymous and privacy-enhancing, the reality is more complex. For example, blockchain-based

---

26 Danny Bradbury, *BitGo Safe Aims to Secure Bitcoin Wallets with Multi-Signature Transactions*, Coindesk (Dec. 19, 2013), https://www.coindesk.com/bitgo-safe-aims-secure-Bitcoin-wallets-multi-signature-transactions/.

27 Lily Hay Newman, *Why It's so Easy to Hack Cryptocurrency Startup Fundraisers*, Wired (Sept. 7, 2017), https://www.wired.com/story/why-its-so-easy-to-hack-cryptocurrency-startup-fundraisers/.

28 *Coindash: Into the Future of Trading*, Coindash, https://www.coindash.io/; Wolfie Zhao, *$7 Million Lost in CoinDash ICO Hack*, Coindesk (July 17, 2017), https://www.coindesk.com/7-million-ico-hack-results-coindash-refund-offer/.

29 Alexandria Arnold, *CoinDash CEO Says Ignore the Conspiracies After Coin-Sale Hack*, Bloomberg Markets (July 20, 2017), https://www.bloomberg.com/news/articles/2017-07-20/coindash-ceo-says-ignore-the-conspiracies-after-coin-sale-hack.

cryptocurrencies may often be pseudonymous rather than anonymous— observers may know that a purchase is associated with the particular address of a Bitcoin wallet, though not who, in the real world, controls that wallet. Even that pseudonymity may be illusory. Researchers have shown that Bitcoin transactions in particular can often be connected to purchases in the real world.[30] For example, if an observer knows the amount and time of a real-world purchase made by a particular individual (perhaps by using internet cookies that track online behavior), she can convert the cost of that purchase to Bitcoins and search for the transaction on the public blockchain ledger. At that point, the address associated with the transaction can be linked to the individual, along with all of the other transactions that were made using that address as recorded on the blockchain ledger.

Various tools can make it harder to link individuals to their Bitcoin transactions. For instance, "mixing" services that connect users who want to make similar-sized payments and mix their payments together make it harder to determine who paid for what. With these mixing services, users hope, an observer may know who the depositors are but be unable to make connections between senders.[31] But researchers have found that if people use a mixing service just a handful of times, it may be possible for an observer to know who made which transactions with near-perfect accuracy.[32] These concerns have led to the development of new, nominally more secretive currencies like Monero and Zcash, the latter of which JP Morgan Chase is using to help develop its own open source blockchain project.[33] Nevertheless, developing privacy-centric cryptocurrencies has proved a difficult task, and developers have faced repeated instances in which they

---

30 *Bitcoin Transactions Aren't as Anonymous as Everyone Hoped,* MIT Technology Review (Aug. 23, 2017), https://www.technologyreview.com/s/608716/bitcoin-transactions-arent-as-anonymous-as-everyone-hoped/.

31 *Survey of Bitcoin Mixing Services: Tracing Anonymous Bitcoins,* Novetta 4 (2015), http://www.novetta.com/wp-content/uploads/2015/10/NovettaBiometrics_BitcoinCryptocurrency_WP-W_9182015.pdf.

32 MIT Technology Review, *supra* note 30.

33 Patrick Howell O'Neill, As Cryptocurrencies Grow, So Does the Demand to Track Their Users, CyberScoop (Nov. 13, 2017), https://www.cyberscoop.com/bitcoin-trackingzcash-monero-cryptocurrency/; Laura Shin, JPMorgan Chase to Integrate Zcash Technology to Its Enterprise Blockchain Platform, Forbes (May 22, 2017), https://www.forbes.com/sites/laurashin/2017/05/22/jpmorgan-chase-to-integrate-zcash-technology-to-its-enterprise-blockchain-platform/#6e9483b57a33.

have been forced to make corrections through hard forks in their blockchains because of vulnerabilities identified by privacy researchers.[34]

In addition to questions about the degree to which blockchains can preserve anonymity or even pseudonymity, there are significant issues about whether and how blockchain-based products will be able to comply with a range of potentially applicable privacy obligations. In many cases, the laws imposing those obligations did not anticipate technologies with characteristics that are inherent to blockchain implementations, such as decentralized storage of data and immutability. As a result, blockchain operators and their users will be forced to fit square blockchain pegs into round regulatory holes.

Consider, for example, one of the most significant recent developments in privacy law—the European Union's General Data Protection Regulation (GDPR) that came into force in May 2018. The extensive obligations that the GDPR imposes fall largely on the "data controller," which generally refers to those who control the "purposes and means" of processing personal data.[35] But it may not be clear who the data controller is in the case of a blockchain; the answer may depend on the particular governance arrangements of a given blockchain. In the case of a public blockchain, each of the numerous nodes may be a separate and distinct data controller.

Further, some of the GDPR's obligations do not translate clearly to the blockchain context. For example, the GDPR mandates a "right to erasure," under which a data controller must delete "personal data" about subjects of the European Union in certain circumstances, such as when the person concerned objects and there is otherwise no overriding reason to keep the data.[36] But that right cannot be easily implemented on a decentralized blockchain for which immutability is a defining characteristic. Although there may be solutions (such as not storing personal data directly in the blockchain or doing so only in encrypted form and then deleting the key),

---

34   In September 2017, for example, the cryptocurrency Monero responded with a hard fork to correct vulnerabilities identified in an originally published privacy-research paper only to see many of the same researchers discover additional issues in a second paper published in March 2018. *See* Rachel O'Leary, *Broken Privacy? The Allegations Against Monero Are Old News*, CoinDesk (March 30, 2018); *see also* Malte Moser, et al., *An Empirical Analysis of Traceability in the Monero Blockchain*, Proceedings on Privacy Enhancing Technologies 1–21 (Mar. 28, 2018).

35   MailControl, *Controller vs. Processor*, https://www.gdpreu.org/the-regulation/key-concepts/data-controllers-and-processors/.

36   Regulation (EU) 2016/679 Art. 17; Stefan Wilke & Dennis Krings, *Blockchain from a Perspective of Data Protection Law*, Deloitte, https://www2.deloitte.com/dl/en/pages/legal/articles/blockchain-datenschutzrecht.html.

it remains unclear whether they are both feasible and will pass regulatory muster.

In the United States, most privacy laws are sector-specific and applicable requirements will vary depending on the use case. For example, a number of companies are building blockchain applications for various financial services, and financial services institutions must comply with a range of regulatory obligations. The Federal Trade Commission's (FTC) Financial Privacy Rule limits a financial institution's ability to disclose a consumer's "nonpublic personal information" to third parties.[37] Covered institutions must give clear notice describing their practices for sharing information with third parties and provide customers an opportunity to opt out of their information being shared.[38] At the same time, banks have data retention obligations that require, for example, the retention of information on past customers for five years after their accounts are closed.[39] Blockchain applications will have to be designed to enable compliance with these privacy safeguards. In some cases, blockchain technology may provide better or more efficient ways to do so. For example, a distributed ledger system can help track customers' opt-in and opt-out consent choices and records of disclosures to consumers. In other cases, just as with the erasure right under GDPR, there may not be a clear means of compliance because the applicable rule did not anticipate technology with blockchain characteristics.

Similarly, companies that are building blockchain products to store medical health records will have to ensure compliance with applicable privacy requirements. The Health Insurance Portability and Accountability Act (HIPAA) Privacy Rule requires health care providers, among others, to use and share only the minimum amount of protected health information necessary to accomplish the objective of the given use.[40] Further, the rule requires that individuals be given the right to review and obtain

---

37 *How to Comply with the Privacy of Consumer Financial Information Rule of the Gramm-Leach-Bliley Act,* FEDERAL TRADE COMMISSION (July 2002), https://www.ftc.gov/tips-advice/business-center/guidance/how-comply-privacy-consumer-financial-information-rule-gramm.

38 *Id.*

39 *Bank Secrecy Act/Anti-Money Laundering Examination Manual,* FEDERAL FINANCIAL INSTITUTIONS EXAMINATION COUNCIL 49 (Aug. 24, 2007), https://www.fdic.gov/regulations/examinations/bsa/ffiec_cip.pdf.

40 *Summary of the HIPAA Privacy Rule,* U.S. DEPARTMENT OF HEALTH AND HUMAN SERVICES (July 26, 2013), https://www.hhs.gov/hipaa/for-professionals/privacy/laws-regulations/index.html.

copies of their protected health information.[41] States impose additional obligations. Most, for instance, regulate how long health institutions must keep information on their patients.[42]

Finally, in addition to privacy, blockchain operators will have to comply with a range of potentially applicable federal, state, and industry data security requirements. At the federal level, under HIPAA, covered health care entities must protect against reasonably anticipated security threats. Under the FTC's Safeguards Rule, covered financial institutions must identify reasonably foreseeable security risks and design plans to address them.[43] At the state level, states such as Massachusetts have enacted detailed data protection requirements for organizations that handle personal information of Massachusetts residents, requiring employee training, third-party oversight, and encryption, among other things.[44] As with privacy, the industry likely will need to translate how these security obligations apply to blockchain implementations, perhaps with guidance from regulators.

Blockchain developers may also have to comply with various industry security standards. For instance, the Payment Card Industry Data Security Standards set security standards for organizations that handle bank cards.[45] Banks often pass fines for violations of this standard onto merchants, which could include blockchain operators that handle credit card purchases.[46]

3. LEGAL CONSEQUENCES

Developers of blockchain technologies can face civil and criminal exposure relating to data security and privacy lapses when their products fail or are misused. In general, the civil claims that have been or may be asserted against blockchain technologies are similar to the claims brought against

---

41   *Id.*

42   *State Medical Record Laws: Minimum Medical Record Retention Periods for Records Held by Medical Doctors and Hospitals,* HEALTHIT, https://www.healthit.gov/sites/default/files/appa7-1.pdf

43   *FTC Financial Information Safeguards Rule Takes Effect,* FEDERAL TRADE COMMISSION (May 23, 2003), https://www.ftc.gov/news-events/press-releases/2003/05/ftc-financial-information-safeguards-rule-takes-effect.

44   Standards for the Protection of Personal Information of Residents of the Commonwealth, 201 C.M.R. 17.

45   Gina Stevens, *Data Security Breach Notification Laws,* CONGRESSIONAL RESEARCH SERVICE 8 (Apr. 10, 2012), https://fas.org/sgp/crs/misc/R42475.pdf.

46   PCI Compliance Guide, *PCI FAQs,* https://www.pcicomplianceguide.org/faq/.

other products and services that suffer from security or privacy compromises. These include claims of negligence, breach of contract, unjust enrichment, and breach of fiduciary duty, among others. The criminal claims that blockchain developers may face include those related to money laundering and to illegally retaining or distributing sensitive information.

(a) Civil Liability

Despite the number of blockchain-related companies in existence, and despite the number of blockchain-related mishaps (Mt. Gox, DAO, and others), there has been little litigation brought against the owners and developers of blockchain-related companies. This will almost certainly change. Users of blockchain technologies, shareholders in the companies that make them, and the U.S. government itself will increasingly bring claims against blockchain owners whose products are compromised from a privacy or data security standpoint.

(i) Consumer Claims

Consumers may potentially assert a range of civil claims against the developers and operators of blockchain technologies when those technologies fail. Those claims likely will be similar to those brought against companies after significant data breaches, including negligence, negligent misrepresentation, breach of contract, unjust enrichment, invasion of privacy, breach of fiduciary duty, and conversion and trespass to chattels. When a blockchain product fails, perhaps because it does not perform its intended function (e.g., it becomes permanently inaccessible due to loss of a crypto key) or because someone inappropriately accesses data contained in it, a user of that product may assert a claim of ordinary negligence. To prevail on such a claim, the user must show that the defendant owed a duty to the user, that there was some breach of that duty and that damages resulted.[47] The challenge for plaintiffs in such cases is often overcoming the "economic loss" doctrine, the requirement that the negligence caused actual harm to the plaintiff's person or property.[48] Nevertheless, plaintiffs have brought many negligence claims against companies after ordinary data breaches.[49] At least one group of plaintiffs have sued for negligence

---

47   Douglas H. Meal, *Private Data Security Breach Litigation in the United States*, 2014 WL 10442 at *6.

48   *Id.* at *4.

49   In re TJX Companies Retail Sec. Breach Litig., 564 F.3d 489, 498 (1st Cir. 2009), *as amended on reh'g in part* (May 5, 2009).

after the failure of a blockchain-based business: former customers of Mt. Gox brought a negligence claim against the site's owner, among others. The plaintiffs claimed that the owner had a duty to exercise reasonable care to prevent the misuse of their Bitcoins and fiat currency and that he breached that duty by failing to implement industry-standard protocols to protect the site.[50] Litigation in that case remains ongoing.

A user of a blockchain product may also bring a claim of negligent misrepresentation. To succeed on such a claim, the plaintiff must show that the defendant made a material misrepresentation without reasonable grounds for believing it to be true, that the plaintiff justifiably relied on this misrepresentation, and that injury resulted.[51] Plaintiffs have brought this claim in other data breach cases. For instance, in *Cumins v. Merrick Bank*, plaintiffs sued a bank after a security breach resulted in the theft of customers' account information, alleging both intentional and negligent misrepresentation.[52] Users of blockchain technologies could similarly claim intentional or negligent misrepresentation if the technology fails or if data is stolen.

Users of blockchain technologies could also claim a breach of express or implied contract, just as plaintiffs have done in other data breach cases. These claims may be more viable as commercially available blockchain software programs come on the market. To succeed on such a claim, the plaintiff must show that a contract between the plaintiff and defendant exists, that the plaintiff complied with the terms of the contract, but that without excuse the defendant did not, and that damages resulted.[53] In *In re: Zappos*, customers sued after a data breach of the shoe store's website, alleging that certain security-related statements on Zappos's website were part of the contracts between Zappos and its customers. The Ninth Circuit, reversing a lower court's decision, held that the customers had standing to sue, at least at the motion-to-dismiss stage, as the plaintiffs faced a "substantial risk of identity theft."[54] Similarly, a data security or privacy compromise of a blockchain technology could result in a meritorious breach of

---

50 Greene et al. v. Mizuho Bank et al., 1:14-cv-01437, Fourth Amended Class Action Complaint, ECF No. 245, ¶¶ 98–99, Mar. 7, 2017 at ¶ 103.

51 Meal, *supra* note 47 at *6.

52 Cumis Ins. Soc., Inc. v. Merrick Bank Corp., 2008 WL 4277877, at *10 (D. Ariz. Sept. 18, 2008).

53 Meal, *supra* note 47 at *5.

54 In re Zappos.com, Inc., 884 F.3d 893 (9th Cir. 2018).

contract claim if the product owner makes assurances about the security or reliability of its product and if users rely on that assurance.[55]

A user of a blockchain product might also assert a claim of unjust enrichment when such a product fails. To succeed in an unjust enrichment claim, a plaintiff must generally show that a benefit was knowingly conferred on the defendant by the plaintiff and that it would be unjust for some reason to allow the defendant to keep the benefit without some compensation to the plaintiff.[56] Such claims often arise when a data breach or product failure reduces the value of a customer's purchase and when customers cannot sue under ordinary contract law. Plaintiffs have already brought one unjust enrichment suit against a blockchain company, the cryptocurrency exchange CoinBase.[57] In *Leidel et al. v. Coinbase*, plaintiffs argued that that the company unjustly benefited from doing business with a sham cryptocurrency exchange called Cryptsy that stole plaintiffs' assets.

A user of a blockchain product may also bring a claim of invasion of privacy if sensitive data stored on the blockchain is exposed. To succeed on such a claim, the plaintiff must generally show that the defendant publicized a matter from the plaintiff's private life, that the matter is not of public concern, and that its release would be highly offensive to the reasonable person.[58] Plaintiffs have brought such a claim in response to other data breaches. In *Randolph v. ING Life Ins. & Annuity Co.*, for instance, plaintiffs claimed an invasion of privacy after a company laptop containing their personal information was stolen. In that particular case, the court rejected the claim, as the plaintiffs were unable to show that their information was actually disclosed to anyone.[59] Nevertheless, users of a blockchain technology could claim an invasion of privacy if information they store with the product is disclosed to others without authorization.

A user of a blockchain product may also claim a breach of fiduciary duty. To succeed on such a claim, a plaintiff must demonstrate the existence of a duty by the defendant and damages flowing from its breach.[60] Plaintiffs have already made such claims against developers of blockchain technologies. Plaintiffs in *CoinBase* argued that CoinBase aided and

---

55   *Id.*
56   66 Am. Jur. 2d Restitution and Implied Contracts § 11.
57   Leidel et al. v. Coinbase, 9:16-cv-81992 (S.D. Fla. Dec. 13, 2016), Complaint, ECF No. 1.
58   *What Is Invasion of Privacy?*, Findlaw, http://injury.findlaw.com/torts-and-personal-injuries/what-is-invasion-of-privacy-.html.
59   Randolph v. ING Life Ins. & Annuity Co., 973 A.2d 702 (D.C. 2009).
60   Crusselle v. Mong, 59 So. 3d 1178, 1181 (Fla. Dist. Ct. App. 2011).

abetted a sham cryptocurrency's breach of fiduciary duties as it allegedly stole users' cryptocurrency.[61]

A user of a blockchain product may also claim impermissible conversion or trespass to chattels. To succeed on a conversion claim, a plaintiff must show that the defendant wrongfully assumed control of plaintiff's property to such an extent that the defendant must pay the value of the property itself.[62] To succeed on the lesser claim of trespass to chattels, the plaintiff must show only the defendant's partial control over the property; the resulting damages are commensurably lesser. Plaintiffs have already brought conversion and trespass claims in blockchain-related suits. For instance, in the case against Mt. Gox operator Mark Karpeles, plaintiffs alleged that Mr. Karpeles was liable for either conversion or trespass to chattels for wrongfully assuming control over their cryptocurrencies. Similarly, in *CoinBase*, plaintiffs claimed that CoinBase aided and abetted Cryptsy's conversion of their cryptocurrencies as the company stole their assets.[63]

In addition to the range of claims listed above, a plaintiff may also bring a claim under any number of consumer protection statutes against a blockchain owner for a faulty product. The specific elements of these consumer fraud statutes vary from state to state. But often the plaintiff must show that the defendant intentionally deceived the plaintiff in the course of trade or commerce and that the plaintiff was damaged as a result.[64] For instance, in the consumer fraud case against Mr. Karpeles, plaintiffs alleged that he deceptively represented that he would keep the plaintiffs' Bitcoins safe, when in fact he neither intended to nor actually did so.[65]

(ii) Shareholder Claims

In addition to the range of claims that plaintiffs could bring for a faulty blockchain technology, shareholders in the company that makes or operates a faulty blockchain technology can sue as well. In these shareholder derivative suits, plaintiffs sue the officers and directors of the defendant company, alleging various failures in their responsibilities as managers.

---

61   Coinbase, 9:16-cv-81992 at ECF No. 1, ¶¶ 71–85.

62   7 American Law of Torts § 23:25.

63   Coinbase, 9:16-cv-81992 at ECF No. 1, ¶¶ 158–60.

64   *See, e.g.*, In re Heartland Payment Sys., Inc. Customer Data Sec. Breach Litig., 834 F. Supp. 2d 566, 606 (S.D. Tex. 2011), *rev'd in part sub nom.* Lone Star Nat. Bank, N.A. v. Heartland Payment Sys., Inc., 729 F.3d 421 (5th Cir. 2013) (describing New York consumer fraud statute).

65   Greene et al. v. Mizuho Bank et al., 1:14-cv-01437, Fourth Amended Class Action Complaint, ECF No. 245, ¶¶ 98–99, Mar. 7, 2017 at ¶¶ 111–13.

For instance, after a data breach at Wyndham Worldwide Corporation in which the personal information of 600,000 customers was disclosed, shareholders brought suit and alleged a breach of fiduciary duty, a waste of corporate assets, and unjust enrichment. Shareholders similarly sued Target and Home Depot after their own data breaches, alleging between the two cases breach of fiduciary duty[66] and breach of corporate loyalty, corporate waste, and violation of the Securities Exchange Act's proxy statement requirement.[67] Ultimately, the claims in all three cases were dismissed.[68] With Wyndham, the court found that the plaintiffs failed to raise a reasonable doubt that the defendants acted in bad faith.[69] With Target, the court concluded that it would not be in the best interests of the company to pursue actions against its directors or officers.[70] And with Home Depot, the court concluded that plaintiffs failed to demonstrate that the Board of Directors failed to act on the security risk with a conscious knowledge that it had a duty to do so.[71] Nevertheless, it is entirely possible that shareholders in companies that build blockchain products will bring similar suits if those products have their data security compromised or otherwise fail.

(iii) Government Actions

In addition to user and shareholder suits, government agencies may bring civil claims or otherwise levy fines against the owners of blockchain technologies for their failure to comply with various security and privacy requirements. For instance, the Federal Trade Commission, among other government agencies, may bring suit for a blockchain owner's failure to comply with the Gramm-Leach-Bliley Act. The statute requires that financial institutions, which may include owners of blockchain technologies, identify reasonably foreseeable internal and external risks to the security of a customer's information and implement information

---

66   12 No. 2 In-House Def. Q. 12.

67   1 Data Sec. & Privacy Law § 8:55 (2017).

68   Davis et al. v. Steinhafel et al., No. 14-CV-0203, [Dkt. 99] (D. Minn. Aug. 29, 2016) (Dismissing derivative action against Target executives); Palkon v. Holmes, 2014 WL 5341880, at *1 (D.N.J. Oct. 20, 2014) (Dismissing case against Wyndham executives); In re The Home Depot, Inc. S'holder Derivative Litig., 223 F. Supp. 3d 1317 (N.D. Ga. 2016), *appeal dismissed sub nom.* Bennek v. Ackerman, No. 16-17742-DD, 2017 WL 6759075 (11th Cir. Oct. 24, 2017).

69   Palkon v. Holmes, 2014 WL 5341880, at *1 (D.N.J. Oct. 20, 2014).

70   Ronald W. Breaux et al., *Target Data Breach Derivative Suit Dismissed* (July 19, 2016), http://www.haynesboone.com/alerts/target-data-breach-derivative-suit-dismissed.

71   12 No. 2 In-House Def. Q. 12.

safeguards to control against those risks.[72] And as mentioned above, the Federal Trade Commission and Department of Health and Human Services can unilaterally levy a range of fines against companies that fail to comply with data security obligations. Blockchain services in the finance and health care industries may well fall under these agencies' jurisdiction and be subject to such fines.

(b) Criminal Liability

In addition to the various civil liabilities discussed above, blockchain users and owners may face a range of criminal liabilities for the misuse of their products. Most prominently, people who use blockchain-based cryptocurrencies as part of broader criminal activities may be charged with money laundering. To be guilty of domestic money laundering, a defendant must attempt to conduct a financial transaction, knowing that the property involved was the product of some crime, with one of several specific intents (for instance, to promote a crime or to evade taxes). In the most publicized example of criminal prosecution involving cryptocurrency, the U.S. Department of Justice charged Ross Ulbricht, the operator of the Silk Road online marketplace for illegal goods, of exactly that. Authorities alleged that Ulbricht, by maintaining the Silk Road site and facilitating the purchase of illegal drugs with Bitcoins, laundered money in order to promote illegal activities. Ulbricht was found guilty, and as part of his case, a court determined that Bitcoins were "funds" within the meaning of the criminal money laundering statute.[73]

In addition to money laundering, operators of blockchain technologies can be charged for operating unlicensed money transfer businesses. To be guilty of such a crime, the defendant must, among other things, operate a money transferring business without federal or state registration or with knowledge that the money is derived from a criminal offense or is intended to be used to promote an unlawful activity.[74] In July 2017, the Justice Department charged Alexander Vinnik, an operator of the cryptocurrency exchange BTC-e with exactly this, as well as engaging in unlawful monetary transactions, transactions involving criminally derived property, and money laundering and conspiracy to do the same.[75] The prosecution remains ongoing.

---

72 Guin v. Brazos Higher Educ. Serv. Corp., 2006 WL 288483, at *3 (D. Minn. Feb. 7, 2006).
73 U.S. v. Ulbricht, 31 F. Supp. 3d 540 (S.D.N.Y. 2014).
74 18 U.S.C. § 1960.
75 U.S. v. Vinnik, 16-cr-00227, Superseding Indictment, Jan. 21, 2017.

Blockchain operators who store or share sensitive information may face additional forms of criminal liability. For instance, federal statutes prohibit knowingly receiving, possessing, or distributing child pornography,[76] and the operator of blockchain technology could face criminal liability if the blockchain product were used to store or share that information. While such an example may seem outlandish, distributed anonymous information networks like Tor have been used to share this sort of information before, and distributed blockchain technologies could be used to do the same.

Defendants found guilty of a crime using a blockchain-based cryptocurrency can also have that cryptocurrency seized. Under federal civil forfeiture law, the government may confiscate property involved in an illegal money laundering transaction or a transaction involving an unlicensed money transfer business. The federal government has used these authorities to seize blockchain-based cryptocurrencies already, for instance by taking the Bitcoins held on both Silk Road and BTC-e servers after their operators' arrests.[77] It is likely that the government will seek similar forfeitures in the future.

4. CONCLUSION

Blockchain technologies present unique—and as yet not fully known—security and privacy concerns. Security concerns can range from the existential (for instance, majority attacks) to the ordinary (thefts of individual cryptocurrency users' wallets). Privacy concerns can range from the inherent ability to track actions on public ledgers to requirements to comply with "right to erasure" regulations. Mismanagement of blockchain technology data security or privacy can result in civil and criminal liability. As blockchain technology evolves, developers will apply it to different industries to accomplish new ends. The application of applicable civil and criminal laws will surely evolve as well.

---

76 18 U.S.C § 2252A.

77 U.S. v. Ulbricht, 13-cv-06919, Partial Judgment by Default and Order of Forfeiture, ECF No. 19, Jan. 15, 2014; Jamie Redman, *BTC-e on Refunds, the FBI and Alexander Vinnik*, Bitcoin.com (July 31, 2017), https://news.bitcoin.com/btc-e-on-refunds-the-fbi-and-alexander-vinnik/.

CHAPTER 5

Antitrust Regulation and Blockchain Technology

Ryan C. Thomas
Thomas D. York
Peter A. Julian

Government antitrust agencies and courts that enforce and interpret antitrust laws regularly confront dynamic and evolving technologies. At its core, blockchain technology is simply an alternative—albeit a potentially disruptive one—to more traditional interactions between buyers and sellers who want to conduct financial or other transactions. Although less than a decade old, blockchains and blockchain-inspired distributed ledgers have been deployed across a number of industries around the world, and many companies are evaluating whether, when, and how to implement the technology. Some of these efforts involve market participants at different levels of the supply chain (manufacturers, distributors, customers); others involve direct competitors (rival buyers or sellers); still others involve collaborations in which the participating companies may be competitors or customers for different transactions.

By enabling collaboration in new and different ways, blockchain technology offers the potential for significantly more efficient and secure transactions. This technology, however, also raises the potential for competitive harm. Some of the same attributes that could lead to significant efficiencies, such as real-time information exchanges about price and self-executing "smart contracts," also could facilitate collusive behavior among participating members. Similarly, a distributed ledger controlled by a single company or a group of companies could deny rivals access to all or important parts of the blockchain platform. Armed with such power, a single firm or a consortium of firms could potentially exclude rivals, raise rivals' costs, or create conditions under which market participants find it easier to collude on price, output, or quality.

Because blockchain is not a unitary concept, there is no one-size-fits-all answer for how best to eliminate or reduce antitrust risk. As discussed in Chapter 1, blockchain is simply a descriptive term for technology by which (i) connected computers (ii) reach agreement over (iii) shared data.[1] Already many different blockchain configurations exist that can be customized to serve the needs of its participants. In general, antitrust risk will vary depending on the purpose (efficiency-enhancing or not) of the collaboration, business relationship of the participants (competitors or suppliers/customers), membership restrictions (open or exclusive), industry structure (concentrated or unconcentrated), and information exchanged (competitively sensitive or not).

Antitrust enforcers around the world, including in the United States, are closely monitoring blockchain issues.[2] To the extent that a blockchain has international dimensions, it is likely subject to the competition laws of multiple jurisdictions. As of this writing, there have been no antitrust enforcement actions or significant judicial decisions on the subject, which is not especially surprising given that the technology remains relatively new. The nascent nature of the

---

1 *See* Chapter 1; *see also* Blockchain, A briefing from Coin Center, Peter van Valkenburgh, presentation at FTC FinTech Forum: Artificial Intelligence and Blockchain (Mar. 23, 2017), https://www.ftc.gov/news-events/audio-video/video/fintech-forum-artificial-intelligence-blockchain-peter-van-valkenburgh.

2 *See* Press Release, U.S. Dep't of Justice, Justice Department Convenes Summit on Digital Currency and the Blockchain (Nov. 9, 2015), https://www.justice.gov/usao-ndca/pr/justice-department-convenes-summit-digital-currency-and-blockchain; *It's Time for a FTC Blockchain Working Group*, FED. TRADE COMM'N (Mar. 16, 2018), https://www.ftc.gov/news-events/blogs/techftc/2018/03/its-time-ftc-blockchain-working-group; *FinTech Forum: Artificial Intelligence and Blockchain*, FED. TRADE COMM'N (Mar. 9, 2017), https://www.ftc.gov/news-events/events-calendar/2017/03/fintech-forum-blockchain-artificial-intelligence; *see also* Speech, Johannes Laitenberger, Director-General for Competition, European Commission, Striking the right balance in the enforcement of competition rules (Sept. 20, 2017), http://ec.europa.eu/competition/speeches/text/sp2017_14_en.pdf; *Report of Study Group on Data and Competition Policy*, Japan FAIR TRADE COMM'N (JFTC) (June 6, 2017), https://www.jftc.go.jp/en/pressreleases/yearly-2017/June/170606_files/170606-3.pdf (summarizing potential antitrust issues involving collection and utilization of various data and application under Japanese law).

technology, however, will not shield it from antitrust scrutiny. Going forward, similar to the introduction of other new technologies, such as business-to-business (B2B) purchasing exchanges in the late 1990s and early 2000s,[3] businesses should expect that, to the extent distributed ledger technology raises competition concerns, traditional antitrust principles will apply.

1. ANTITRUST FRAMEWORK: FORMATION AND OPERATION OF BLOCKCHAIN

Antitrust laws fundamentally seek to protect competition. There are four U.S. federal antitrust laws that could potentially implicate issues related to distributed ledger technology:

- Section 1 of the Sherman Act, which prohibits agreements that unreasonably restrain trade;[4]
- Section 2 of the Sherman Act, which prohibits monopolization and attempted monopolization;[5]
- Section 5 of the Federal Trade Commission Act (FTC Act), which prohibits unfair competition;[6] and
- Section 7 of the Clayton Act, which prohibits anticompetitive transactions, including certain joint ventures and competitor collaborations.[7]

---

3 *See, e.g.,* Press Release, Fed. Trade Comm'n, FTC Terminates HSR Waiting Period for Covisint B2B Venture (Sept. 11, 2000), https://www.ftc.gov/news-events/press-releases/2000/09/ftc-terminates-hsr-waiting-period-covisint-b2b-venture ("Covisint is the first B2B venture to be reviewed by the Commission. It is a proposed joint venture that plans to operate an internet-based business-to-business exchange providing services for firms in the automotive industry supply chain. The venture's core offerings will include services to assist in product design, supply chain management, and procurement functions performed by auto manufacturers and their direct and indirect suppliers."); *see also Entering the 21st Century: Competition Policy in the World of B2B Electronic Marketplaces,* Fed. Trade Comm'n (Oct. 2000), https://www.ftc.gov/system/files/documents/reports/entering-21st-century-competition-policy-world-b2b-electronic-marketplaces/b2breport.pdf.

4   15 U.S.C. §§ 1, 2.

5   15 U.S.C. §§ 1, 2.

6   15 U.S.C. § 45.

7   15 U.S.C. § 18.

Other jurisdictions worldwide generally enforce similar prohibitions on collusion,[8] monopolization/abuse of dominance,[9] and transactions that may substantially lessen competition.[10] Although similarities exist across jurisdictions in terms of prohibited conduct, there are some important differences in the legal standards to establish violations.[11] Companies that

---

8   Europe: EU law contains a prohibition on anticompetitive agreements and concerted conduct and in practice prohibits a similar range of horizontal restraints to those covered by Section 1 of the Sherman Act. *See* Consolidated Version of the Treaty on the Functioning of the European Union art. 101(1), Sept. 5, 2008, 2008 O.J. (C 115) 47 [hereinafter TFEU]; *see also* Treaty of Lisbon Amending the Treaty Establishing the European Communities, Dec. 13, 2007, 2007 O.J. (C 306) 1 (introduced a renumbering of the articles in the TFEU, renumbering former art. 81 to art. 101).

China: Articles 13 and 14 of the Anti-Monopoly Law of the People's Republic of China (Anti-Monopoly Law) prohibit "monopoly agreements," defined as any agreement, decision, or concerted practice that eliminates or restricts competition. Presidential Decree No. 68 (Promulgated by the Standing Comm. Nat'l People's Cong., Aug. 30, 2007, effective Aug. 1, 2008) [hereinafter *Anti-Monopoly Law*], http://english.mofcom.gov.cn/article/policyrelease/Businessregulations/201303/20130300045909.shtml.

Japan: Article 3 of Antimonopoly Act prohibits "unreasonable restraint of trade," which is any agreement or concerted practice that substantially restricts competition in a market, https://www.jftc.go.jp/en/legislation_gls/amended_ama09/index_files/The_Antimonopoly_Act.pdf.

9   Similar to the Sherman Act, Section 2, Article 102 of the Treaty on the Functioning of the European Union (Article 102 TFEU) prohibits firms holding a dominant position in a relevant market from abusing that position. TFEU, *supra* note 8, Art. 102 ("Any abuse by one or more undertakings of a dominant position within the internal market or in a substantial part of it shall be prohibited as incompatible with the internal market in so far as it may affect trade between Member States."). In China, Anti-Monopoly Law similarly prohibits a firm from abusing its dominant market position. *Anti-Monopoly Law, supra* note 8, Art. 17. In Japan, the Antimonopoly Act prohibits monopolization as well as certain exclusionary conduct, such as exclusive dealing and refusal to deal, which are prohibited as unfair trade practices even if a firm does not have a dominant position and no substantial anticompetitive effect is found.

10   Similar to the Clayton Act, the 2004 EU Merger Regulation (EUMR) applies to a wide array of transactions, including mergers, acquisitions, and joint ventures. *See* Council Regulation (EC) No 139/2004 of 20 January 2004 on the control of concentrations between undertakings, 2004 O.J. (L 24) 1-22 [hereinafter EU Merger Regulation], http://eur-lex.europa.eu/legal-content/en/ALL/?uri=CELEX:32004R0139. The China *Anti-Monopoly Law* includes a merger control regime requiring preclosing clearance by the Ministry of Commerce (MOFCOM) of reportable transactions. *Anti-Monopoly Law, supra* note 8, Art. 21. Also, the Japanese Antimonopoly Act regulates various forms of merger transactions which require preclosing merger filing and review of transactions exceeding certain filing thresholds by the JFTC.

11   In China, for example, alleged "concerted practices" may be proven merely by showing parallel conduct (e.g., regarding price) combined with an opportunity to communicate, a standard that would appear to endanger many blockchain-style collaborations in which price or other commercial terms are captured and communicated within the distributed ledger. Vertical agreements, too, are subject to a higher level of scrutiny in China than in the United States, with particularly aggressive enforcement of resale price maintenance—another potential risk

participate in blockchain initiatives that cross international borders must be mindful that their business activities are likely subject to the competition laws of multiple countries.

The unifying theme that generally applies across all U.S. antitrust laws (with the exception of certain naked restraints on competition) is whether, on balance, a business activity helps or harms competition. Indeed, many collaborations between competitors, which typically raise more potential antitrust issues than purely unilateral conduct, often survive antitrust scrutiny. Enforcement agencies and courts often conclude that competitor collaborations, including those designed to develop and implement new technology, can generate significant procompetitive benefits.[12] Certain other business practices between competitors, however, such as fixing prices, allocating markets, and rigging bids, are found to always or almost always harm competition. Such conduct is presumed unlawful without any inquiry into claimed procompetitive benefits (per se analysis).[13]

---

for blockchain platforms given the potential for the communication and preservation of pricing information. For companies with significant market positions, China has a lower threshold for a finding of market dominance, including a presumption of dominance for market shares over 50 percent. Dominant firms are prohibited from engaging in a long list of "abusive" conduct, including, for example, setting unfairly high prices, refusing to deal, requiring exclusivity, and discriminating between similarly situated customers. Most of these prohibitions may technically be offset by proof of sufficient procompetitive justifications, but in practice, there has been little consideration given to efficiency claims. For example, the agencies gave scant attention to such claims in two-high profile abuse of dominance cases—*Qualcomm* (2015) and *Tetra Pak* (2016).

    12 *See* Princo Corp. v. ITC, 616 F.3d 1318, 1334-35 (Fed. Cir. 2010) (en banc) (noting that "research joint ventures . . . can have significant procompetitive features, and it is now well settled that an agreement among joint venturers to pool their research efforts is analyzed under the rule of reason" (citing Addamax Corp. v. Open Software Found., 152 F.3d 48, 52 (1st Cir. 1998))); Realcomp II Ltd. v. FTC, 635 F.3d 815, 830 (6th Cir. 2011) (applying rule of reason to policy that "limited access to internet marketing and imposed additional costs on the marketing of discount listings"); United States v. Nat'l Ass'n of Realtors, 2006 WL 3434263, at *3, *13 (N.D. Ill. 2006) (applying rule of reason to policies that "allegedly single out Internet access, allegedly without any legitimate basis, for unique treatment vis-a-vis all other methods by which a broker can provide information to a client"). *But see, e.g.,* United States v. Apple Inc., 952 F. Supp. 2d 638, 694 (S.D.N.Y. 2013) (reviewing a horizontal agreement on pricing for electronic books under the per se rule); Fiona Scott-Morton, Deputy Ass't Att'y Gen., Antitrust Div., U.S. Dep't of Justice, Antitrust Enforcement in High-Technology Industries: Protecting Innovation and Competition, Remarks as Prepared for the 2012 NYSBA Annual Antitrust Forum 2 (Dec. 7, 2012), http://www.justice.gov/atr/public/speeches/290876.pdf (noting that "[i]nteroperability is key" in technology industries because, among other reasons, they often "rely on numerous technology standards in order to ensure basic compatibility.").

    13 Leegin Creative Leather Prods. v. PSKS, Inc., 551 U.S. 877, 885 (2007); *see also* Business Elecs. Corp. v. Sharp Elecs. Corp., 485 U.S. 717, 723 (1988) ("Certain categories of agreements . . . have been held to be per se illegal, dispensing with the need for case-by-case

In the United States, antitrust violations can be subject to civil and criminal penalties. The Antitrust Division of the U.S. Department of Justice (DOJ), Federal Trade Commission (FTC) and private plaintiffs can bring civil antitrust actions, seeking treble damages and injunctions to prevent or to halt ongoing anticompetitive conduct.[14] The DOJ may also prosecute price fixing, market allocation, and bid rigging criminally. Such per se violations are subject to criminal fines and imprisonment.[15]

(a) Sherman Act Section 1

Antitrust laws treat concerted actions between parties differently than unilateral actions taken by a single party. Section 1 of the Sherman Act addresses concerted activity, prohibiting "[e]very contract, combination . . . or conspiracy, in restraint of trade."[16] Courts have interpreted this language to prohibit agreements that *unreasonably* restrain trade.[17]

A threshold issue in any Section 1 inquiry is whether there is an unlawful "agreement," as Section 1 does not prohibit independent conduct, and the courts have long wrestled with what amounts to an "agreement" under the antitrust laws.[18] An unlawful agreement need not be express; companies could instead tacitly coordinate their pricing behavior, such as by taking the same actions after sharing competitively sensitive information.[19] If competing firms did so with the common understanding that other competitors would follow suit, that could form the basis of a tacit

---

evaluation. We have said that per se rules are appropriate only for 'conduct that is manifestly anticompetitive,' that is, conduct 'that would always or almost always tend to restrict competition and decrease output.'" (citations omitted)).

14   15 U.S.C. § 15. Additionally, state attorneys general can bring civil and criminal actions under state antitrust laws. State antitrust laws are usually identical to the federal antitrust laws, but in some cases can be broader.

15   15 U.S.C. § 1; *see, e.g.,* Arizona v. Maricopa Cty. Med. Soc'y, 457 U.S. 332, 344 n.15 (1982); Press Release, U.S. Dep't of Justice, E-Commerce Exec and Online Retailer Charged with Price Fixing Wall Posters (Dec. 4, 2015), www.justice.gov/opa/pr/e-commerce-exec-and-online-retailer-charged-price-fixing-wall-posters (online retailers using algorithms to fix prices).

16   15 U.S.C. § 1.

17   *See, e.g.,* Leegin Creative Leather Prods. v. PSKS, Inc., 551 U.S. 877, 885 (2007) (quoting State Oil Co. v. Khan, 522 U.S. 3, 10 (1997)).

18   *E.g.,* Bell Atl. Corp. v. Twombly, 550 U.S. 544, 561 n.7 (2007) ("[N]either parallel conduct nor conscious parallelism, taken alone, raise the necessary implication of conspiracy . . ."); *In re* Graphics Processing Units Antitrust Litig., 527 F. Supp. 2d 1011, 1011 (N.D. Cal. 2007) (noting that "even conscious parallel behavior is not, by itself, unlawful" (quoting Bell Atl. Corp. v. Twombly, 550 U.S. 544 (2007)).

19   Theatre Enters., Inc. v. Paramount Film Distributing Corp., 346 U.S. 537 (1954).

anticompetitive agreement.[20] For example, as described further below, one potentially significant risk with blockchain technology is that barring procedural safeguards, a distributed ledger could allow competitors to access each other's competitively sensitive information, such as current pricing data. These actions, in turn, could be used to reduce competition between the participating firms.[21]

Agreements among competitors not to deal with a rival can also violate Section 1. Consider, for example, a successful blockchain collaboration by manufacturers and their customers that refuses to permit access to a rival manufacturer. To the extent that the rival cannot set up its own competing blockchain with sufficient numbers of customers—for example, if network effects preclude the rival's competing blockchain from gaining traction with customers—such a boycott could potentially drive the rival manufacturer out of the market, eliminating an important source of price competition. Alternatively, instead of boycotting a rival manufacturer, a blockchain consortium could agree among themselves to force their customers to use the platform for all of their purchases, depriving those customers of alternative sources of supply.

The DOJ and FTC have issued joint *Competitor Collaboration Guidelines* to provide guidance concerning the agencies' analytical approach to competitor collaborations.[22] These guidelines recognize that joint ventures and other less formal collaborations can result in substantial consumer

---

20 The European Court of Justice (ECJ) has adopted the same approach in several cases, holding that direct or indirect contacts between competitors to signal or influence business conduct, thereby facilitating a collusive outcome on the market, may be precluded by article 101 TFEU. *See* Case C-7/95 P, John Deere, ECLI:EU:C:1998:256, ¶¶ 86 *et seq.* and Cases 40/73 and others, Suiker Unie, ECLI:EU:C:1975:174, ¶ 173 *et seq.*

21 As explained above, in several non-U.S. jurisdictions such as China, distributed ledgers, which involve the exchange of competitively sensitive information among competitors, run a substantial risk of being challenged as a prohibited "concerted practice." Anti-Monopoly Law, *supra* note 8, art. 13. Additionally, other ministry-level regulations provide relevant guidance. For example, according to Article 6 of NDRC's Anti-Price Monopoly Rules, a finding of concerted practices shall be based on (1) uniformity between the pricing conducts of undertakings and (2) communication between the undertakings.

22 U.S. Dep't of Justice & Fed. Trade Comm'n, Antitrust Guidelines for Collaborations Among Competitors 1–2 (2000) [hereinafter Competitor Collaboration Guidelines], https://www.jftc.go.jp/en/legislation_gls/amended_ama09/index_files/The_Antimonopoly_Act.pdf. The European Commission has similar guidelines for assessments under Article 101 TFEU. *See* European Comm'n, Guidelines on the Applicability of Article 101 of the Treaty on the Functioning of the European Union to Horizontal Co-Operation Agreements, 2011 O.J. (C 11) [hereinafter EC Co-Operation Guidelines], http://eur-lex.europa.eu/legal-content/EN/ALL/?uri=CELEX%3A52011XC0114%2804%29.

benefits, but also can raise prices, reduce output, or result in other anti-competitive harm. As a result, if a particular collaboration is deemed likely to cause competitive harm, the agencies require the parties to demonstrate that such harm will be offset by efficiencies—such as cost savings or improved R&D—that cannot be achieved through less restrictive means.[23]

The *Competitor Collaboration Guidelines* also establish "safety zones" under which collaborations are not likely to result in anticompetitive harm.[24] Generally, the antitrust agencies will not challenge a collaboration when the collaboration and its participants collectively account for less than 20 percent of the relevant market.[25] This "safety zone" should provide some comfort to start-up and smaller firms seeking to establish a block-chain platform to achieve procompetitive benefits.

(b) Sherman Act Section 2

The antitrust laws also generally prohibit the abuse of monopoly power. Section 2 of the Sherman Act makes it unlawful to monopolize, or attempt to monopolize, any part of trade or commerce.[26] A Section 2 monopolization claim has two basic elements: (1) possession of monopoly power in a relevant market and (2) the willful acquisition or maintenance of that power through exclusionary conduct.[27] "Exclusionary conduct" can

---

23   The *Competitor Collaboration Guidelines* identify a number of factors the agencies consider when analyzing a collaboration, including the extent to which the relevant agreement is nonexclusive (and, thus, whether participants can continue to compete independently outside the collaboration), the extent to which participants retain independent control of assets necessary to compete, the nature and extent of participants' financial interests in the collaboration or in each other, the control of the collaboration's competitively significant decision making, the likelihood of anticompetitive information sharing, and the duration of the collaboration. Competitor Collaboration Guidelines, *supra* note 22, § 3.34(d). In China, a similar rule-of-reason type analysis is available for companies with otherwise prohibited monopoly agreements to seek, and prove their eligibility for, exemption under Article 15 of the *Anti-Monopoly Law*.

24   Under EU law, several block exemption regulations are premised on the belief that the combination of complementary skills or assets can be the source of substantial efficiencies in research and development and specialization agreements. These efficiencies provide a "safe harbor" from the application of Article 101 TFEU, provided that the combined market shares of the parties do not exceed the threshold set out the relevant block exemption. *See* EC Co-Operation Guidelines, *supra* note 22, ¶¶ 284–86.

25   Competitor Collaboration Guidelines, *supra* note 22, § 4.2. This safety zone does not apply to agreements that are per se illegal or to collaborations subject to a merger analysis.

26   15 U.S.C. § 2.

27   United States v. Grinnell Corp., 384 U.S. 563, 570-71 (1966); *see also* Verizon Commc'ns v. Law Offices of Curtis V. Trinko, LLP, 540 U.S. 398, 407 (2004) ("mere possession of monopoly power, and the concomitant charging of monopoly prices, is not only not unlawful; it is an

include refusals to deal, exclusive dealing, or denying rivals' access to essential facilities.[28]

Blockchain platforms may implicate Section 2 if, for example, a manufacturer has significant market share over an important input or end-product and forces its customers to use its blockchain for all of their upstream or downstream purchases. Such a requirement could force customers to effectively abandon its competitor's blockchain, which could qualify as exclusionary conduct.[29]

(c) Section 5 of the FTC Act

Section 5 of the FTC Act prohibits "[u]nfair methods of competition in or affecting commerce."[30] The FTC has interpreted this language expansively, asserting that Section 5 makes illegal any "deceptive, collusive, coercive, predatory, unethical or exclusionary conduct" that causes harm to competition, including conduct that the Sherman Act does not reach.[31] Some courts have agreed with the FTC's expansive reading of Section 5, holding that it gives the FTC "broad powers designed to enable it to cope with new

---

important element of the free-market system," and in order to "safeguard the incentive to innovate, the possession of monopoly power will not be found unlawful unless it is accompanied by an element of anticompetitive *conduct*").

28   The same framework generally applies in the EU and China. In China, this begins with an assessment of whether a firm is market-dominant (presumed for market shares over 50 percent) and then whether the firm has engaged in certain prohibited "abusive" conduct.

29   The FTC has adopted the "minimum efficient scale" test into its exclusive dealing analysis. Under this test, the FTC looks at whether an exclusive dealing contract denies rivals "access to customers or supplies" such that it "driv[es] their costs up and render[s] them less effective competitors." Jonathan M. Jacobson & Scott A. Sher, *"No Economic Sense" Makes No Sense for Exclusive Dealing*, 73 Antitrust L.J. 779, 791 (2006); *see, e.g.*, In the Matter of McWane, Inc., 2014 WL 556261, *28 (F.T.C. 2014) ("The FTC found that McWane's exclusive dealing contract with its distributors harmed competition because it deprived rivals of sufficient distribution to achieve efficient scale of operations.").

30   15 U.S.C. § 45(a).

31   *See e.g.*, Complaint at 31, FTC v. Qualcomm Inc., No. 5:17-cv-00220, 2017 WL 242848 (N.D. Cal. 2017) (bringing a stand-alone Section 5 count in its complaint suggesting it would catch conduct beyond the reach of Sherman Act Section 2: "Qualcomm's practices, regardless of whether they constitute monopolization or unreasonable restraints of trade, harm competition and the competitive process and therefore constitute unfair methods of competition in violation of Section 5(a) of the FTC Act."). *But see* Dissenting Statement of Commissioner Maureen K. Ohlhausen, FTC File No. 141-0199 (Jan. 17, 2017) ("It is no answer to an unsupported Sherman Act theory to bring an amorphous standalone Section 5 claim based on the same conduct.").

threats to competition as they arise."[32] Only the FTC can bring a claim under the FTC Act; there is no private cause of action.

Section 5 of the FTC has been used in a number of different contexts, but its primary target has been to challenge invitations to collude—private or public invitations by one firm to one or more of its competitors soliciting them to enter into unlawful price fixing or market allocation agreements.[33] Blockchain platforms could potentially be employed as a means to invite competitors to collude, either explicitly or implicitly. For example, providing forward-looking pricing information could be interpreted as a "signal" to competitors to follow suit.

(d) Clayton Act Section 7

Finally, the Clayton Act may apply to companies that formally combine their resources to establish a blockchain platform. Section 7 of the Clayton Act prohibits transactions, such as acquisitions, mergers, and joint ventures, if the transaction may substantially lessen competition or tend to create a monopoly.[34] Section 7 is typically enforced by the DOJ and FTC, though private party enforcement is possible as well.[35]

Under Section 7, the focus turns on the likely anticompetitive effects that may result from a transaction. This includes the loss of direct current or future (e.g., R&D, pipeline) competition between the parties as well as the potential for increased coordination between the combined firm and the remaining competitors in the market after closing. The DOJ and FTC also consider a transaction's potential for efficiencies. The agencies will not challenge a merger if the efficiencies "are of a character and magnitude such that the merger is not likely to be anticompetitive in any relevant market."[36]

Section 7 analysis necessarily requires an evaluation of competition in the future and how the transaction might help or hinder that competition.

---

32 E.I. Du Pont De Nemours & Co. v. FTC, 729 F.2d 128, 137 (2d Cir. 1984).

33 Such unilateral behavior fails to meet the required "agreement" element of Sherman Act Section 1 or the "monopoly power" element of Section 2. *See* Joshua D. Wright & Angela M. Diveley, *Unfair Methods of Competition After the 2015 Commission Statement*, Antitrust Source 7–8 (Oct. 2015), http://www.americanbar.org/content/dam/aba/publishing/antitrust_source/oct15_wright_10_19f.authcheckdam.pdf ("[O]nly a single form of business conduct—invitations to collude—has been generally accepted as a relatively uncontroversial [unfair competition method] violation.").

34 *Id.*

35 The legal basis for EU Merger Control is the EU Merger Regulation, *supra* note 10.

36 U.S. Dep't of Justice & Fed. Trade Comm'n, Horizontal Merger Guidelines 29–31 (2010).

This can be a challenging task even in many traditional industries in which competition is relatively static, there are relatively few changes in buyers and sellers, and there are limited variations in market shares over time. Under the agencies' merger guidelines, "[a] merger is not likely to enhance market power if entry into the market is so easy that the merged firm and its remaining rivals in the market, either unilaterally or collectively, could not profitably raise price or otherwise reduce competition compared to the level that would prevail in the absence of the merger."[37] Dynamic "high-tech" products such as blockchain technology often present greater predictive challenges because the nature of competition can change so rapidly. Indeed, roughly 1,300 blockchain startups and 300 corporate blockchain ventures[38] have launched in recent years, and even more are expected in the coming years.[39] To the extent they have not adopted it already, most Fortune 500 companies are evaluating the technology for its potential benefits in business operations and security.[40]

(i) Reportability of Blockchain Under the Hart-Scott-Rodino Antitrust Improvements Act

Formation of a blockchain initiative or collaboration may be subject to the Hart-Scott-Rodino Antitrust Improvements Act of 1976 (HSR Act), which establishes procedures for the review of certain transactions that meet its jurisdictional thresholds regarding the size of the transaction, size of the parties involved, and effect on U.S. commerce.[41] If reportable, the parties

---

37   *Id.* at 23.

38   *See* Outlier Ventures, Startup Tracker, https://outlierventures.io/startup-tracker/ #ecosystem (listing 1,349 blockchain startups as of March 29, 2018); Outlier Ventures, Corporate Research Tracker, https://outlierventures.io/corporate-tracker/#ecosystem (listing 293 corporate blockchain ventures as of March 29, 2018).

39   Jonathan Tyce, *Blockchain Is Coming Everywhere, Ready or Not*, BLOOMBERG INTELLIGENCE (Feb. 1, 2018), https://www.bloomberg.com/professional/blog/blockchain-coming-everywhere-ready-not; Ben Schiller, *2018 Is Going to Be a Massive Year for Blockchains, The Tech Behind Bitcoins*, FAST COMPANY (Dec. 27, 2017), https://www.fastcompany.com/40502720/2018-is-going-to-be-a-massive-year-for-the-blockchain-the-tech-behind-bitcoins.

40   Ashley Lannquist, *Blockchain in Enterprise: How Companies Are Using Blockchain Today*, Blockchain at Berkeley (Jan. 18, 2018), https://blockchainatberkeley.blog/a-snapshot-of-block-chain-in-enterprise-d140a511e5fd ("Most major Fortune 500 companies, from retail and finance to automobiles and airlines, are exploring blockchain technology for its possible benefits in business operations and security.").

41   15 U.S.C. § 18a. Many countries in Europe have generally similar merger control regimes. Under EU law, the European Commission reviews mergers that have a Community dimension, which is determined by reference to the turnover of the undertakings concerned. The EC assesses whether the merger could significantly impede effective competition in the

must submit a premerger notification form to the FTC and DOJ and abide by certain waiting periods prior to closing.[42] The HSR Act process allows the antitrust enforcement agencies to review proposed transactions and take appropriate action (including litigating to enjoin the transaction) prior to closing and provides a mechanism for the agencies to obtain information relevant to such review.

HSR Act reporting requirements may apply to certain blockchain collaborations. For example, if one or more manufacturers in an industry contribute assets to form a joint venture among themselves or with an independent third party to operate a blockchain for the industry, the transaction could be subject to HSR Act reporting requirements if it meets the then-prevailing filing thresholds.[43] But regardless of whether a transaction is reportable under the HSR Act, the collaboration remains subject to antitrust scrutiny under the substantive provisions of the Clayton Act (as well as the Sherman Act and the FTC Act). The agencies can at any time review nonreportable transactions that raise potential antitrust concerns.

2. KEY ANTITRUST ISSUES FOR BLOCKCHAIN

While distributed ledger technology may deliver significant efficiencies, companies should consider the potential antitrust risks associated with blockchain platform formation and operation. Blockchain technology presents three primary antitrust concerns: "naked" collusion, improper exchanges of information, and exclusion of rivals. Each is discussed in detail below.

(a) Collusion

First, blockchain platforms could be used as a tool by competitors to facilitate a per se unlawful conspiracy in violation of Section 1 of the Sherman

---

common market or a substantial part of it, employing wide-ranging authority, including the powers to request information, to impose remedies, and to prohibit a merger.

42 The initial waiting period for most transactions under the HSR Act is thirty days following submission of the parties' notification. *Id.* § 18a(b)(1). Either agency can trigger a second waiting period by issuing within the initial period a request for additional information, commonly referred to as a "second request." *Id.* § 18a(e)(2). A complete response to a second request can take several months or more.

43 In the EU, parties must notify as a concentration joint ventures whose parents' turnover exceeds the relevant notification thresholds when such joint ventures are "full function"—i.e., the venture performs on a lasting basis all the functions of an autonomous economic entity. *See* EU Merger Regulation, *supra* note 10, at 1, ch. IV. The formation of such a joint venture may also be subject to required premerger notification in China.

Act. Because it provides businesses a comprehensive, perfect transaction ledger, that record of transactions could potentially allow conspirators to implement and police a conspiracy across several different metrics, including, for example, current prices, output restrictions, and territory or customer restrictions. This information could allow coconspirators to ensure that no one is "cheating"—e.g., selling below the agreed on prices. In this sense, blockchain platforms are not inherently different from other communication tools that are available to facilitate collusion today. It is important to note that interdependent pricing, without more, is not illegal under U.S. antitrust law; an antitrust violation requires an agreement among the competitor conspirators.

Although no antitrust enforcement actions have been brought against firms or individuals for using blockchain technologies to carry out an anticompetitive activity to date, the DOJ has brought actions against parties in the past for colluding through common platforms.

- In 1994, the DOJ settled allegations that six airlines had fixed prices through a common airfare computer system provided by Airline Tariff Publishing Company (ATP). According to the DOJ, ATP's platform allowed the airlines to "carry on conversations just as direct and detailed as those traditionally conducted by conspirators over the telephone or in hotel rooms" by, for example, floating "trial balloon" price increases and making and receiving counterproposals.[44] The DOJ agreed to allow airlines to continue to use ATP for legitimate purposes; however, it required ATP to eliminate features that allowed airlines to negotiate prices with each other. In addition, airlines were no longer allowed to announce fares before making them public, which gave competitors time to "signal" their intentions regarding fare adjustments.[45]

- In 2015, the DOJ criminally prosecuted two executives and an e-commerce retailer in a price-fixing conspiracy through which the conspirators employed pricing algorithms to fix the prices of wall décor posters sold on Amazon. According to the DOJ, the conspirators used the same commercially available algorithm-based pricing software. That software collected competitor pricing information and priced products based on

---

44 *See, e.g.,* Press Release, U.S. Dep't of Justice, Justice Department Settles Airlines Price Fixing Suit, May Save Consumers Hundreds of Millions of Dollars (Mar. 17, 1994), https://www.justice.gov/archive/atr/public/press_releases/1994/211786.htm.

45 *See id.*

rules set by the seller. The conspirators allegedly agreed to set their respective pricing rules to match one another at the lowest price offered by one of their (nonconspiring) competitors, thereby effectively eliminating competition between themselves. The conspirators monitored and enforced their agreement by spot-checking prices. Once implemented, according to the DOJ, the conspiracy was largely self-executing.[46]

Similar to the common airline software program in *ATP* and the algorithms in *Wall Décor*, blockchain technology platforms could potentially be used to structure, implement, and police a conspiracy. At the same time, the same data that would facilitate the conspiracy could serve to undo it. Blockchains typically provide meticulous records of every transaction, showing exactly who did what and when. If antitrust authorities or private civil plaintiffs gained access to a blockchain used by cartel members, they could use ledger records to evaluate the relationship between conspirators' prices, to analyze whether evidence of coordination can be explained by other market factors, and to estimate potential overcharges.

(b) Improper Information Exchanges

Second, even in the absence of a cartel, blockchain technology could be used to facilitate improper exchanges of competitively sensitive information among competitors. Unlike naked collusion (which is always per se unlawful), many information exchanges occur for legitimate business purposes and are therefore analyzed under the rule of reason.[47] (Note, however, that "unreasonable" information exchanges are frequently used as evidence to establish a per se illegal conspiracy.)[48]

---

46 *See, e.g.,* Press Release, U.S. Dep't of Justice, E-Commerce Exec and Online Retailer Charged with Price Fixing Wall Posters (Dec. 4, 2015), https://www.justice.gov/opa/pr/e-commerce-exec-and-online-retailer-charged-price-fixing-wall-posters; *see also* Plea Agreement, United States v. Topkins, No. 15-cr-00201 (N.D. Cal. Mar. 30, 2015), https://www.justice.gov/atr/case-document/file/628891/download.

47 *See* United States v. U.S. Gypsum Co., 438 U.S. 422, 441 (1978).

48 *See* Eastern States Retail Lumber Dealers' Ass'n v. United States, 234 U.S. 600 (1914); *see also* In re Medical X-Ray Film Antitrust Litig., 946 F. Supp. 209, 221 (E.D.N.Y. 1996) (association served as "clearinghouse" from which competitors could gather current and future price information to coordinate pricing activities); United States v. FMC Corp., 306 F. Supp. 1106, 1143 (E.D. Pa. 1969) (information exchange formed part of price-fixing conspiracy). *Compare* American Column & Lumber Co. v. United States, 257 U.S. 377 (1921) (enjoining a trade association's "open price plan," under which the association collected extensive price information and disseminated detailed, prospective reports to its members predicting future prices), *with* Maple

A key feature of public distributed ledger technology is that information can be accessed by any of the participants and nodes on the system. While this decentralization potentially improves operational efficiency, it can create antitrust risk to the extent it facilitates exchanges of competitively sensitive information among competitors. Thus, if the ledger contained price, margin, cost, or other competitively sensitive data, the information exchange itself could result in less vigorous competition on prices, even in the absence of an anticompetitive "agreement" to do so.[49]

The reasonableness of information exchanges under the rule of reason considers several factors:

- *Information Sources.* Sharing information between actual or potential competitors is more likely to draw antitrust scrutiny than exchanges that involve noncompetitors. Vertically integrated firms, however, could potentially misuse information by sharing competitively sensitive information obtained by a customer of one division with another division that competes downstream with that same customer.

- *Nature of Information.* Generally, exchanges of price, output, and cost information are more likely to raise concerns than exchanges of other information. Likewise, courts consider the currency of the information, its specificity, whether it is publicly available, and the frequency of the exchanges.[50] Current price information raises greater concerns than dated information because it has a greater potential to facilitate collusion.[51] Likewise, the more specific the information exchanged, the greater potential the exchange will be viewed as anticompetitive.[52] Information that

---

Flooring Mfrs. Ass'n v. United States, 268 U.S. 563 (1925) (reversing an injunction against a trade association that merely collected historic price data and disseminated to members aggregated, nonspecific, and retrospective reports of price trends).

49 As noted earlier, under the antitrust laws of many non-U.S. jurisdictions such as China, these sorts of blockchain scenarios might constitute a prohibited "concerted practice" if the blockchain represents (and memorializes) (a) parallel business conduct among competitors combined with (b) an opportunity for them to communicate.

50 *See, e.g.,* United States v. Container Corp. of Am., 393 U.S. 333, 334–36 (1969); Todd v. Exxon Corp., 275 F.3d 191, 211–13 (2d Cir. 2001); In re Currency Conversion Fee Antitrust Litig., 773 F. Supp. 2d 351, 369 (S.D.N.Y. 2011).

51 *See U.S. Gypsum,* 438 U.S. at 441 n.16; *Todd,* 275 F.3d at 211.

52 *See* In re Currency Conversion, 773 F. Supp. 2d at 369 (specific fee amounts discussed, which raised inference of collusion).

is dated and aggregated and compiled by a third party is rarely subject to challenge.[53]

- *Industry Structure.* If an industry is highly concentrated (relatively few competing buyers or sellers), the information exchange is more likely to have anticompetitive effects.[54] By contrast, if the industry is not particularly concentrated, courts have recognized that information sharing may enhance competition.[55] This is consistent with the FTC and DOJ's *Competitor Collaboration Guidelines*, which establish "safety zone" guidelines for competitor collaborations where the participants have less than 20 percent combined market share.[56]

Through the use of a distributed ledger that is available to all participants and nodes, blockchain platforms provide an attractive means of sharing information. If used to exchange competitively sensitive information such as prices, margins, or cost data, especially between horizontal competitors, the use of blockchain platforms may suggest a violation of the Sherman Act's prohibition on express or tacit coordination based on improper information exchanges.[57] As a result, firms considering implementation of a distributed ledger must closely consider the types of information being exchanged through the blockchain, the parties to whom the information

---

53 *See* Dep't of Justice & Fed. Trade Comm'n, Antitrust Guidance for Human Resource Professionals 5 (2016), https://www.justice.gov/atr/file/903511/download; *see also Todd*, 275 F.3d at 212. But aggregation and dissemination by a third party is not a safe harbor where, for example, aggregated data consists of only a few competitors, thereby more easily allowing for attribution or where defendants use other sources, such as in-person meetings, to obtain more specific information. *See Todd*, 275 F.3d at 212–13.

54 *See, e.g.*, United States v. Container Corp. of Am., 393 U.S. 333, 337 (1969) (finding 18 firms controlling 90 percent of the market was sufficient concentration to support information-exchange claim); Sugar Inst. v. United States, 297 U.S. 553, 572 (1936) (information-exchange violation involving 15 companies holding 70–80 percent of the market); *Todd*, 275 F.3d at 199 (finding 14 companies sharing an 80–90 percent market share sufficient to support data-exchange claim on motion to dismiss).

55 *See U.S. Gypsum*, 438 U.S. at 443 n.16 ("The exchange of price data and other information among competitors does not invariably have anticompetitive effects; indeed such practices can in certain circumstances increase economic efficiency and render markets more, rather than less, competitive.").

56 Competitor Collaboration Guidelines, *supra* note 22, §§ 3.31(b), 4.2.

57 This conduct may also result in a violation of antitrust laws outside the United States. For example, to determine whether the exchange of information violates EU law, the Commission examines the characteristics of the market in which it takes place (such as concentration, transparency, stability, symmetry, complexity) as well as the type of information that is exchanged. *See* EC Co-Operation Guidelines, *supra* note 22, ¶ 58 *et. subs.*

BLOCKCHAIN INFORMATION EXCHANGE

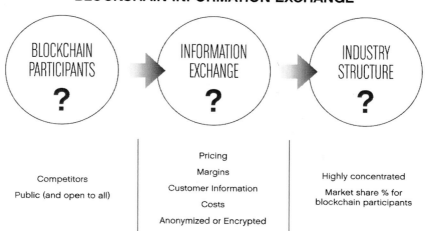

Figure 5.1: Blockchain Information Exchange

will be exchanged, and the potential for anticompetitive harm in doing so, as shown in Figure 5.1.

Today, there are two general types of blockchain ledgers: public (open or permissionless) ledgers and private (permissioned) ledgers. Each raises potential information-sharing concerns.

(i) Anonymity and Public Ledger Exchanges

Public blockchains are open, distributed ledgers that are available to everyone to participate. Anyone can be a node, and every transaction is accessible to every node. As a consequence, all information recorded on the ledger is available to everyone.

To protect user privacy—even for transactions that are publicly accessible—public blockchains often use anonymity to conceal user information. For example, while Bitcoin users can register account information,[58] the Bitcoin platform does not require users to provide any personally identifying information—only their public encryption keys.[59] To record a transaction in the distributed ledger, Bitcoin allows disclosure only of the sender's and recipient's public encryption keys and the amount of a transaction, with the latter being necessary to enable other parties to confirm that a particular public key has funds for a subsequent transaction.

---

58 *See* http://bitcoinwhoswho.com.

59 "The [Bitcoin] blockchain doesn't need to know who anybody is." DON TAPSCOTT & ALEX TAPSCOTT, BLOCKCHAIN REVOLUTION 42 (2016).

Despite its relative anonymity, a public ledger can nevertheless reveal competitively sensitive information. For example, Bitcoin has millions of unique public encryption keys for different users. Anyone can see any transaction tied to a public transaction key. As a result, once a user (say, Seller) has transacted in Bitcoin with another user (Buyer), Seller can track all of Buyer's other transactions using the same public key.[60] If Buyer later transacts with another user whose public key Seller also knows (say, Competing Seller), Seller can determine how much value was exchanged between Buyer and Competing Seller. If Competing Seller sells only one product, Seller may be able to discern Competing Seller's pricing. This scenario may not be particularly likely in Bitcoin, where millions of other users are simultaneously exchanging value. But in a business application involving significantly fewer counterparties, Seller may be able to determine the real-world identity of Competing Seller relatively easily and thus discern the prices at which Competing Seller is selling real-world goods. The potential ability to identify transacting parties would be especially high in industries where companies are vertically integrated, acting as both suppliers and competitors to other companies. In such cases, the anonymity offered by public blockchains may quickly disappear.[61]

Public blockchains can use other means to conceal information on a distributed ledger, such as encryption and hybrid on- and off-chain solutions. Today, a number of ledgers have implemented some degree of encryption or encoding. However, despite the availability of cryptographic tools to conceal data, encryption can be computationally expensive, especially for data-rich applications like complex smart contracts.[62] Blockchain developers may face pressure to limit how much information is encrypted

---

60 The Bitcoin developers provide the ability to create a new public key for each transaction in which Bitcoins are received, which would pose some obstacles to the kind of tracking discussed here.

61 This assumes that a blockchain could be anonymous in the first place. Many businesses, especially financial institutions, are subject to "Know Your Customer," antimoney laundering, and antiterrorism financing regulations that require customers to prove their identity. Such regulations may prohibit the use of anonymous blockchain in the first place.

62 *See* Vitalik Buterin, Privacy on the Blockchain (Jan. 15, 2016), https://blog.ethereum .org/2016/01/15/privacy-on-the-blockchain. Smart contract encryption is also difficult to implement in a way that still permits smart contracts to execute on the blockchain, which typically requires all information to be accessible to miners. *See* Andrew Elmore, Smart Contracts on Ethereum—Solidity & Privacy, Gresham Tech (June 13, 2016), https://www.greshamtech.com/ blog/smart-contracts-on-ethereum-solidity-privacy.

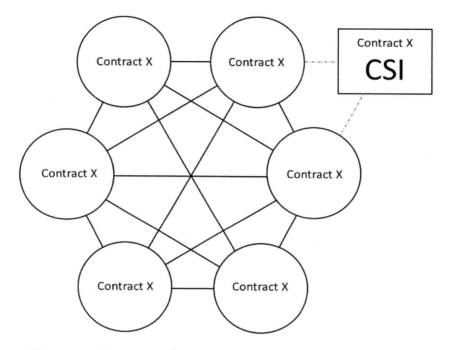

Figure 5.2: Competitively Sensitive Information Stored Off-Chain

and must balance those demands against the risk of exposing competitively sensitive information.

Companies can also use hybrid on-chain and off-chain solutions, which can pair on-chain records of the completed transaction with off-chain storage of confidential or competitively sensitive data. This approach could, for example, record the existence of a consummated contract across the distributed ledger, while giving only the contracting parties off-chain access to competitively sensitive contract information, like pricing, trade secret specifications, or other sensitive contract terms, as shown in Figure 5.2.

These hybrid solutions have the advantage of keeping certain information private without requiring as much computational expense, but the tradeoff is limiting the ability of users to maintain a comprehensive record on the blockchain or execute a smart contract on-chain, which may undermine blockchains' value proposition of transparency and traceability.

In sum, public blockchains have a variety of methods to potentially limit improper information exchanges despite all distributed ledger information being publicly accessible, but there are tradeoffs. "Anonymity" may be illusory given the smaller nature of business blockchains. Although

OPEN vs. PERMISSIONED BLOCKCHAIN

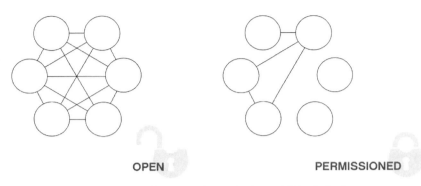

Figure 5.3: Open vs. Permissioned Blockchain

encryption and other methods of concealing competitively sensitive information may reduce the antitrust risk of improper information exchanges, they come at a significant tradeoff that may limit the value of adopting blockchain in the first place.

(ii) Permissioned-Ledger Information Exchanges

While public blockchains are entirely open, permissioned blockchains, by contrast, can, in addition to the masking and encryption tools available on public blockchains, employ additional restrictions to protect competitively sensitive information based on a user's credentials.[63] Permissioned blockchains are hosted by a defined set of nodes and editable by a defined set of users. The ledger may be publicly viewable, or it may be partially or completely private and restricted to particular users, with different users having only specified access. Figure 5.3 demonstrates the difference between these basic types of blockchain.

Most blockchains for business involve permissioned blockchains. Permissioned blockchain examples include:

- Factom, a publishing blockchain platform on which users pay to store data. Factom Harmony is a Factom application for tracking documents used for processing mortgages. The documents are encrypted and securely stored, providing an authoritative record that is accessible to authorized users.[64]

---

63   Tapscott & Tapscott, *supra* note 59, at 67.
64   https://www.factom.com/products/harmony.

- Ripple is a global financial settlement permissioned block-chain that acts as middleware between financial institutions and financial products. The platform allows users to assign value to assets such as real estate and trade them online without intermediaries.[65]
- IBM Blockchain offers a distributed ledger platform-as-a-service.[66] Walmart has tested using IBM Blockchain for tracking Chinese pork and Mexican mangoes and is now partnering with large food suppliers on a food supply chain distributed ledger to track how food is grown, handled, stored, and inspected.[67]
- R3's Corda platform is a blockchain-inspired platform created for the financial services industry.[68] Corda was developed by a consortium of more than seventy financial institutions.[69] Banks have tested using Corda for cross-border transactions like sight letters of credit for shippers and carriers.[70]

Permissioned blockchains can restrict outside access to competitively sensitive information, whereas a permissioned blockchain that is established and overseen by a market participant may present additional antitrust concerns. For example, a company that oversees smart contracts for competitors may need to ensure that competitively sensitive information is not internally accessible to its employees or that it is appropriately "walled off" from individuals involved in pricing or other competitive strategies

---

65   TAPSCOTT & TAPSCOTT, *supra* note 59, at 67, 262.

66   IBM Blockchain Platform, https://www.ibm.com/cloud/blockchain-platform.

67   Roger Aitken, *IBM & Walmart Launching Blockchain Food Safety Alliance in China with Fortune 500's JD.com*, FORBES (Dec. 14, 2017), https://www.forbes.com/sites/rogeraitken/2017/12/14/ibm-walmart-launching-blockchain-food-safety-alliance-in-china-with-fortune-500s-jd-com/#5a6adf3a7d9c (partners include Dole, Driscoll's, Golden State Foods, Kroger, McCormick and Company, McLane Company, Nestlé, Tyson Foods, and Unilever); Robert Hackett, *Walmart and 9 Food Giants Team Up on IBM Blockchain Plans*, Forbes (Aug. 22, 2017), http://fortune.com/2017/08/22/walmart-blockchain-ibm-food-nestle-unilever-tyson-dole.

68   R3, *Eleven Banks Develop Trade Finance App on R3's Corda DLT Platform*, FINEXTRA (Aug. 7, 2017), https://www.finextra.com/pressarticle/70297/eleven-banks-develop-trade-finance-app-on-r3s-corda-dlt-platform.

69   Jemima Kelly, *Exclusive: Blockchain Platform Developed by Banks to Be Open-Source*, REUTERS UK (Oct. 20, 2016), https://uk.reuters.com/article/us-banks-blockchain-r3-exclusive/exclusive-blockchain-platform-developed-by-banks-to-be-open-source-idUKKCN12K17E.

70   R3, *Eleven Banks Develop Trade Finance App on R3'S Corda DLT Platform*, Finextra (Aug. 7, 2017), https://www.finextra.com/pressarticle/70297/eleven-banks-develop-trade-finance-app-on-r3s-corda-dlt-platform.

to limit access. Likewise, a permissioned blockchain that is used by horizontal competitors could facilitate a hub-and-spoke conspiracy, such as an agreement by retailers not to offer similar contract terms to suppliers who did not participate on the permissioned blockchain.[71]

(c) Excluding Rivals

Unreasonably limiting another company's access to a distributed ledger could also trigger antitrust scrutiny. Although companies are generally free to do business (or not do business) with whomever they please, exceptions exist that apply to consortia or individual companies that possess market power. If a particular distributed ledger became a standard for an industry's transactions, the party or parties controlling access to the blockchain could risk running afoul of the antitrust laws if they unreasonably or inconsistently refused to grant access to rivals.[72]

(i) Concerted Refusal to Deal

A permissioned blockchain that is controlled by a consortium of firms could become the industry standard or a "must have" to compete in the industry. If a rival firm is denied access to the blockchain, the consortium's refusal to give a rival access to the distributed ledger may be challenged as a group boycott under Section 1 of the Sherman Act.

In the analogous context of trade association membership, decisions to exclude rivals have drawn antitrust scrutiny. Authorities evaluate whether membership requirements are consistent with, and related to, the legitimate goals of the organization and are applied in a fair, consistent, and

---

71 *Cf.* United States v. Apple, Inc., 791 F.3d 290 (2d Cir. 2015) (finding a noncompetitor, vertical participant liable for its role in orchestrating an anticompetitive horizontal agreement among book publishers), *cert. denied*, 136 S. Ct. 1376 (2016).

72 The European Commission, for example, maintains that refusals by (a) dominant undertaking(s) to grant access to an essential facility or a network may constitute an infringement to article 102 TFEU, provided the refusal relates to a product or service that is objectively necessary to compete effectively in a downstream market, the refusal is likely to lead to the elimination of effective downstream market competition, and the refusal is likely to lead to consumer harm. *See* European Comm'n, Guidance on the Commission enforcement priorities in applying Article 82 of the EC Treaty to abusive exclusionary conduct by dominant undertakings, ¶ 50 (2009/C 45/02), http://eur-lex.europa.eu/legal-content/EN/TXT/PDF/?uri=CELEX:52009XC0224(01)&from=EN.

nondiscriminatory manner.[73] The same is true for decisions to expel members.[74]

Courts recognize the need for organizations to establish and enforce membership criteria, and they typically apply the rule of reason in determining whether a decision to deny membership or to expel a current member is anticompetitive.[75] The threshold issue is whether the association possesses both market power and exclusive access to an element essential to effective competition.[76] If so, the court will analyze whether the membership restrictions are substantially related to the procompetitive efficiencies of the organization and whether those procompetitive benefits outweigh the anticompetitive effects of excluding rivals.[77]

For distributed ledger technology, the reasons for excluding rivals must be weighed against the procompetitive justification for limiting membership.[78] There may be legitimate reasons for limiting membership, such as maintaining platform security, keeping out fraudulent actors, or permitting only highly trusted firms to participate in a blockchain to enable high-trust transaction verification measures that keep transaction costs low. Blockchain administrators would likely face greater scrutiny if they treated similarly situated parties inconsistently, such as granting access to

---

73 *See* ABA Section of Antitrust Law, Antitrust and Ass'ns Handbook 68 (2009) ("Criteria should not be susceptible to subjective or discriminatory application.").

74 *Id.*

75 *See, e.g.,* Northwest Wholesale Stationers v. Pac. Stationery & Printing Co., 472 U.S. 284, 296–97 (1985) ("Unless the cooperative possesses market power or exclusive access to an element essential to effective competition, the conclusion that expulsion is virtually always likely to have an anticompetitive effect is not warranted. . . . Absent such a showing with respect to a cooperative buying arrangement, courts should apply a rule of reason analysis.").

76 GSI Tech. v. Cypress Semiconductor Corp., No. 5:11-cv-03613 EJD, 2012 WL 2711040, at *6 (N.D. Cal. 2012) (denying motion to dismiss antitrust claim alleging a computer-memory-production company was repeatedly excluded from membership in a memory-standard consortium that supplied "two-thirds" of the SRAM worldwide); *see also Northwest Wholesale Stationers*, 472 U.S. at 295–96; S&S Commc'ns v. Local Exch. Carriers Ass'n, No. CIV 02–1028, 2006 WL 519651, at *10–11 (D.S.D. 2006) (granting summary judgment of dismissal where there was no showing of market power and membership decision did not prevent plaintiff from competing in market or increase rates in the market).

77 Northwest Wholesale Stationers, 472 U.S. at 296 n.7.

78 *See, e.g.,* North Carolina State Bd. of Dental Exam'rs v. FTC, 717 F.3d 359 (4th Cir 2013) (applying quick look and full rule of reason analysis to condemn dental board's issuance of cease-and-desist letters to prevent nondentists from practicing teeth-whitening services), *aff'd on other grounds*, 135 S. Ct. 1101 (2015); Realcomp II, Ltd. v. FTC, 635 F.3d 815 (6th Cir. 2011) (discussing various restraints and finding substantial evidence to support FTC's contention that association restriction limiting distribution of MLS listing through MLS data feeds was illegal under rule of reason).

a trusted firm that is a preferred business partner while blocking access to a rival trusted firm known for low pricing strategies.

The composition of a distributed ledger's participants is an important element to evaluate anticompetitive purpose.[79] Again, by way of analogy, trade association membership decisions in associations that include the members' customers and suppliers are less likely to be challenged than associations that include only competitors, as the competing interests of vertically aligned groups are likely to offset members' desire to derive a competitive advantage from association decisions.[80]

Similarly, a blockchain consortium that includes companies at different levels in the supply chain is less likely to invite antitrust scrutiny. Conversely, while additional members and liberal access policies generally create fewer antitrust concerns,[81] adding "too many" members to a group may give the association market power, which would increase the likelihood the consortium's action could be found to be anticompetitive under the rule of reason.[82]

---

79   *See* Consolidated Metal Prods. v. Am. Petroleum Inst., 846 F.2d 284, 294–95 (5th Cir. 1988).

80   *See id.*

81   *See, e.g.*, Charley's Taxi Radio Dispatch Corp. v. SIDA of Haw., Inc., 810 F.2d 869, 877–78 (9th Cir. 1987) (declining to apply per se treatment when membership remained open and members continued to compete with each other).

82   *See, e.g.*, In re Titanium Dioxide Antitrust Litig., 959 F. Supp. 2d 799 (D. Md. 2013) (alleging addition of DuPont would provide access to 80–90% of the worldwide production data and create additional anticompetitive effects); *Northwest Wholesale Stationers*, 472 U.S. at 297; *see also* U.S. Dep't of Justice & Fed. Trade Comm'n, Statements of Antitrust Enforcement Policy in Health Care (1996), Statement 7 ("Joint purchasing arrangements are unlikely to raise antitrust concerns unless (1) the arrangement accounts for so large a portion of the purchases of a product or service that it can effectively exercise market power in the purchase of the product or service. . . ." (footnote omitted)); XIII Phillip Areeda & Herbert Hovenkamp, Antitrust Law ¶ 2221 (3d. ed. 2012); *cf.* Craftsmen Limousine v. Ford Motor Co., 491 F.3d 380, 392 (8th Cir. 2007) ("Because neither Ford nor American Coach has the ability to wield market power on their own, we must assume that Craftsmen's theory of the case depends on the concerted actions of Ford, GM, and the members of their QVM and CMC programs, including American Coach. Acting together, these businesses could conceivably exercise market power in the industry."); United States v. Realty Multi-List, Inc., 629 F.2d 1351, 1372–74 (5th Cir. 1980) (analyzing market power of organization because the association "is directly involved in the business of its members"; refusing to "set strict mathematical standards regarding the level of market power which must be shown; in any given case, the question whether the association has the requisite power may turn on a number of different factors relevant to the structure of the market"); GSI Tech. v. Cypress Semiconductor Corp., No. 5:11–cv–03613 EJD, 2012 WL 2711040, at *5–6 (N.D. Cal. 2012) (finding market power for a consortium that provided "'two-thirds' of Fast SRAM worldwide").

(ii) Unilateral Refusal to Deal

If access to a blockchain is controlled by an individual firm, a refusal to provide access to the firm's competitors may be unlawful under Section 2 of the Sherman Act under certain circumstances. The threshold to find an antitrust violation would be higher for a single entity that controls a blockchain than for a group of competitors. This is because a firm (including one with monopoly power, if lawfully obtained) is generally free to choose with whom it will do business.[83] There are two general exceptions to this rule: (1) if a firm terminates a prior course of dealing and (2) if a firm controls facilities that are essential to compete.[84]

First, a firm with monopoly power may risk an antitrust violation if it has a prior course of dealing with a competitor and it terminates the business relationship. In *Aspen Skiing Co. v. Aspen Highlands Skiing Corp.*, for example, the Supreme Court upheld antitrust liability for a ski company that terminated a profitable multi-ticket relationship with a rival ski company and then refused to sell tickets to its rival even at retail prices or honor vouchers from its rival as it had in the past.[85] Courts have since extracted from *Aspen Skiing* a rule that if a monopolist terminates a previously profitable relationship with a horizontal competitor at a short-term financial loss to the monopolist, then that may be actionable under Section 2.[86]

Thus, if a blockchain platform operator holds monopoly power in a relevant market, it could face antitrust scrutiny if it terminates an ongoing course of dealing with a competitor.[87] For example, if a manufacturer with

---

83 Verizon Communications v. Law Offices of Curtis V. Trinko, LLP, 540 U.S. 398, 408 (2004).

84 Similar concepts are generally understood to exist in other jurisdictions, including China, although in many of those jurisdictions, these distinctions and exceptions are not yet clearly articulated or utilized publicly in enforcement practice.

85 472 U.S. 585 (1985).

86 *Id.* at 601 ("The high value that we have placed on the right to refuse to deal with other firms does not mean that the right is unqualified."). Prior to *Trinko*, the First Circuit held that "[i]n essence, a unilateral refusal to deal is prima facie exclusionary if there is evidence of harm to the competitive process; a valid business justification requires proof of countervailing benefits to the competitive process." Data Gen. Corp. v. Grumman Sys. Support Corp., 36 F.3d 1147, 1183 (1st Cir. 1994) (affirming that the Chicago Stadium was an essential facility to a party with agreement to buy the Bulls contingent on obtaining a stadium lease.

87 In the United States, a single actor's market share of 65–70 percent in a cognizable relevant market generally constitutes compelling evidence of monopoly power. *See, e.g.*, Spirit Airlines v. Nw. Airlines, 431 F.3d 917, 935–36 (6th Cir. 2005) (finder of fact can find monopoly power based on evidence of 70–89 percent market share); Image Technical Servs. v. Eastman Kodak

monopoly power over widgets also managed a critical blockchain for all upstream and downstream participants in the widget industry but abruptly terminated access to the blockchain from its competitors, the termination could be analyzed as a potentially unlawful exclusionary act.

Likewise, if use of a blockchain became so pervasive in an industry that it became impossible to compete without it and it could not reasonably be duplicated, the blockchain operator may be required to provide access to this "essential facility" to its rivals on nondiscriminatory terms, regardless of whether it had previously provided access to its competitors.[88] While this doctrine is typically applied to transportation facilities (e.g., railroad tracks) and utilities (e.g., power and water), lower courts have at times applied the doctrine outside these industries.[89]

(iii) Exclusionary Membership Requirements

Blockchain access terms and conditions can also be potentially anticompetitive if the blockchain is controlled by a consortium of competitors or a single competitor with market power in a relevant market that engages in exclusionary conduct. If, for example, users are required to exclusively use a dominant blockchain platform, then that could raise Section 2 concerns if it would foreclose members from joining a rival blockchain. Of course, not all exclusivity restrictions harm competition. It may be necessary and reasonable to require exclusivity, for example, when a startup blockchain platform is working to reach a threshold scale of users necessary to be viable. If the hypothetical startup is a marketplace blockchain platform, it will need enough buyers to attract sellers and vice versa. Requiring users to buy or sell on only the startup platform may help it obtain a critical mass of users to allow the platform to compete with other online marketplaces.

Co., 125 F.3d 1195, 1206 (9th Cir. 1997) ("Courts generally require a 65 percent market share to establish a prima facie case of market power."). By contrast, a market share that permits an inference of monopoly power is lower in China, Japan, and the European Union.

88   MCI Commc'ns Corp. v. AT&T, 708 F.2d 1081, 1132–33 (7th Cir. 1983).

89   Fishman v. Estate of Wirtz, 807 F.2d 520, 539 (7th Cir. 1986) (affirming findings that "the Chicago Stadium . . . was the only Stadium in the Chicago Metropolitan area during the relevant time period which was suitable for the exhibition of professional basketball"); Colonial Penn Group v. Am. Ass'n of Retired Persons, 698 F. Supp. 69, 73 (E.D. Pa. 1988) (denying dismissal of essential facilities claim contending "advertising in the AARP publications is the only effective means to market its products to persons over the age of fifty, or the more discrete market of AARP members").

3. CONCLUSION

Although blockchain technology represents an innovative way for companies to decentralize data and secure transactions, antitrust enforcers will apply existing antitrust principles to evaluate the potential for competitive harm. For example, competing firms that (i) fix prices, (ii) allocate customers, (iii) engage in exclusionary conduct to foreclose rivals from access to important inputs or customers, or (iv) exchange competitively sensitive information will face scrutiny under the antitrust laws, regardless of how they carry out that conduct. The antitrust laws are agnostic as to whether parties reach an unlawful agreement to restrain trade through in-person meetings in a smoke-filled room or through nodes in a blockchain. The same dynamic applies to unilateral conduct—antitrust authorities will investigate dominant firms that use their market power to keep out rivals, whether by denying them access to a key market or by denying them access to a dominant supply chain blockchain platform.

Figure 5.4 below illustrates the general spectrum of antitrust risk for firms that are considering whether to form or to participate in a blockchain initiative.

RISK OF ANTITRUST INVESTIGATION

More Risk   **Less Risk**

- Two or more competitors participating
- Highly concentrated industry
- Pricing, cost, or other competitively-sensitive data
- No encryption of data
- Restricted access to blockchain
- Few efficiency justifications

- No competitors participating
- Unconcentrated industry
- No competitively-sensitive data
- Encrypted data
- Open access to blockchain
- Significant efficiency justifications

Figure 5.4: Risk of Investigation Factors

CHAPTER 6

Cryptocurrencies and the Regulation of Money Transmission

Lisa M. Ledbetter
Colin C. Richard
Kayla M. Davis

Federal laws and many state laws regulate money transmitters. The laws that apply to money transmission were enacted for purposes of consumer protection and to prevent money laundering and fraud. Subject to limited exceptions, a nonbank business that provides money transmission services or that is engaged in the transfer of funds is generally considered a money transmitter under federal law.[1] However, the meaning of "money transmitter" and the rules that apply are not uniform across jurisdictions.

As the concepts of money and currency have continued to evolve and technology has enabled new means for storing and transmitting value, federal and state authorities have implemented administrative rules and/ or guidance that apply specifically to virtual currency. Because federal and state money transmission laws are both broad and evolving, it is imperative for a business that engages in virtual-currency activities, including administering or exchanging virtual currency, to ensure compliance with these laws, to the extent applicable, in order to avoid civil and criminal penalties that may be imposed for noncompliance.

---

1   *See* 31 C.F.R. § 1010.100(ff)(5) ("money transmitter" definition). For this purpose, "[t]he term 'money transmission services' means the acceptance of currency, funds, or other value that substitutes for currency from one person *and* the transmission of currency, funds, or other value that substitutes for currency to another location or person by any means." *Id.*

Money transmitters are subject to federal and state regulation and generally must register with the Financial Crimes Enforcement Network (FinCEN), a bureau of the U.S. Department of the Treasury (the Treasury) established in 1990, and obtain a state license to operate, implement an anti-money laundering program, report certain events, and retain relevant records. For purposes of the federal money transmission requirements, "users" of virtual currency are generally not considered money transmitters, while "administrators" and "exchangers" of virtual currency generally would be considered money transmitters if such entities accept and transmit virtual currency or buy or sell virtual currency in exchange for currency or another virtual currency (unless one of several regulatory exceptions apply). By contrast, state laws vary regarding the application of money transmission requirements to virtual-currency businesses, and a uniform act to regulate virtual-currency businesses is under consideration in some states.

As financial institutions are an essential component of international, federal, and state efforts to deter illicit financial transactions, it is important for a business exploring possible new business models, products, or services involving virtual currencies to understand how money transmitter requirements may apply.[2]

1. FEDERAL REGULATION OF MONEY TRANSMITTERS

(a) The Bank Secrecy Act and FinCEN

Beginning in 1970 with enactment of the Currency and Foreign Transactions Reporting Act (commonly known as the Bank Secrecy Act, or BSA) and continuing through a series of legislative actions in subsequent years, Congress has developed a framework designed to inhibit illicit financial transactions, including money laundering and terrorist financing.[3]

FinCEN administers many of the requirements of the BSA.[4] FinCEN's stated mission is to "safeguard the financial system from illicit use and combat money laundering and promote national security through the collection, analysis, and dissemination of financial intelligence and strategic

---

2 Certain relevant topics of state regulation are discussed further in Chapter 7 of this book.

3 *See* 12 U.S.C. § 1829b; 12 U.S.C. §§ 1951–59; 31 U.S.C. §§ 5311–14; and 31 U.S.C. §§ 5316–32.

4 In addition to its regulatory and enforcement roles, FinCEN also facilitates the sharing of financial transaction information with U.S. law enforcement agencies, financial intelligence units in more than 140 countries, and the private sector.

use of financial authorities."[5] FinCEN executes this mission through the pursuit of two strategic goals: (i) "[s]afeguard the financial system from evolving money laundering and national security threats" and (ii) "[m]aximize sharing of financial intelligence by and between FinCEN and its domestic and foreign partners in government and private industry."[6]

The BSA requirements establish an audit trail that permits law enforcement agencies to "follow the money" in an effort to inhibit and prosecute illicit financial transactions. Over the years, FinCEN has expanded application of the BSA requirements to apply to a wide range of financial institutions—both banks and certain nonbank financial institutions such as money services businesses (MSBs), broker-dealers, and credit card systems. FinCEN promulgated BSA rules covering MSBs in 1999, which require MSBs to register with FinCEN, establish anti-money laundering programs and policies, issue reports, and retain records.

It is important for a business operating in the virtual-currency space to understand BSA and FinCEN obligations and expectations that relate to the business's activities, including the exchange or movement of real currency, virtual currency, or other funds for customers.

(b) Money Transmitters

Pursuant to FinCEN regulations, an MSB is an entity "wherever located doing business, whether or not on a regular basis or as an organized or licensed business concern, wholly or in substantial part within the United States, in one or more of the [following] capacities": foreign exchange dealers, check cashers, issuers and sellers of monetary instruments such as money orders, providers and sellers of prepaid access, the U.S. Postal Service, and money transmitters.[7] This chapter focuses on money transmitters.

The FinCEN regulations generally define a "money transmitter" as any entity that provides money transmission services or any other entity engaged in the transfer of funds.[8] Money transmission services are a broad

---

5 *Strategic Plan for Fiscal Years 2014–2018*, Financial Crimes Enforcement Network, 3.

6 *Id.* at 6–10.

7 31 C.F.R. § 1010.100(ff) (definition of "money services business"). The definition excludes banks, SEC- or CFTC-regulated entities, and individuals who engage in certain of these activities on an infrequent basis and not for gain or profit. A virtual currency business that is not a MSB may have similar BSA compliance obligations under rules applicable to other financial institutions.

8 *Id.* at § 1010.100(ff)(5)(i). States generally also regulate money transmitters, and each state's definition may be similar to the FinCEN definition, but not necessarily the same. State money transmission regulation is discussed in Section 2 of this chapter.

concept and refer to "the acceptance of currency, funds, or other value that substitutes for currency from one person *and* the transmission of currency, funds, or other value that substitutes for currency to another location or person by any means."[9] Accordingly, businesses that accept a customer's currency, funds, or other value and transmit currency, funds, or other value to another location or another person by any means or any other business engaged in the transfer of funds may fall within the scope of this definition.

Whether a business meets this definition "is a matter of facts and circumstances," and the FinCEN regulations provide six express exceptions to the definition of money transmitter.[10] A business that only engages in the following activities is *not* a "money transmitter":

- *Certain Service Providers*—"Provides the delivery, communication, or network access services used by a money transmitter to support money transmission services."

- *Payment Processors*—"Acts as a payment processor to facilitate the purchase of, or payment of a bill for, a good or service through a clearance and settlement system by agreement with the creditor or seller." FinCEN has considered this exception with regard to a virtual-currency trading platform and a virtual-currency payment system and requires four conditions to be met for this exception to apply.[11] FinCEN requires that (i) "the entity providing the service must facilitate the purchase of goods or services, or the payment of bills for goods or services (other than money

---

9   *Id.*

10   31 C.F.R. § 1010.100(ff)(5)(ii). These express exceptions reflect a clarification of the prior version of FinCEN's money transmitter definition. In 2009, FinCEN proposed a rule to amend the prior money transmitter definition. The prior definition included a single exception that FinCEN has described as "difficult for potential money transmitters to apply"; therefore, FinCEN added the current six exceptions to "reflect[] policy developed through administrative ruling letters and guidance" in the years since the initial definition was introduced. 74 Fed. Reg. 22129, 22137–22138 (May 12, 2009) (Notice of Proposed Rulemaking). FinCEN explained that the revisions, implemented by the final rule issued in 2011, "more clearly delineate the scope of entities regulated as MSBs, so that determining which entities are obligated to comply is more straightforward and predictable." 76 Fed. Reg. 43585, 43585 (July 21, 2011) (Final Rule).

11   See *Request for Administrative Ruling on the Application of FinCEN's Regulations to a Virtual Currency Trading Platform*, Financial Crimes Enforcement Network, 4–5, FIN-2014-R011 (Oct. 27, 2014), and *Request for Administrative Ruling on the Application of FinCEN's Regulations to a Virtual Currency Payment System*, Financial Crimes Enforcement Network, 4, FIN-2014-R012 (Oct. 27, 2014).

transmission itself)";[12] (ii) "the entity must operate through clearance and settlement systems that admit only BSA-regulated financial institutions"; (iii) "the entity must provide the service pursuant to a formal agreement"; and (iv) "the entity's agreement must be at a minimum with the seller or creditor that provided the goods or services and receives the funds."[13]

• *Clearance and Settlement Systems*—"Operates a clearance and settlement system or otherwise acts as an intermediary solely between BSA regulated institutions. This includes but is not limited to the Fedwire system, electronic funds transfer networks, certain registered clearing agencies regulated by the Securities and Exchange Commission ('SEC'), and derivatives clearing organizations, or other clearinghouse arrangements established by a financial agency or institution."

• *Transporters of Currency*—"Physically transports currency, other monetary instruments, other commercial paper, or other value that substitutes for currency as a person primarily engaged in such business, such as an armored car, from one person to the same person at another location or to an account belonging to the same person at a financial institution, provided that the person engaged in physical transportation has no more than a custodial interest in the currency, other monetary instruments, other commercial paper, or other value at any point during the transportation."

• *Prepaid Providers*—"Provides prepaid access."

• *Sale of Goods or Services*—"Accepts and transmits funds only integral to the sale of goods or the provision of services, other than money transmission services, by the person who is accepting and transmitting the funds." FinCEN has considered this exception with regard to a virtual-currency trading platform and a virtual-currency payment system and requires three conditions to be met for this exception to apply.[14] FinCEN requires that (i) "[t]he money transmission component must be part of the provision of goods or services distinct from money transmission

---

12 Regarding this first condition, FinCEN explained that it "does not consider providing virtual currency for real currency or vice versa as a non-money transmission related service." FIN-2014-R011 at 5.

13 *See, e.g., id.* at 4–5.

14 *See* FIN-2014-R011 at 4 and FIN-2014-R012 at 4–5.

itself"; (ii) "[t]he exemption can only be claimed by the person that is engaged in the provision of goods or services distinct from money transmission"; and (iii) "[t]he money transmission component must be integral (that is, necessary) for the provision of the goods or services."[15]

(c) FinCEN's Rules in the Virtual Currency Context

As virtual currencies have become more prevalent, FinCEN has issued interpretive guidance and several administrative rulings and taken enforcement actions against businesses that have failed to comply with applicable requirements.

In March 2013, FinCEN published interpretive guidance regarding the application of the FinCEN regulations to administrators, exchangers, and users of convertible virtual currencies. This guidance distinguishes "currency" from "virtual currency"; FinCEN generally defines "currency" as the circulating legal tender of a jurisdiction that is customarily used and accepted in that jurisdiction and defines "virtual currency" as a medium of exchange that operates similarly to a currency but lacks some attributes of currency. The March 2013 guidance focuses specifically on "convertible" virtual currency—virtual currency that "either has an equivalent value in real currency, or acts as a substitute for real currency."[16]

The guidance considers three roles within the virtual currency market: an administrator, an exchanger, and a user.[17] These roles are not mutually exclusive; a business can act in one or more of these capacities.

- *Administrator*—"a person engaged as a business in issuing (putting into circulation) a virtual currency, and who has the authority to redeem (to withdraw from circulation) such virtual currency."
- *Exchanger*—"a person engaged as a business in the exchange of virtual currency for real currency, funds, or other virtual currency."
- *User*—"a person that obtains virtual currency to purchase goods or services," by mining, purchasing, or otherwise.

FinCEN concluded that "[a] user who obtains convertible virtual currency and uses it to purchase real or virtual goods or services is not an

---

15 *See, e.g.*, FIN-2014-R011 at 4.

16 *Application of FinCEN's Regulations to Persons Administering, Exchanging, or Using Virtual Currencies*, Financial Crimes Enforcement Network, 1, FIN-2013-G001 (Mar. 18, 2013).

17 *Id.* at 2.

MSB under FinCEN's regulations."[18] An administrator or exchanger, on the other hand, may be a money transmitter, to the extent such an entity:

> (1) accepts and transmits a convertible virtual currency or (2) buys or sells convertible virtual currency in exchange for currency of legal tender or another convertible virtual currency for any reason (including when intermediating between a user and a seller of goods or services the user is purchasing on the user's behalf) . . . unless a limitation to or exemption from the definition applies . . .[19]

As of February 2018, approximately 100 virtual currency administrators and exchangers were registered with FinCEN.[20]

Through examples in the March 2013 guidance and numerous administrative rulings, FinCEN has provided to administrators and exchangers of convertible virtual currencies several factors for determining whether a business is a money transmitter and, thereby, subject to the FinCEN regulations.

(i) Centralized and Decentralized Virtual Currencies

FinCEN refers to convertible virtual currencies that have a centralized repository as "centralized virtual currencies" and has stated that an administrator of such a repository that allows transfers of value between persons or locations is considered a money transmitter.[21] A business that accesses the convertible virtual currency services of the administrator to accept and transmit the virtual currency on behalf of others is considered an exchanger and a money transmitter. An exchanger's money transmission activities may include transmitting value to another *location*, which, FinCEN explains, expressly includes transmitting value from a user's bank account to the user's convertible virtual-currency account with the administrator.[22] The exchanger's money transmission activities may also include the transmission of value to a third party, including by "accept[ing] currency or its equivalent from a user and privately

---

18 *Id.* at 2.

19 *Application of FinCEN's Regulations to Virtual Currency Mining Operations,* Financial Crimes Enforcement Network, 1, FIN-2014-R001 (Jan. 30, 2014). *See also* FIN-2013-G001 at 3.

20 Letter from Assistant Secretary for Legislative Affairs, U.S. Department of the Treasury, to Senator Wyden (Feb. 13, 2018).

21 FIN-2013-G001 at 4.

22 *Id.*

credit[ing] the user with an appropriate portion of the exchanger's own convertible virtual currency held with the administrator of the repository ... [and] then transmit[ting] that internally credited value to third parties at the user's direction."[23]

FinCEN refers to a convertible virtual currency "(1) that has no central repository and no single administrator and (2) that persons may obtain by their own computing or manufacturing effort" as a decentralized virtual currency.[24] With regard to decentralized virtual currencies, a business acts as a money transmitter when it (i) "creates units of convertible virtual currency and sells those units to another person for real currency or its equivalent"[25] or (ii) "accepts such de-centralized convertible virtual currency from one person and transmits it to another person as part of the acceptance and transfer of currency, funds, or other value that substitutes for currency."[26]

While the March 2013 guidance explains that a business that creates and sells units of a decentralized "convertible virtual currency" to another entity for "real currency or its equivalent" is generally considered a money transmitter,[27] to date, FinCEN has not issued specific interpretive guidance or administrative rulings that expressly address the application of the money transmitter definition to initial coin offerings (ICOs). The Treasury, however, has commented on the issue in response to a December 2017 letter to FinCEN requesting information about FinCEN's oversight and enforcement capabilities, including specifically how FinCEN will "apply existing anti-money laundering laws such as the Bank Secrecy Act to participants in the ICO market, like token developers."[28] The Treasury's Assistant Secretary for Legislative Affairs explained that "Treasury expects businesses involved in ICOs to meet the BSA obligations that apply to them" and stated:

> Generally, under existing regulations and interpretations, a developer that sells convertible virtual currency, including in the form of ICO coins or tokens, in exchange for another type of value

---

23 *Id.* at 4–5.

24 *Id.* at 5.

25 *Id.* The business would be considered a user of the virtual currency and not a money transmitter, however, if it were to create units of the virtual currency and use the virtual currency to purchase goods or services.

26 *Id.*

27 *See id.*

28 Letter from Senator Wyden to Acting Director, Financial Crimes Enforcement Network (Dec. 14, 2017).

that substitutes for currency is a money transmitter and must comply with AML/CFT requirements that apply to this type of MSB. An exchange that sells ICO coins or tokens, or exchanges them for other virtual currency, fiat currency, or other value that substitutes for currency, would typically also be a money transmitter.[29]

(ii) Brokers, Dealers, and Issuers of Digital Certificates

In the March 2013 guidance, FinCEN stated that a broker or dealer in e-currency or e-precious metals (e.g., by electronically distributing digital certificates of ownership of real currencies or precious metals, respectively) is not a money transmitter to the extent it "accepts and transmits funds solely for the purpose of effecting a *bona fide* purchase or sale of the real currency or other commodities for or with a customer."[30] This does not apply if funds are transferred between the customer and a third party.[31]

FinCEN concluded in an August 2015 administrative ruling, however, that a company that issues freely transferable digital certificates evidencing custody of precious metals for buyers would be considered an administrator of a convertible virtual currency and a money transmitter.[32] FinCEN stated that "when the [c]ompany issues a freely transferable digital certificate of ownership to buyers, it is allowing the unrestricted transfer of value from a customer's commodity position to the position of another customer or a third-party, and it is no longer limiting itself to the type of transmission of funds that is a fundamental element of the actual transaction necessary to execute the contract for the purchase or sale of the currency or the other commodity."[33]

---

29 Letter from Assistant Secretary for Legislative Affairs, U.S. Department of the Treasury, to Senator Wyden (Feb. 13, 2018).

30 FIN-2013-G001 at 3.

31 *Id.* at 3–4.

32 *Application of FinCEN's Regulations to Persons Issuing Physical or Digital Negotiable Certificates of Ownership of Precious Metals*, Financial Crimes Enforcement Network, 4, FIN-2015-R001 (Aug. 14, 2015). The company's activities, in relevant part, included that it "holds precious metals in custody for buyers that purchase this service ('Customers'), opening a digital wallet for the Customer and issuing a digital proof of custody (a 'digital certificate') that can be linked to the Customer's wallet on the Bitcoin blockchain ledger. The Customer then can trade or exchange its precious metals holdings at the Company by any means it could trade or exchange bitcoin via the rails of the blockchain ledger." *Id.* at 1.

33 *Id.* at 4.

(iii) Virtual Currency Mining Operations

In a January 2014 administrative ruling, FinCEN concluded that a company that mines a convertible virtual currency would not be considered a money transmitter when it uses the mined convertible virtual currency solely for its own purposes and not for the benefit of another party.[34] FinCEN explained that the company may, without being considered a money transmitter, use the convertible virtual currency it has mined:

- "to pay for the purchase of goods or services";
- "pay debts it has previously incurred (including debts to its owner(s))";
- "make distributions to owners"; or
- "purchase real currency or another convertible virtual currency, so long as the real currency or other convertible virtual currency is used solely in order to make payments (as set forth above) or for [the company]'s own investment purposes."[35]

Similarly, in an April 2014 administrative ruling, FinCEN explained that the FinCEN regulations do not apply to the rental of computer systems to third parties for mining virtual currency.[36] The money transmitter definition expressly exempts delivery, communication, or network data access services. Accordingly, FinCEN concluded that "even if the [c]ompany rents a computer system to third parties that will use it to obtain convertible virtual currency to fund their activities as exchangers, such rental activity, in and of itself, would not make the [c]ompany a money transmitter."[37]

(iv) Investments in Virtual Currency for a Company's Own Account

FinCEN stated in a January 2014 administrative ruling that a company that "limits its activities strictly to investing in virtual currency for its own account" would not be considered a money transmitter, because it is

---

34 FIN-2014-R001 at 3.

35 See id.

36 *Application of Money Services Business Regulations to the Rental of Computer Systems for Mining Virtual Currency*, Financial Crimes Enforcement Network, 2, FIN-2014-R007 (Apr. 29, 2014).

37 *Id.* at 2–3.

acting as a user, not an exchanger, of virtual currency.[38] FinCEN similarly concluded that the company's production and distribution of software to facilitate the company's virtual currency purchases "does not constitute acceptance and transmission of value, even if the purpose of the software is to facilitate the sale of virtual currency," and therefore, the company would not be considered a money transmitter due to such activities.[39]

(v) Virtual Currency Trading Platforms

In an October 2014 administrative ruling, FinCEN concluded that a business that intended to implement a convertible virtual currency trading and booking platform would be a money transmitter.[40] The platform, in relevant part, would attempt to match one customer's purchase order of a virtual currency to one or more sell orders of the virtual currency. FinCEN explained that the business would be an exchanger and money transmitter because it would accept virtual currency and transmit the same; "[t]he fact that such a transmission sometimes may not occur in [the company's] business model if no match is found does not remove the [c]ompany from the scope of the regulations for those transactions that do occur."[41]

(vi) Virtual Currency Payment Systems

FinCEN concluded in an October 2014 administrative ruling that a company would be considered a money transmitter if it implements a convertible virtual currency payment system, pursuant to which the company would receive payment from a buyer in real currency, and transfer an equivalent amount of virtual currency from the company's reserves to a seller, less a transaction fee.[42] FinCEN would consider the company an exchanger and explained that it is not relevant whether the company would fund each individual transaction or would make payments from an existing virtual currency inventory that the company maintains.[43]

---

38 *Application of FinCEN's Regulations to Virtual Currency Software Development and Certain Investment Activity*, Financial Crimes Enforcement Network, 4, FIN-2014-R002 (Jan. 30, 2014).

39 *Id.* at 2.

40 FIN-2014-R011.

41 *Id.* at 3.

42 FIN-2014-R012.

43 *See id.* at 2–3.

(d) Registration and Compliance

Money transmitters must register with FinCEN and are subject to compliance obligations under the FinCEN regulations.[44] A money transmitter is generally required to register with FinCEN within 180 days from the date the business is established.[45] Additionally, a money transmitter is generally required to develop, implement, and maintain an anti-money laundering program (AML program) that is reasonably designed to prevent the company from being used to facilitate money laundering and the financing of terrorist activities.[46] The AML program must, at a minimum:

- "Incorporate policies, procedures, and internal controls reasonably designed to assure compliance with" the FinCEN regulations;
- "Designate a person to assure day to day compliance with" the AML program and the FinCEN regulations;
- "Provide education and/or training of appropriate personnel concerning their responsibilities under the program, including training in the detection of suspicious transactions"; and
- "Provide for independent review to monitor and maintain an adequate program."[47]

A money transmitter is also subject to reporting and recordkeeping requirements. For example, such a company is required to report large currency transactions[48] and suspicious transactions[49] and to maintain certain records related to compliance with the FinCEN regulations.[50]

(e) Enforcement and Liability

FinCEN has overall enforcement authority for the FinCEN regulations and coordinates the enforcement activity of other federal agencies that exercise delegated authority to examine institutions for compliance with

---

44 *See* 31 C.F.R. Part 1010 (General Provisions) and Part 1022 (Rules for MSBs).
45 *See id.* at § 1022.380.
46 *See id.* at § 1022.210.
47 *See id.* at § 1022.210(d).
48 *See id.* at § 1022.310.
49 *See id.* at § 1022.320.
50 *See id.* at § 1022.400.

the FinCEN regulations.[51] Compliance examination authority regarding money transmitters is delegated to the Commissioner of Internal Revenue. Both FinCEN and the Internal Revenue Service have the authority to examine the books and records of a money transmitter with regard to the FinCEN regulations' recordkeeping and reporting requirements. The FinCEN regulations authorize civil penalties, which may be imposed on the business and/or its partners, directors, officers, and employees; the regulations also authorize criminal penalties, which similarly may be brought against the business and individuals.

FinCEN has enforced the BSA rules against several virtual currency businesses. In May 2015, FinCEN issued a $700,000 civil money penalty against a virtual currency company and its wholly owned subsidiary, for violations of the BSA's registration, program, and reporting requirements.[52] FinCEN described the companies as acting as virtual-currency exchangers when selling premined convertible virtual currency to third parties.[53] The companies also entered into a settlement agreement with the U.S. Attorney's Office for the Northern District of California, which agreed not to pursue criminal prosecution based on the companies' conduct, and the companies paid a forfeiture of $450,000 and agreed to implement various remedial steps.[54]

In July 2017, FinCEN issued a $110,003,314 civil money penalty against a virtual currency company and a $12,000,000 penalty against an individual acting as an operator of the company, related to FinCEN determinations of violations of the BSA's registration, program, reporting, and recordkeeping requirements.[55] FinCEN stated that the company operated as an exchanger of convertible virtual currencies, and the individual "participated in the direction and supervision of [the company's] operations and finances and controlled multiple [company] administrative accounts

---

51 *See id.* at § 1010.810 generally regarding enforcement of the FinCEN regulations.

52 "Assessment of Civil Money Penalty," *In the Matter of Ripple Labs Inc. and XRP II, LLC*, Financial Crimes Enforcement Network, 2015-05 (May 5, 2015).

53 *See* "FinCEN Fines Ripple Labs Inc. in First Civil Enforcement Action Against a Virtual Currency Exchanger," Financial Crimes Enforcement Network (May 5, 2015).

54 *Settlement Agreement*, U.S. Attorney's Office for the Northern District of California, U.S. Department of Justice (May 5, 2015). The FinCEN penalty was partially satisfied by the forfeiture.

55 "Assessment of Civil Money Penalty," *In the Matter of BTC-E a/k/a Canton Business Corporation and Alexander Vinnik*, Financial Crimes Enforcement Network, 2017-03 (July 26, 2017).

used in processing transactions."[56] The company and the individual were also indicted in the Northern District of California.[57]

(f) Additional Regulatory Considerations

In addition to FinCEN regulatory requirements, other federal regulatory provisions may be relevant to certain virtual-currency businesses that act as money transmitters.[58] The FinCEN regulations are a core component of money transmission regulation, but money transmission activities can be relevant to other frameworks as well, including economic sanctions and consumer protection. The FinCEN regulations are an important starting point and a money transmitter must comprehensively evaluate its compliance obligations.

The Secretary of the Treasury is authorized, pursuant to Section 311 of the USA PATRIOT Act, to designate a financial institution operating outside of the United States as a primary money-laundering concern.[59] The designation permits the Secretary of the Treasury to require U.S. financial institutions to take special measures against the designated company, such as additional recordkeeping, information collection, and information-reporting requirements. The Treasury stated that its May 2013 designation of an online moneytransfer system was its "first use of Section 311 authorities by Treasury against a virtual currency provider."[60]

Additionally, businesses that are considered remittance transfer providers are subject to certain disclosure, error-resolution procedure, and other requirements.[61] Larger participants in the international moneytransfer market are also subject to supervision by the Bureau of Consumer

---

56   *Id.* at 2.

57   *Id.*

58   This section includes several examples only and is not a comprehensive discussion of all potentially applicable requirements.

59   *See* 31 U.S.C. § 5318A.

60   "Treasury Identifies Virtual Currency Provider Liberty Reserve as a Financial Institution of Primary Money Laundering Concern under USA Patriot Act Section 311," U.S. Department of the Treasury (May 28, 2013). *See also Notice of Finding That Liberty Reserve S.A. Is a Financial Institution of Primary Money Laundering Concern*, Financial Crimes Enforcement Network, 78 Fed. Reg. 34169 (June 6, 2013); *Withdrawal of Finding and Notice of Proposed Rulemaking Regarding Liberty Reserve S.A.*, Financial Crimes Enforcement Network, 81 Fed. Reg. 9139 (Feb. 24, 2016).

61   *See* 12 C.F.R. Part 1005, Subpart B (Requirements for Remittance Transfers).

Financial Protection.[62] These considerations are relevant to businesses that provide such financial services to consumers.

Finally, the Office of Foreign Assets Control, an office within the Treasury, administers U.S. economic sanctions, and a money transmitter should ensure that its activities are consistent with any applicable sanctions requirements.

2. STATE REGULATION OF MONEY TRANSMITTERS

In addition to federal regulation of money transmitters, most states have money transmitter regulatory frameworks. This section discusses the various approaches to state money transmission regulation with regard to virtual currency businesses. The spectrum of state approaches to the emergence of virtual currency spans from no specific action to the establishment of a new regulatory framework: (i) some states have neither enacted any legislation nor issued any administrative rules regarding virtual currencies, (ii) some states have revised existing statutory and/or regulatory frameworks and/or issued guidance addressing whether virtual currencies are within the scope of the state's existing money transmitter regulatory framework, and (iii) one state has established a new regulatory framework to govern virtual-currency businesses.

Rules and orders issued by FinCEN generally do not preempt the regulatory and enforcement frameworks adopted by the states. Variation in state regulatory approaches may increase compliance costs for companies that operate nationally. Companies must consider both the FinCEN regulations and state frameworks in each jurisdiction in which the company expects to operate to ensure that they comply with all applicable laws and rules.

(a) State Money Transmitter Acts

Most states regulate money transmitters by requiring a state license, regular examinations, reporting, and recordkeeping. A May 2016 report by the Conference of State Bank Supervisors and the Money Transmitter Regulators Association explains the state licensing approach: a primary purpose "of licensing is credentialing the entities and individuals seeking to engage in money transmission. The credentialing process serves two complementary purposes: 1) ensuring MSBs are responsible and qualified to do business, and 2) as an ongoing measure of accountability for

---

62 *See id.* at Part 1090, Subpart A and § 1090.107 (International Money Transfer Market).

the public."[63] As of May 2016, approximately forty-four states have issued licenses to virtual currency-related businesses.[64]

States have varied, however, in their approach to virtual currencies. Some states have addressed virtual-currency businesses within the framework of existing state money transmitter acts or regulations. For example, North Carolina revised its Money Transmitter Act in 2017 by broadening the scope of activities covered under the act to include certain virtual-currency businesses. The revised act defines "money transmission" to expressly include "maintaining control of virtual currency on behalf of others."[65] Many states that have modified their money transmitter laws or regulations have decided to broaden those laws to include virtual currency.[66]

By contrast, New Hampshire passed a law in 2017 that exempts from the state money transmitter license requirement "[p]ersons who engage in the business of selling or issuing payment instruments or stored value solely in the form of convertible virtual currency or receive convertible virtual currency for transmission to another location."[67] Wyoming enacted similar legislation in 2018 to add a virtual-currency exemption to the Wyoming Money Transmitter Act.[68]

(b) The Uniform Regulation of Virtual-Currency Businesses Act

The Uniform Law Commission "provides states with non-partisan, well-conceived and well-drafted legislation that brings clarity and stability to critical areas of state statutory law."[69] In July 2017, the Uniform Law Commission approved and recommended for enactment the Uniform Regulation of Virtual-Currency Businesses Act (Uniform Regulation Act) to provide states with a uniform framework for regulating entities involved in "virtual currency business activity." The Uniform Regulation Act would

---

63 *The State of State Money Services Businesses Regulation & Supervision*, Conference of State Bank Supervisors and Money Transmitter Regulators Association, 7 (May 2016).

64 *See id.* at 9.

65 N.C. Gen. Stat. § 53–208.42(13)(b).

66 Such states include, but are not limited to, Alabama, Connecticut, Georgia, North Carolina, and Washington.

67 N.H. Rev. Stat. Ann. § 399-G:3, VI-a. Such businesses are instead subject to New Hampshire's regulation of business practices for consumer protection.

68 *See* Wyoming H.B. 0019 (signed Mar. 7, 2018).

69 *About the ULC*, Uniform Law Commission, http://www.uniformlaws.org/Narrative .aspx?title=About%20the%20ULC.

"require licensure of and impose prudential regulations and customer protection requirements on businesses whose products and services include" the exchange or transfer of virtual currencies or certain custodial or fiduciary services regarding virtual currencies.[70]

If adopted by a state, the Uniform Regulation Act could decrease compliance costs and burden by providing a licensee two methods to obtain a license—application or reciprocity. A license by reciprocity would be available for "a person licensed by another state to conduct virtual-currency business activity in that state."[71] In the alternative, a state could choose to make a license by reciprocity available for entities that are licensed in a state that has substantially similar virtual-currency laws.[72]

The Uniform Regulation Act includes several exemptions.[73] For example, a business with $5,000 or less of aggregate activity with residents of an enacting state would be exempt from the Uniform Regulation Act.[74] The purpose of the Uniform Regulation Act's scope section is to ensure that the act does not regulate virtual currencies, but instead focuses on entities that issue virtual currencies or provide virtual-currency services.[75] The Uniform Regulation Act would also allow companies to register in lieu of receiving a license if the entity's volume of virtual-currency business activity does not exceed $35,000.[76]

To date, the Uniform Regulation Act has not been enacted by any state and has been introduced in only three state legislatures—Connecticut, Hawaii, and Nebraska.[77] As the Uniform Regulation Act is still relatively new, the impact, if any, that the act will have on state regulation of virtual-currency businesses remains unclear.

(c) New York

Unlike some states that have modified existing money transmitter frameworks to address virtual currencies, New York took more direct measures

---

70 Uniform Regulation Act, Prefatory Note.

71 *See, e.g., id.* at § 203, Alternative A (a).

72 *Id.* at § 203, Alternative B (a).

73 *See id.* at § 103.

74 *Id.*

75 *Id.* at § 103, comment 1.

76 *Id.* at § 207 (a).

77 *Regulation of Virtual-Currency Businesses Act*, UNIFORM LAW COMMISSION, http://www.uniformlaws.org/Act.aspx?title=Regulation%20of%20Virtual-Currency%20Businesses%20Act.

by enacting a new regulatory framework. In June 2015, the New York Department of Financial Services published a regulatory framework for virtual currencies and licensing of virtual-currency businesses, referred to as the BitLicense Regulatory Framework.[78] The New York BitLicense Regulatory Framework requires entities engaged in virtual-currency business activity to obtain a license. Virtual-currency business activity is defined broadly to cover a range of activities, including issuing virtual currencies, holding virtual currencies for others, and transmitting virtual currencies.[79]

The BitLicense Regulatory Framework requires a licensee to have a compliance officer and maintain compliance policies that focus on anti-fraud, anti-money laundering, cybersecurity, privacy, and information security.[80] A licensee must implement programs and internal controls to protect the safety of its transactions.[81] The BitLicense Regulatory Framework also covers capital requirements[82] and requirements regarding the custody and protection of customer assets.[83] Licensees must submit quarterly financial statements[84] and audited annual financial statements with an opinion and attestation from an independent certified public accountant on the effectiveness of the licensee's internal control structure.[85]

(d) California

California's Money Transmission Act is administered by the California Department of Business Oversight (DBO), and California has not yet

---

78   23 NYCRR Part 200 (Virtual Currencies). For further information on the market effects of the BitLicense regulation, please refer to Chapter 7 of this book.

79   The regulation defines virtual-currency business activities as "the conduct of any one of the following types of activities involving New York or a New York Resident: (1) receiving Virtual Currency for Transmissions or Transmitting Virtual Currency, except where the transaction is undertaken for non-financial purposes and does not involve the transfer of more than a nominal amount of Virtual Currency; (2) storing, holding, or maintaining custody or control of Virtual Currency on behalf of others; (3) buying and selling Virtual Currency as a customer business; (4) performing Exchange Services as a customer business; or (5) controlling, administering, or issuing a Virtual Currency. The development and dissemination of software in and of itself does not constitute Virtual Currency Business Activity." 23 NYCRR § 200.2(q).

80   *Id.* at § 200.7.

81   Section 200.15 sets forth the requirements for the licensee's anti-money laundering program, and Section 200.16 sets forth the requirements for the licensee's cybersecurity program.

82   *Id.* at § 200.8.

83   *Id.* at § 200.9.

84   *Id.* at § 200.14(a).

85   *Id.* at § 200.14(b).

directly addressed virtual-currency businesses within this framework. In April 2014, the DBO published an advisory to "provide the basics" about virtual currencies, including "the risks to contemplate if you're considering exchanging and investing in virtual currencies."[86] The advisory described virtual currency exchanges as "unregulated."[87] In January 2015, DBO reiterated that "[t]he California Department of Business Oversight has not decided whether to regulate virtual currency transactions, or the businesses that arrange such transactions, under the state's Money Transmission Act."[88]

California lawmakers, however, have considered legislation regarding virtual-currency businesses.[89] In February 2015, a bill was introduced that would have required digital-currency businesses to enroll in a Digital Currency Business Enrollment Program to be administered by the DBO.[90] The bill stated that the program was intended to enable the DBO to identify the businesses providing digital-currency services in California, collect information from such businesses, and require consumer disclosures.[91] The bill was not enacted into law.

In February 2017, a bill was introduced to prohibit an entity from engaging in any virtual-currency business in California unless licensed by the DBO.[92] This bill was referred to the California State Assembly's Committee on Banking and Finance, but did not pass within the applicable time period. The bill would have required a license applicant to, among other things, provide a description of any virtual-currency services previously provided by the business, the virtual-currency services that the business intends to provide in California, and a list of the other states in which the entity is licensed to engage in virtual-currency business.

---

86 *What You Should Know About Virtual Currencies*, CALIFORNIA DEPARTMENT OF BUSINESS OVERSIGHT (Apr. 30, 2014).

87 *Id.* at 1.

88 *DBO Commissioner Owen Clarifies Coinbase Exchange's Regulatory Status in California*, CALIFORNIA DEPARTMENT OF BUSINESS OVERSIGHT (Jan. 27, 2015).

89 For additional information regarding the California legislature's attempts to regulate virtual currency, please refer to Chapter 7 of this book.

90 *See* California Assembly Bill 1326 (Aug. 8, 2016 amended version), California Legislature, 2015–2016 Regular Session.

91 *See id.*

92 *See* California Assembly Bill 1123 (Mar. 30, 2017 amended version), California Legislature, 2017–2018 Regular Session.

3. INTERNATIONAL REGULATORY CONSIDERATIONS

A virtual-currency business may have money transmitter regulatory considerations in multiple countries, depending on the company's activities. FinCEN facilitates financial transaction information sharing with financial intelligence units in more than 140 countries.[93] Additionally, the intergovernmental Financial Action Task Force (FATF) has issued guidance related to virtual currencies.[94]

In June 2014, FATF published a preliminary assessment of the money-laundering and terrorist-financing risks arising from virtual-currency payment products and services[95] and, in June 2015, issued guidance to address convertible virtual-currency exchangers.[96] This June 2015 guidance was intended, in part, to "help national authorities understand and potentially develop regulatory responses including the need to amend their national laws in order to address the [money-laundering and terrorist-financing] risk of [virtual-currency payment products and services]."[97] The guidance discusses the application of FATF standards to convertible virtual-currency exchanges, including recommendations regarding applying a risk-based approach, registration or licensing, AML program requirements, customer due diligence, and reporting and recordkeeping.[98]

4. CONCLUSION

Companies exploring possible new business models, products, or services involving virtual currencies should be alert to applicable money transmitter requirements and regulatory expectations. Subject to limited exceptions, FinCEN has generally applied federal money transmission requirements to administrators and exchangers of virtual currency that accept and transmit virtual currency or buy or sell virtual currency in exchange for currency or another virtual currency.

---

93 *See, e.g., The Egmont Group of Financial Intelligence Units*, Financial Crimes Enforcement Network, https://www.fincen.gov/resources/international/egmont-group-financial-intelligence-units.

94 The FATF is an intergovernmental organization consisting of 35 member jurisdictions and two regional organizations.

95 *See Virtual Currencies: Key Definitions and Potential AML/CFT Risks*, FATF Report, Financial Action Task Force (June 2014).

96 *See Guidance for a Risk-Based Approach to Virtual Currencies*, Financial Action Task Force (June 2015).

97 *Id.* at 3.

98 *See id.* at 12.

Over several decades, federal and state regulators have developed frameworks to inhibit and prosecute illicit financial transactions, protect consumers, and diminish money-laundering risks. International standards have also been developed to address these issues. These frameworks necessarily require the involvement of financial institutions, such as money transmitters, to implement anti-money laundering programs, report information, and retain records to assist in this effort. This frameworks continue to evolve as new technologies emerge, and recent updates regarding virtual currencies are only the latest example.

CHAPTER 7

State Laws Addressing Blockchain Technology

Margaret I. Lyle
Gwendolyn R. Higley
Jared R. Kelley

Today's wide spectrum of state blockchain legislation reflects the different conclusions that state legislatures reach when they evaluate the technology's potential benefits and risks. When states make policy choices about blockchain and distributed ledger technology, they typically look to a set of hoped-for gains: economic growth, efficiency and cost savings for businesses and government, and a competitive edge in attracting business vis-à-vis other states. But state policymakers also consider some potential negatives: the new technology may be overpromoted, fail to live up to expectations, attract bad actors, or harm consumers and markets. As the technology matures, the states may reach a consensus on the right way to balance these considerations—but as yet no such consensus has emerged.[1]

At one end of the spectrum are states that have embraced blockchain as an engine of economic growth. Wyoming, for example, has enacted sweeping legislation: five new statutes (1) exempt utility blockchain tokens from state securities laws; (2) exempt virtual currency from the state's money transmitter statute; (3) authorize corporate recordkeeping by distributed or electronic records; (4) exempt virtual currency from state property taxation; and (5) authorize "series" LLC's, a corporate form considered especially conducive to blockchain-related business. Arizona has enacted legislation validating "smart contracts" and creating a "sandbox"

---

1 The discussion in this chapter of the states' laws governing blockchain technology is current as of early 2018.

that would allow "FinTech" businesses to form and develop in a protected environment. Nevada has amended its electronic-records statute to make clear that blockchain records qualify and has forbidden any local taxation of the technology. New Hampshire was the first state to exempt virtual currency from its money-transmission licensing laws. Both Delaware and Illinois have invested in blockchain initiatives to improve government services. And a Delaware statute authorizes the use of blockchain for corporate recordkeeping—a move meant to keep the state at the forefront of corporate law.

At the other end of the spectrum is New York State, which has taken the lead in regulating virtual currency by adopting a rigorous licensing requirement with a strong compliance component. New York's regulatory approach—which has come under severe criticism from the virtual-currency industry—serves the state's policy of protecting the integrity of its financial industry and markets, thus preserving public confidence in them.

In contrast to the blockchain activism demonstrated by these states, others have either staked out a middle ground or remained silent on the issue. Vermont has expressly given blockchain records evidentiary force while it considers whether other legal changes would bring new business to the state. California adopted a wait-and-see approach after initially considering virtual-currency legislation in 2015. It reconsidered the question in 2017–2018 but has not yet enacted oversight legislation directed toward virtual-currency businesses. Many states have limited themselves to clarifying how virtual currency fits within their money-transmission laws. Their goal is to prevent the use of virtual currency for criminal purposes like money laundering while providing some consumer protections. The Uniform Regulation of Virtual Currency Businesses Act promulgated by the Uniform Law Commission in 2017—which as of early 2018 has only been introduced in Hawaii, Nebraska, and Connecticut—also takes this middle approach.

As Justice Louis Brandeis recognized, under our federal form of government, a "state may, if its citizens choose, serve as a laboratory; and try novel social and economic experiments without risk to the rest of the country."[2] The current environment for blockchain and distributed ledger

---

2 *See* New State Ice Co. v. Liebmann, 285 U.S. 262, 311 (1932) (Brandeis, J., dissenting). In recent years, economic, legal, and political commentators have reexamined the extent to which the concept of the states as "laboratories of democracy" works in practice. *See, e.g.,* Edmund Andrews, *Steven Callander: How to Make States "Laboratories of Democracy,"* Stanford Graduate School of Business (May 19, 2015), https://www.gsb.stanford.edu/insights/

technology may serve as just such a state-law laboratory. Nevertheless, the blockchain landscape has also been derided as a "patchwork" of different state laws and regulations,[3] where the lack of uniformity imposes high costs of compliance for those doing business in multiple states. As the law begins to engage with this new technology, the benefit of state experimentation necessarily brings with it a corresponding burden of fragmented regulation.

1. STATE LAWS GOVERNING THE USE OF BLOCKCHAIN IN CORPORATE RECORDS, INCLUDING THE STOCK LEDGER

(a) Delaware—Authorizing Corporate Recordkeeping by Blockchain

Delaware's Senate Bill 69, signed into law in August 2017,[4] amended the Delaware General Corporation Law to allow corporations to use blockchain technology to maintain their stock ledgers.[5] Drafted with the help and expertise of the Corporate Law Council of the Delaware State Bar in response to Governor Jack Markell's 2016 call for the state to embrace blockchain technology through legislation,[6] the bill was designed to ensure that businesses incorporated in Delaware could track outstanding shares using the technology to verify current ownership and record changes in ownership at the time of the transaction.[7]

The most important amendments were the changes to section 224 of Title 8 of the Delaware code. Prior to Senate Bill 69, section 224 had

---

steven-callander-how-make-states-laboratories-democracy; Steven Callander and Bard Harstad, *Experimentation in Federal Systems*, The Quarterly Journal of Economics 130, No. 2 (2015), https://academic.oup.com/qje/article/130/2/951/2330892; Brian D. Galle and Joseph K. Leahy, *Laboratories of Democracy? Policy Innovation in Decentralized Governments*, Emory Law Journal 58, No. 6 (2009), https://lawdigitalcommons.bc.edu/cgi/viewcontent.cgi?referer=https://www.google.com/&httpsredir=1&article=1544&context=lsfp; Michael S. Greve, *Laboratories of Democracy: Anatomy of a Metaphor*, American Enterprise Institute (Mar. 31, 2001), http://www.aei.org/publication/laboratories-of-democracy/.

3 *See, e.g.*, Rob Marvin, *Blockchain, The Invisible Technology That's Changing the World*, PCMag.com (Aug. 29, 2017), https://www.pcmag.com/article/351486/blockchain-the-invisible-technology-thats-changing-the-wor (criticizing "patchwork state-by-state regulations and the ever more muddled role of federal agencies").

4 S. 69, 149th Gen. Assem., 1st Reg. Sess. (Del. 2017).

5 *See id.*

6 *See* CoinDesk, *Introducing the Delaware Blockchain Initiative*, YouTube (Sept. 30, 2016) https://www.youtube.com/watch?v=-mgxEhIvSTY.

7 *See* S. 69, 149th Gen. Assem., 1st Reg. Sess. (Del. 2017) (synopsis).

provided that a corporation's records, including its stock ledger, could "be kept on, or by means of, or be in the form of, any information storage device, or method, provided that the records so kept [could] be converted into clearly legible paper form within a reasonable time."[8] Senate Bill 69 modified that already-broad statute to make it clear that such records could be kept "on one or more electronic networks or databases (including one or more distributed electronic networks or databases)."[9] The amendments expressly allow stock ledgers stored in blockchains to perform important corporate functions such as preparing lists of stockholders entitled to vote or recording stock transfers.[10] Section 224 requires, however, that records kept in blockchains be converted to a legible paper format in response to any valid request.[11] Moreover, the amendments to section 224 give these records (when converted to paper format) the same evidentiary standing as if the records had been kept on paper.[12]

The bill's synopsis indicates that these changes, together with those described below, were "intended to provide specific statutory authority for Delaware corporations to use networks of electronic databases (examples of which are described currently as 'distributed ledgers' or a 'blockchain')."[13] It is worth noting that unlike other states, Delaware neither defines nor uses the term *blockchain* within the operative legislative text of its statutes.

Other sections of Delaware's Title 8 were modified slightly to ensure that notices given by electronic transmission have the same statutory protection as traditional written forms of communication.[14] "Electronic transmission"—previously defined to mean any communication that did not involve the transmission of paper[15]—now explicitly includes "the use of, or participation in, one or more electronic networks or databases (including

---

8 Del. Code Ann. tit. 8, § 224 (West 2017) (amended Aug. 2017).

9 Del. Code Ann. tit. 8, § 224 (West 2017).

10 *See id.* In particular, the amendments provide that blockchain "(i) can be used to prepare the list of stockholders specified in §§ 219 and § 220," covering stockholders entitled to vote and inspection of books and records; to "(ii) record the information specified in §§ 156, 159, 217(a) and 218," covering partly paid shares, share transfer for collateral, voting rights of fiduciaries, pledgors and joint owners of stock, and voting trusts and agreements; and to "(iii) record transfers of stock as governed by Article 8 of subtitle I of Title 6." *See id.*

11 *See id.*

12 *See id.*

13 S. 69, 149th Gen. Assem., 1st Reg. Sess. (Del. 2017) (synopsis).

14 *See* Del. Code Ann. tit 8, §§ 151(f), 202(a), 364 (West 2017).

15 *See* Del. Code Ann. tit. 8, § 232(c) (West 2017) (amended Aug. 2017).

one or more distributed networks or databases)."[16] This change appears to allow for ledgers kept using blockchain technology to incorporate smart-contract properties by which corporations can automate notices to stockholders.

The value of Delaware's endorsement of blockchain technology should be understood against the backdrop of the problems that attend traditional methods of recordkeeping. A recent Delaware class-action settlement, *In re Dole Food Co.*, illustrates the difficulty of maintaining an up-to-date stock ledger by traditional means.[17] After Dole went private in 2013, stockholders sued Dole's fiduciaries.[18] The parties reached a settlement that would pay the stockholders an additional $2.74 per share. The number of claims presented for payment, however, was far greater than the number of shares in the settlement class (by more than 10 million), and the difference could not be reconciled.[19] Frustrated, the court—cognizant of Delaware's blockchain agenda—observed that distributed ledger technology, once implemented, could offer "a potential technological solution by maintaining multiple, current copies of a single and comprehensive stock ownership ledger."[20]

(b) Wyoming—Authorizing Corporate Recordkeeping by Distributed or Electronic Records

A March 2018 amendment to the Wyoming Business Corporations Act allows corporations to use distributed ledger technology (such as blockchains) as a recognized corporate recordkeeping system.[21] This amendment expands the definition of "electronic transmission" to include "a process of communication that uses one (1) or more distributed or other electronic networks or databases."[22] The new law also expands the definitions of *shareholder* and *signature* and adds definitions for the terms *identity, data address, network signature,* and *record of shareholders,* enabling a corporation to use the features of blockchain technology for corporate

---

16   DEL. CODE ANN. tit. 8, § 232(c) (West 2017).

17   *See* In re Dole Food Co., 2017 WL 624843 (Del. Ch. Feb. 2, 2017).

18   *See id.* at *1.

19   *See id.* at *1–*4 ("At the conclusion of the claims process, claimants had submitted facially eligible claims for 49,164,415 shares. That figure substantially exceeded the 36,793,758 shares in the class." *Id.* at *2.).

20   *Id.* at *7 n. 1.

21   2018 Wyo. Sess. Laws HEA No. 0022, http://legisweb.state.wy.us/2018/Enroll/HB0101 .pdf.

22   *Id., codified at* WYO. STAT. ANN. § 17-16-140(a)(ix) (West 2018).

recordkeeping.[23] In other words, a corporation can use blockchain techno-logy as its only means of recordkeeping,[24] without the obligation to main-tain an add-on or legacy system in order to comply with the law. A data address can be used as the name of a shareholder,[25] and notice is effect-ive "[w]hen an electronic transmission has been made to a data address provided by the shareholder."[26]

(c) Arizona—Authorizing Blockchain as a Writing for Purposes of the Corporation Law

In April 2018, Arizona amended the definitions in its corporations statute to include blockchain technology as a "writing," meaning that blockchain will qualify when the statute specifies a "writing" or "written" form.[27]

---

23 *Id., codified at* Wyo. Stat. Ann. §§ 17-16-140(a)(xxxvii), (xxxix), (xlvi), (xlvii), (xlviii), & (xlix) (West 2018). The new language in the statutory definitions appears below in italics: (xxxvii) "Shareholder" means the person in whose name shares are registered in the records of a corporation, or the beneficial owner of shares to the extent of the rights granted by a nominee certificate on file with a corporation *or the owner of a private key that is uniquely associated with a data address that facilitates or records the sending and receiving of shares*; (xxxix) "Sign" or "signature" includes any manual, facsimile, conformed or electronic signature *or a network signature; (xlvi) "Identity" means the name of a shareholder or the data address for which the share-holder has knowledge or possession of the private key uniquely associated with the data address; (xlvii) "Data address" means the string of alphanumeric characters on one (1) or more distributed or other electronic networks or databases that may only be accessed by knowledge or possession of a private key in order to facilitate or record transactions on the distributed or other electronic network or database; (xlviii) "Network signature" means a string of alphanumeric characters that when broad-casted by a shareholder to the data address's corresponding distributed or other electronic network or database provides reasonable assurances to a corporation that the shareholder has knowledge or possession of the private key uniquely associated with the data address; (xlix) "Record of shareholders" means one (1) or more records administered by or on behalf of a corporation that records the identity of all the corporation's shareholders and the number and class of shares held by each shareholder in accordance with W.S. 17-16-1601. "Record of shareholders" includes a record of all issuances and transfers of shares of a corporation at the discretion of the corporation.*

24 *See also id., codified at* Wyo. Stat. Ann. § 17-16-1601(d) (West 2018).

25 *Id., codified at* Wyo. Stat. Ann. § 17-16-142(a)(iv) and Wyo. Stat. Ann. § 17-16-1601(c) (West 2018).

26 *Id., codified at* Wyo. Stat. Ann. § 17-16-141(c)(ii) (West 2018).

27 *See* Arizona House Bill 2603, signed into law on April 3, 2018, *available at* https://legiscan.com/AZ/text/HB2603/id/1771532/Arizona-2018-HB2603-Engrossed.html (amend-ing Ariz. Rev. Stat. § 10-140, but not yet codified; providing that "'writing' or 'written' includes blockchain technology as defined in section 44-7061," for chapters 1–17 of Title 10, Corpora-tions and Associations).

2. STATE LAWS GOVERNING SMART CONTRACTS AND BLOCKCHAIN AS ELECTRONIC RECORDS

(a) Vermont—Making Blockchain Records Self-Authenticating and Admissible

After a collaborative planning effort between the Vermont Law School, Vermont legislators, the Uniform Law Commission, and the state court system, Vermont introduced its first blockchain technology bill in March 2016.[28] Governor Phil Scott signed it into law in June 2016. Vermont's statute embraced a number of different aspects of blockchain technology within one section of the state's laws governing court procedures—"Blockchain Enabling" Title 12, Section 1913 of the Vermont Statutes.

The first subsection of this new statute defines "blockchain technology."[29] The remainder of section 1913 addresses, for evidentiary purposes, the authentication, admissibility, and certain presumptions for a "digital record electronically registered in blockchain;" it also provides some examples of the types of blockchain records to which section 1913 applies.[30]

A blockchain record is self-authenticating[31] if accompanied by "a written declaration of a qualified person, made under oath."[32] The declaration must also state the "qualification of the person to make the certification;" the date and time the record was both entered and received into the blockchain; that the record was maintained in the blockchain as a "regular conducted activity;" and that the record was made as a "regular practice."[33] A blockchain record accompanied by such a declaration is treated something like a business record.[34] It is "presumed that the fact or record verified through blockchain technology is authentic, that the date and time of

---

28   Higgins, Stan, *Vermont is Close to Passing a Law That Would Make Blockchain Records Admissible in Court*, Coindesk (May 17, 2016), https://www.coindesk.com/vermont-blockchain-timestamps-approval/.

29   "'[B]lockchain technology' means a mathematically secured, chronological, and decentralized consensus ledger or database, whether maintained via Internet interaction, peer-to-peer network, or otherwise." Vt. Stat. Ann. tit. 12 § 1913(a) (West 2016).

30   *See* Vt. Stat. Ann. tit. 12 § 1913(b)–(c) (West 2016).

31   Self-authenticating documents do not require "[e]xtrinsic evidence of authenticity as a condition precedent to admissibility." *See* Vt. R. Evid. 902.

32   Vt. Stat. Ann. tit. 12 § 1913(b)(1) (West 2016).

33   *See id.*

34   *See* Vt. Stat. Ann. tit. 12 § 1913(b)(2) (West 2016) (citing Vt. R. Evid. 803(b), the business-records exception to the hearsay rule).

blockchain recordation are true, and that the person the blockchain shows as making the recordation is the person who made it.[35] However, "[a] presumption does not extend to the truthfulness, validity, or legal status of the contents of the fact or record."[36] In addition, the statute assigns burdens of production and persuasion that apply to blockchain evidence.[37]

Section 1913(c) provides many examples of the types of blockchain records to which the statute can apply. These include, among other things, the ownership or transfer of money or property; the identity and status of interactions with government agencies or interactions in private transactions; and contractual parties or provisions.[38] Although these examples suggest the legislature's expectation that the adoption of blockchain technology will benefit business efficiency and accurate recordkeeping, section 1913(d) makes clear that the statute neither creates nor negates a duty to adopt or implement blockchain technology.[39] Nor does the statute affect, one way or the other, the legality of the underlying activity verified through the blockchain.[40]

(b) Arizona—Authorizing Blockchain Signatures as Electronic Records and Authorizing Smart Contracts

In March 2017, Arizona passed its first blockchain statute, creating a new section within the state's electronic transactions statute. The new law defines "blockchain technology" and makes it clear that blockchain records qualify as electronic records; it also defines and authorizes "smart contracts."[41]

Under the Arizona statute, blockchain technology means "distributed ledger technology that uses a distributed, decentralized, shared and replicated ledger," where "the data on the ledger is protected with cryptography, is immutable and auditable and provides an uncensored truth."[42] The distributed ledger "may be public or private, permissioned or permissionless, or driven by tokenized crypto economics or tokenless."[43] Thus defined, any signature, record, or contract "secured through blockchain technology is

---

35   *See* Vт. Sтат. Ann. tit. 12 § 1913(b)(3) (West 2016).
36   Vт. Sтат. Ann. tit. 12 § 1913(b)(4) (West 2016).
37   *See* Vт. Sтат. Ann. tit. 12 § 1913(b)(5) (West 2016).
38   *See* Vт. Sтат. Ann. tit. 12 § 1913(c) (West 2016).
39   *See* Vт. Sтат. Ann. tit. 12 § 1913(d) (West 2016).
40   *See id.*
41   *See* Arız. Rev. Sтат. Ann. § 44-7061(E)(1)–(2) (West 2017).
42   Arız. Rev. Sтат. Ann. § 44-7061(E)(1) (West 2017).
43   *Id.*

considered to be in an electronic form" and therefore to be an electronic signature or electronic record.[44]

Arizona defines a smart contract as "an event-driven program, with state,[45] that runs on a distributed, decentralized, shared and replicated ledger and that can take custody over and instruct transfer of assets on that ledger."[46] Such smart contracts are considered as valid as regular contracts.[47]

Although the Arizona legislature gave statutory legitimacy to blockchain technology and smart contracts, it also took some steps to limit their use. The most significant limitation appears in section 44-7003 (among the other general restrictions for electronic transactions under Chapter 26, the Arizona Electronic Transactions Act). This section limits blockchain and smart-contract technology "only to" the portions of Title 47 (Arizona's UCC) that deal with sales, leases, and certain documents of title[48] and by an April 2018 amendment to Title 10, Arizona's Corporations and Associations Statute.[49] Another Arizona statute, also passed in 2017, prohibits the use of blockchain technology to track gun ownership without the owner's written consent, except for certain permitted law enforcement uses.[50]

(c) Nevada—Authorizing Blockchains as Electronic Records

In June 2017, a new Nevada statute recognized a blockchain as an electronic record and incentivized businesses to use the technology by preventing local county or city authorities from taxing it. Senator Ben Kieckhefer, who first introduced the legislation, described this blockchain work as an

---

44 ARIZ. REV. STAT. ANN. § 44-7061(A)–(B) (West 2017).

45 "With state" refers to a program's ability to log and remember interactions with users, other programs, or other external sources. In other words, a program "with state" is designed to remember one or more previous events.

46 ARIZ. REV. STAT. ANN. § 44-7061(E)(2) (West 2017).

47 *See* ARIZ. REV. STAT. ANN. § 44-7061(C) (West 2017) (providing that a contract "may not be denied legal effect, validity, or enforceability solely because [it] contains a smart contract term."). In Florida, similar language that would have authorized blockchain electronic records and smart contracts was legislatively introduced in 2018, but the blockchain provisions were removed even before that bill died. *See* H.B. 1357, Gov. Acct. Comm. (Fla. 2018) (indefinitely postponed and withdrawn from consideration).

48 *See* ARIZ. REV. STAT. ANN. 44-7003(C) (West 2017), as amended by House Bill 2603, signed on April 3, 2018, text of amendment available at https://legiscan.com/AZ/text/HB2603/id/1771532/Arizona-2018-HB2603-Engrossed.html.

49 See the discussion *supra* at § 1(c) of this chapter.

50 *See* ARIZ. REV. STAT. ANN. § 13-3122 (West 2017).

offshoot of efforts to cultivate a welcoming environment in Nevada for start-ups.[51]

The Nevada statute defines a blockchain as "an electronic record of transactions or other data which is (1) [u]niformly ordered, (2) [r]edundantly maintained or processed by one or more computers or machines to guarantee the consistency or nonrepudiation of the recorded transactions or other data, and (3) [v]alidated by the use of cryptography."[52] Nevada also modified its definition of electronic record to include "without limitation, a blockchain."[53]

One of the primary goals of the Nevada legislation was to protect individuals and companies from restrictions on the use of blockchain technology, especially through taxation or other fees.[54] Recognizing that local governments can, and often do, get creative in raising funds, the statute explicitly forbids taxation, licensing, or regulation of blockchains by cities and counties. Boards of county commissioners, city councils, or any other governing body of a city shall not:

(a) Impose any tax or fee on the use of a blockchain by any person or entity;

(b) Require any person or entity to obtain from the incorporated city any certificate, license or permit to use a blockchain; or

(c) Impose any other requirement relating to the use of a blockchain by any person or entity.[55]

Thus, businesses using blockchain technology in Nevada need not concern themselves about local government regulation.

3. STATE LAWS GOVERNING VIRTUAL CURRENCY, MONEY TRANSMISSION, AND MONEY LAUNDERING

(a) New York—Regulating Virtual Currency by Licensing

New York has led the way in state licensing of businesses conducting virtual money transmission. In 2015, New York introduced regulatory rules

---

51 Michael Scott, *Nevada Takes a Chance on Pro-Blockchain Legislation*, Bitcoin Magazine (June 13, 2017) https://bitcoinmagazine.com/articles/nevada-takes-chance-pro-blockchain-legislation/ (quoting Sen. Ben Kieckhefer).

52 Nev. Rev. Stat. Ann. § 719.045 (West 2017).

53 Nev. Rev. Stat. Ann. § 719.090 (West 2017).

54 *See* Michael Scott, *supra* note 51.

55 Nev. Rev. Stat. Ann. §§ 244.3535, 268.0979 (West 2017).

requiring that businesses whose conduct involves virtual currency obtain a BitLicense.[56] For the details of New York's licensing requirements, please refer to Section 2(c) of Chapter 6 of this book.

Shortly after this licensing requirement became law, a number of companies ceased doing business in New York State rather than apply for the license. Strikingly, just a few months after the requirement was put in place, only nine businesses had applied for a BitLicense. That was fewer than the number of businesses—fifteen—that had exited the state because of the licensing requirement.[57]

The application and approval process for BitLicenses has taken considerable time. The State Department of Financial Services (DFS) is the governing body that grants BitLicenses in New York. In September 2015, the DFS announced that it had issued the first BitLicense to Circle Internet Financial. As of the date of that announcement, DFS had received twenty-five applications for BitLicenses.[58] Also in 2015, DFS granted charters to two virtual currency companies, Gemini Trust Company, LLC, and itBit Trust Company.[59] Such charters are issued to virtual currency exchanges under New York banking law pursuant to a DFS order; the exchanges are also expected to "meet the full requirements" of the DFS BitLicense regulatory framework.[60] The next DFS approval of a BitLicense—for XRP II, LLC, an affiliate of Ripple Labs— was announced in June 2016. The approval process had taken almost a full year after XRP had submitted its application in August 2015. DFS described its review of XRP's BitLicense application as rigorous: it reviewed in detail "the company's anti-money laundering, capitalization, consumer protection, and cyber security standards." On that same date in 2016, DFS announced that it had denied BitLicenses to Snapcard Inc. and OKLink PTE. Ltd.[61]

---

56 N.Y. Comp. Codes R. & Regs 79th Reg. Sess. tit. 23, Part 200 (2015).

57 *BitLicense: Who Has Applied and Who Has Left New York*, Coindesk.com (Aug. 15, 2015), https://www.coindesk.com/bitlicense-round-up-whos-left-standing-in-new-york. *See also* Daniel Roberts, *Behind the 'Exodus' of Bitcoin Startups from New York*, Fortune.com (Aug. 14, 2015), http://fortune.com/2015/08/14/bitcoin-startups-leave-new-york-bitlicense.

58 Press Release, *NYDFS Announces Approval of First BitLicense Application from a Virtual Currency Firm* (Sept. 2, 2015), http://www.dfs.ny.gov/about/press/ pr1509221.htm.

59 *See* Press Release, *NYDFS Grants Charter to "Gemini" Bitcoin Exchange Founded by Cameron and Tyler Winklevoss* (Oct. 5, 2015), https://www.dfs.ny.gov/about/press/pr1510051 .htm; Press Release, *NYDFS Grants First Charter to a New York Virtual Currency Company* (May 7, 2015), https://www.dfs.ny.gov/about/press/pr1505071.htm.

60 *See id.; see also* N.Y. Dep't of Fin. Serv. Order In the Matter of Virtual Currency (Mar. 11, 2014), http://www.dfs.ny.gov/about/ea/ea140311.pdf.

61 Press Release, *NYDFS Grants Virtual Currency License to XRP II, LLC, an Affiliate of Ripple* (June 13, 2016), http://www.dfs.ny.gov/about/press/ pr1606131.htm. As of the date of these announcements, DFS had received a total of twenty-six applications for BitLicenses.

More than six months later, in January 2017, DFS made another BitLicense announcement, adding Coinbase, Inc. to the BitLicense list. DFS announced that it had by then approved three firms (Coinbase, Inc.; XRP II; and Circle Internet Financial) for virtual currency licenses and had denied applications that did not meet DFS's standards.[62] In addition, DFS had granted charters to a total of two virtual currency exchanges[63] (referring to the two charters granted in 2015). DFS had also denied BitLicenses to a total of four companies, ordering them to cease New York operations: ChangeCoin Inc., Ovo Cosmico Inc., Snapcard Inc., and OKLink PTE. Ltd. DFS superintendent Maria T. Vullo endorsed strong regulatory safeguards as compatible with a commitment to technological innovation, stating that "[t]hrough the creation and promotion of strong state-based regulation, DFS continues New York's long record of being responsive to technological innovation. New York is committed to fostering and encouraging the long-term growth of new industries throughout the state while enforcing all necessary safeguards to protect our markets and consumers."[64]

Although the pace of the New York approvals has been slow, one benefit for trust companies with virtual currency charters is the potential for reciprocity from other states. In June 2017, Gemini Trust, a company that had been granted a virtual currency charter by New York's DFS, was approved to offer services in Washington State. DFS superintendent Vullo described this as an "example of the demonstrable success of state regulators working together through the Conference of State Bank Supervisors' uniform application process. It also highlight[ed] states' ability to rapidly respond to and effectively foster FinTech business models."[65]

---

62 Press Release, *DFS Grants Virtual Currency License to Coinbase, Inc.* (Jan. 17, 2017), http://www.dfs.ny.gov/about/press/pr1701172.htm.

63 *Id.*

64 Press Release, *DFS Grants Virtual Currency License to Coinbase, Inc.* (Jan. 17, 2017), http://www.dfs.ny.gov/about/press/pr1701172.htm.

65 *Statement by N.Y. Dept. of Fin. Serv. Superintendent Maria T. Vullo on the Approval of Gemini Trust to Open Representative Office in Washington State*, http://www.dfs.ny.gov/about/statements/st1706131.htm (June 13, 2017). *See also* Press Release, *Amendments to Washington's Money Transmitter Regulations Bring Clarification for Virtual Currency Companies*, WA DEPT. OF FIN. INST. (June 14, 2017), https://dfi.wa.gov/news/press/virtual-currency-regulation ("Recently, [Washington State's] DFI had the opportunity to work with another type of regulated entity in the virtual currency space. In concert with the New York Department of Financial Services (NYDFS), [Washington State's] DFI granted authority to Gemini Trust Company, LLC, a New York virtual currency exchange company to do business in the State of Washington. Such authority was permitted through a multi-state reciprocity agreement for trust companies. The company is regulated by the NYDFS and was chartered as a limited purpose trust company

In November 2017, DFS announced another BitLicense. The successful applicant was bitFlyer USA, Inc., a wholly owned subsidiary of a Japanese corporation licensed and registered as a virtual currency exchange by the Japan Financial Services Agency.[66]

As of its November 2017 announcement, DFS had approved six applications for virtual currency charters or licenses in the more than two years since the introduction of the licensing requirements. In February 2018, when DFS announced guidance reminding virtual currency companies to prevent fraud, the approval count remained at six.[67]

DFS has acknowledged that the application process for BitLicenses may be difficult for start-ups. In the BitLicense Frequently Asked Questions section, the DFS website notes the possibility of a conditional license for start-ups:

> Question: Is it possible for my small start-up company to receive a BitLicense even if it does not initially meet all the BitLicense regulatory requirements?

> Answer: After a comprehensive evaluation of, among other things, an applicant's business model and the risks it presents, the Department may, at its discretion, issue a two-year conditional BitLicense. Licensees with conditional BitLicenses may be subject to heightened review.[68]

---

by the NYDFS on Oct. 2, 2015. DFI approved the authority June 9, 2017."); Lalita Clozel, *Are Trust Charters the Key to Simplifying FinTech Regulation?* (Nov. 8, 2016), https://www.americanbanker.com/news/are-trust-charters-the-key-to-simplifying-fintech-regulation (explaining that when "two virtual currency exchanges—Gemini and itBit . . . obtained New York state trust company charters, they appeared to find a readily available antidote to multistate licensing headaches," but cautioning that while "[g]etting a state trust charter can allow exchanges . . . to skip licensing as money transmitters in other states . . . the process doesn't always work and can force a company to change its practices, . . . also potentially resulting in higher capital requirements and more supervision," including the express assumption of fiduciary duties).

66 Press Release, *NYDFS Grants Virtual Currency License to Bitflyer USA, Inc.* (Nov. 28, 2017), http://www.dfs.ny.gov/about/press/pr1711281.htm.

67 *See* Press Release, *DFS Takes Action to Deter Fraud and Manipulation in Virtual Currency Markets* (Feb. 7, 2018), https://www.dfs.ny.gov/about/press/pr1802071.htm.

68 *BitLicense Frequently Asked Questions*, N.Y. Dept. of Fin. Serv., http://www.dfs.ny.gov/legal/regulations/ bitlicense_reg_framework_faq.htm.

(b) Wyoming—Exempting Virtual Currency from Money Transmission Laws and Property Taxation, Exempting Utility Tokens from State Securities Laws, and Fostering Blockchain Business Through a New Form of LLC

In 2018, Wyoming exempted virtual currency from the Wyoming Money Transmitter Act (WMTA).[69] Defining virtual currency as "any type of digital representation of value that: (A) is used as a medium of exchange, unit of account or store of value; and (B) is not recognized as legal tender by the United States government,"[70] the new law exempts those who transact with virtual currency from the licensing requirements of the WMTA.[71] In conjunction with this exemption, Wyoming also exempted virtual currency from state property taxation.[72]

During this same legislative session, Wyoming enacted an open blockchain token exemption that allows "utility" blockchain tokens to be developed and used without being considered a security if certain conditions are met, including notice filing requirements as well as limitations on the purposes and marketing of the tokens.[73] Wyoming also created a "series" LLC,[74] a corporate form considered by proponents of the bill to be especially conducive to blockchain-related businesses.[75]

---

69   Wyo. Stat. Ann. § 40-22-102, § 40-22-104 (West 2018). The text of the amendment is found at 2018 Wyo. Sess. Laws HEA No. 0001, http://legisweb.state.wy.us/2018/Enroll/HB0019 .pdf.

70   Wyo. Stat. Ann. § 40-22-102 (a)(xxii) (West 2018).

71   See Wyo. Stat. Ann. § 40-22-104 (a)(vi) (West 2018) (providing that the WMTA shall not apply to "[b]uying, selling, issuing, or taking custody of payment instruments or stored value in the form of virtual currency or receiving virtual currency for transmission to a location within or outside the United States by any means").

72   See Wyo. Stat. Ann. § 39-11-105(b)(vi)(A) (West 2018). The text of the amendment is found at 2018 Wyo. Sess. Laws SEA No. 0034, http://legisweb.state.wy.us/2018/Enroll/SF0111 .pdf.

73   See Wyo. Stat. Ann. § 17-4-206 (West 2018). The text of the amendment is found at 2018 Wyo. Sess. Laws HEA No. 0027, http://legisweb.state.wy.us/2018/Enroll/HB0070.pdf.

74   2018 Wyo. Sess. Laws HEA No. 0024, http://legisweb.state.wy.us/2018/Enroll/HB0126 .pdf. The new law is to be section 17-29-211 of the Wyoming Statutes but is not yet codified as of this writing.

75   See Gary Miller, *Blockchain Valley: Wyoming Is Posed to Become the Crypto Currency Capital of America*, Newsweek (Mar. 2, 2018), http://www.newsweek.com/wyoming-cowboy-state-poised-today-become-blockchain-valley-828124 (reporting that the Series LLC's bill "allows the creation of "sub-LLCs" compartmentalized . . . to isolate and allocate certain assets or liabilities to specific members," thus allowing a buyer to "purchase a token only offered in Wyoming," with each purchaser being its own Series LLC; reportedly, some suggest the result might be that companies could raise funds using utility tokens rather than issuing securities); *see also* Josiah Wilmoth, *Wyoming House Unanimously Passes Bill Exempting Utility*

(c) California—Legislative Attempts

In June 2014, California governor Jerry Brown signed into law Assembly Bill 129, which repealed section 107 of the Corporations Code. Section 107 had prohibited corporations, associations, and individuals "from issuing or putting into circulation, as money, anything other than the lawful money of the United States."[76] The repeal of this law provided a more favorable environment to conduct business that involved virtual currency.

During the 2015–2016 legislative session, an attempt was made to pass a digital currency act in California, but the bill died in the Senate.[77] Reaction to the bill from the blockchain industry was mixed. As the bill developed, it was first supported, then heavily criticized by Coin Center, a "non-profit research and advocacy center focused on the public policy issues facing cryptocurrency and decentralized computing technologies like Bitcoin and Ethereum."[78] In 2015, Coin Center commented that while the bill was "not perfect," it at least took account of "cryptocurrency's unique attributes" and avoided "unnecessary regulation."[79] The California bill was then seen as "a counterweight to [New York's] BitLicense."[80] From Coin Center's perspective, the alternative to the bill was not an unregulated industry, but instead the application of California's money-transmission statute, which had no exemptions for software development, noncustodial businesses,

---

Tokens from Securities Laws (Feb. 19, 2018), https://www.ccn.com/wyoming-house-unanimously-passes-bill-exempting-utility-tokens-securities-laws/ (describing series LLCs as a type of company structure that proponents in the Wyoming legislature believe will benefit blockchain start-ups and attract blockchain entrepreneurs); Matthew DeSilva, *Wyoming Legislature Goes All in on Blockchain, Cryptocurrency Bills* (Mar. 8, 2018), https://www.ccn.com/wyoming-house-unanimously-passes-bill-exempting-utility-tokens-securities-laws/ (describing series LLCs as useful for developing decentralized governance protocols or to minimize legal risks associated with token ownership); Lewis Cohen, *A Ray of Hope for Utility Tokens* (Feb. 27, 2018), https://www.coindesk.com/ray-hope-utility-tokens/ (describing Series LLC bill as "attractive for issuers to manage myriad token purchasers, or owners to manage their myriad coins").

76 A.B. 129, Assemb., 2013-14 Reg. Sess. (Cal. 2014).

77 A.B. 1326, Assemb., 2015-16 Reg. Sess. (Cal. 2016) (Inactive Bill–Died), https://leginfo. legislature. ca.gov/faces/billStatusClient.xhtml?bill_id=201520160AB1326 (follow "Text" hyperlink).

78 *About Us*, CoinCenter.org, https://coincenter.org/about.

79 Jerry Brito, *EFF's Opposition to California Bill Unwittingly Endangers Bitcoin Innovators*, CoinCenter.org (Aug. 7, 2015), https://coincenter.org/entry/eff-s-opposition-to-california-bill-unwittingly-endangers-bitcoin-innovators. For the Electronic Frontier Foundation's criticisms of the 2015 bill, *see* Rainey Reitman, *A License to Kill Innovation: Why A.B. 1326—California's Bitcoin License—Is Bad for Business, Innovation, and Privacy*, Eff.org (Aug. 7, 2015), https://www.eff.org/deeplinks/2015/08/license-kill-innovation-why-ab-1326-californias-bitcoin-license-bad-business.

80 *Id.*

or currency miners and offered no provisional licenses for start-ups.[81] Moreover, the existing money-transmission statute required the maintenance of eligible securities of a certain market value, a requirement that would make digital currency business models unworkable.[82]

By mid-2016, however, Coin Center had soured on the California bill in its then-current form, pointing out that (1) the bill did not clarify whether digital currency businesses needed money-transmission licenses; (2) the bill was framed as an enrollment requirement, but was essentially the same as a licensing requirement, with a fine of up to $25,000 for failure to enroll; (3) the definition of a "digital currency business" was loose, requiring enrollment by many actors in the industry beyond exchanges and hosted wallet providers; and (4) a business would need to enroll in order to innovate, develop, code, or network.[83]

Ultimately, the bill died in the Senate. The failed attempt to set up a virtual-currency licensing system in California similar to that in New York was seen as a victory for users and creators of virtual currency.

Following that defeat, on February 17, 2017, a new California virtual-currency bill was introduced; this bill would have added a section to the financial code to regulate virtual currency, and it would have required licenses from the Department of Business Oversight.[84] But it, too, did not pass within the applicable time.[85] For the details of the licensing requirements proposed in that latest bill, refer to Section 2(d) of Chapter 6 of this book. In response to the latest legislative efforts in California, Coin Center expressed a preference for the Uniform Law Commission's model act, which had not then been finalized,[86] to promote innovation and uniformity among the states.[87]

---

81 See id.

82 See id. ("Worst of all, the statute . . . would render any digital currency business model unviable if regulated as money transmission.") (emphasis in original).

83 See Peter Van Valkenburg and Jerry Brito, New California Digital Currency Bill Is a Step Backwards, COINCENTER.ORG (Aug. 9, 2016), https://coincenter.org/entry/new-california-digital-currency-bill-is-a-step-backwards.

84 A.B. 1123, Assemb., 2017-18 Reg. Sess. (Cal. 2017), https://leginfo.legislature.ca.gov/faces/billStatusClient. xhtml?bill_id=201720180AB1123 (follow "Text" hyperlink).

85 See id.

86 For more information on the ULC Model Act, see Section 2(b) of Chapter 6 of this book.

87 See Peter Van Valkenburgh, Hot Takes, COINCENTER.ORG (Apr. 12, 2017), https://coincenter.org/link/california-is-back-at-it-a-new-old-virtual-currency-licensing-bill-is-pending-in-the-assembly The "best hope . . . is getting the Uniform Law Commission's model Regulation of Virtual Currency Businesses Act passed into law by as many states as possible. . . . Enacting the ULC model act instead of AB 1123 would be better for consumers and innovators,

(d) New Hampshire—Exempting Virtual Currency from Money-Transmitter Registration Requirements

On the other side of the virtual-currency regulation scale, New Hampshire was the first state to enact a bill that exempted certain businesses whose conduct involved virtual currency from obtaining a money transmitter license. Effective August 1, 2017, "[p]ersons who engage in the business of selling or issuing payment instruments or stored value solely in the form of convertible virtual currency or receive convertible virtual currency for transmission to another location" are classified as exempt from the chapter applicable to money transmitters.[88]

Even prior to its enactment, the virtual-currency community was enthusiastic about this bill. It was seen to "remove[] the decision making power from the bureaucrats and return[] it to consumers."[89] It was also seen as "a positive development for alternative cryptocurrencies gaining traction in the state, including Dash and Ethereum."[90]

(e) Many States in the Middle—Enacting Virtual-Currency Laws or Adding New Regulatory Guidance

Many other states fall in the middle on virtual currency, either by enacting virtual currency laws or by issuing statements of policy, opinion, guidance, letters, warnings, or practices.[91] For a more comprehensive discussion of

---

and would also make California a leader in promoting uniformity and innovation amongst the states.")

88 H.B. 436, 165th Gen. Ct. Sess. (N.H. 2017); N.H. REV. STAT. ANN. § 399-G:3.VI-a (LexisNexis, Lexis Advance through the 2017 Regular Session). Such virtual currency businesses are subject to N.H. REV. STAT. ANN. 358-A (Regulation of Business Practices for Consumer Protection).

89 JP Buntinx, *New Hampshire House Bill 436 Will Effectively Deregulate Bitcoin and Cryptocurrency*, THE MERKLE, https://themerkle.com/new-hampshire-house-bill-436-will-effectively-deregulate-bitcoin-and-cryptocurrency/ (Mar. 11, 2017) ("All things considered, this is by far one of the more positive developments regarding bitcoin regulation we have seen in some time.").

90 *Id.*

91 *See* Justin S. Wales and Matthew E. Kohen, *State Regulations on Virtual Currency and Blockchain Technologies*, Payment Sys Gd 100:400 (Westlaw). In Texas, for example, state banking and securities regulators have recently issued cease-and-desist orders against several companies in relation to their cryptocurrency activities. *See* Press Release, Texas Dept. of Banking, *Texas Department of Banking Commissioner Issues Cease & Desist Order Relating to AriseBank*, (Jan. 26, 2018), *available at* https://www.dob.texas.gov/public/uploads/files/news/press-releases/2018/01-26-18bpr.pdf; Press Release, Texas State Secs. Bd., *$4 Billion Crypto-Promoter Ordered to Halt Fraudulent Sales*, (Jan. 4, 2018), *available at* https://www.ssb.texas.gov/news-publications/4-billion-crypto-promoter-ordered-halt-fraudulent-sales; Press Release,

the regulatory frameworks created by the various states to govern virtual currencies, refer to Section 2 of Chapter 6 of this book.

The Chamber of Digital Commerce, which has been active in lobbying and advocacy efforts in fourteen states, sees "a huge national debate around how states can effectively regulate digital currency and money transmission, and every state has its own opinion and a completely different way of doing things."[92] The Chamber prefers a mid-level approach, like that seen in North Carolina: "New York says businesses need a separate digital currency license to operate in the state. North Carolina said that's way too complicated and regulatory overkill, and decided instead to amend their existing money transmission laws to incorporate digital currency. We prefer the latter approach."[93] Acknowledging the wide variation in the states' treatment of virtual currency, others in the industry also prefer a lighter regulatory touch.[94] The nonprofit Coin Center, for example, urges the states to adopt either its own framework for digital currency or the Uniform Law Commission's act.[95]

4. STATE GOVERNMENT TASK FORCES AND INITIATIVES

(a) Delaware Blockchain Initiative

In his keynote address at the Consensus 2016 technology conference, Delaware Governor Markell announced that the state would officially

---

Texas State Securities Board, *Bitcoin Promoter USI-Tech Hit with Emergency Order*, (Dec. 20, 2017). *available at* https://www.ssb.texas.gov/news-publications/bitcoin-promoter-usi-tech-hit-emergency-order. *See also* Dan Zehr, *After Bitcoin Surges, Texas Regulators Start to Scrutinize Virtual Currency Offers*, 512 TECH BY AUSTIN AMERICAN-STATESMAN, https://www.512tech .com/technology/after-bitcoin-surges-texas-regulators-start-scrutinize-virtual-currency-offers/ hNPRUhbrAQgQQCHJyXxfPM/ (Jan. 10, 2018).

92   *See* Rob Marvin, *Blockchain: The Invisible Technology That's Changing the World*, PCMAG .COM, https://www.pcmag.com/article/351486/blockchain-the-invisible-technology-thats-changing-the-wor (Aug. 29, 2017) (quoting Perianne Boring, President of the Chamber of Digital Commerce).

93   *Id.*

94   Coin Center maintains an interactive map of the State's digital-currency regula-tion. *See* Peter Van Valkenburgh, *Visualizing Digital Currency Regulation State-by-State*, COINCENTER.ORG (Aug. 24, 2017), https://coincenter.org/entry/visualizing-digital-currency-regulation-state-by-state; *see also* https://coincenter.org/page/state-digital-currency-regulatory-tracker (interactive map and chart); *Coin Center's Digital Currency Principles and Framework* (Mar. 2017).

95   Peter Van Valkenburgh, *supra* note 94 (noting that whether digital currency activi-ties now constitute "money transmission" as defined in a particular state "will depend on how broadly the state's legislature drafted that definition" as well as "whether the State has adopted legislation specifically addressing digital currency activities or whether the licensing authority has issued interpretative guidance").

welcome blockchain technology to encourage Delaware corporations to embrace new technologies that make their businesses easier to run.[96] Dubbing this plan the Delaware Blockchain Initiative, Governor Markell announced four key elements:

1. Ensuring that Delaware's regulatory environment is welcoming and enabling by observing the industry as it develops further, rather than immediately enacting laws and regulations regarding licensing of blockchain companies, while working with the industry and consumer groups to determine best practices.

2. Creating an appropriate legal infrastructure for distributed ledger shares in cooperation with the Delaware State Bar Association's Corporation Law Council. Distributed ledger shares hold the promise of dramatic increases in efficiency and speed particularly for multifaceted transactions like incorporation services.

3. Naming an Ombudsperson, Andrea Tinianow, the State Director of Corporate and International Development, to welcome companies in the industry to Delaware.

4. Committing state government to the use of the technology, beginning with the Public Archives project.[97]

In March 2017, Andrea Tinianow[98] published an article that briefly explained three milestones on the Delaware Blockchain Initiative roadmap. The first milestone was achieved when the Delaware Public Archives Department began to use blockchain technology to automate compliance with laws governing the retention and destruction of archival records.[99] The Delaware Public Archives project is considered a successful

---

96   *See* Press Release, *Office of the Governor, Governor Markell Launches Delaware Blockchain Initiative* (May 2, 2016), https://www.prnewswire.com/news-releases/governor-markell-launches-delaware-blockchain-initiative-300260672.html; *See also* CoinDesk, *Introducing the Delaware Blockchain Initiative*, YouTube (Sept. 30, 2016), https://www.youtube.com/watch?v=-mgxEhIvSTY.

97   Press Release, *Office of the Governor, Governor Markell Launches Delaware Blockchain Initiative* (May 2, 2016), https://www.prnewswire.com/news-releases/governor-markell-launches-delaware-blockchain-initiative-300260672.html.

98   In January 2018, Ms. Tinianow resigned her Delaware post to become the chief innovation officer at Global Kompass Strategies, Inc., and she is no longer affiliated with the Delaware Blockchain Initiative. *See* Jason Shueh, *Delaware Blockchain Director Resigns, But the State's Work Will Continue*, StateScoop (Jan. 8, 2018), https://statescoop.com/delaware-blockchain-director-resigns-but-the-states-work-will-continue.

99   *See* Andrea Tinianow and Caitlin Long, *Delaware Blockchain Initiative: Transforming the Foundational Infrastructure of Corporate Finance*, Harv. L. Sch. F. on Corp. Gov. and Fin. Reg. (Mar. 16, 2017), https://corpgov.law.harvard.edu/2017/03/16/delaware-blockchain-initiative-transforming-the-foundational-infrastructure-of-corporate-finance/.

beta test. A second milestone—the only one of the three milestones listed by Director Tinianow that has not been achieved—involves "smart UCC" filings, which, according to Ms. Tinianow, would speed up the "surprisingly paper-based, slow and error-prone" filing process. The third milestone was achieved when Senate Bill 69 was signed into law authorizing Delaware corporations to use distributed-ledger technology to keep corporate records.[100] For more information regarding Senate Bill 69, refer to Section 1(a) of this chapter.

The Delaware Blockchain Initiative did not concern itself with virtual currencies. Instead, as evidenced both by Governor Markell's initial comments on the subject and by the progress that has been made to date, Delaware has focused on enabling companies to embrace new technologies such as blockchain so that they can run their businesses more efficiently. Still, it is noteworthy that the Delaware Department of Justice released a statement in January 2018 warning of the risks of investing in cryptocurrencies and cautioning that cryptocurrency opportunities can be scams.[101]

And as of early 2018, the momentum of the Delaware initiative has slowed.[102] The state administration has paused to examine the technology's potential costs as well as its potential revenue benefits while Secretary of State Jeffrey Bullock's office considers the role of the technology in Delaware.[103]

(b) Illinois Initiatives

(i) Cook County Pilot Program

The state of Illinois has been at the forefront of exploring the use of blockchain technology within state government. The initial push came from the Cook County Illinois Recorder's Office (CCRD). In October 2016, the CCRD announced that it would partner with Velox.re to test use of the Bitcoin blockchain for transferring and tracking property titles as well as other public records. The pilot program was to test the use of blockchain technology for property title transfer, lien filing, and vacant-property conveyance.[104]

---

100   *See id.*

101   *News Release, Investors Should Approach Cryptocurrency with Caution, Delaware's Investor Protection Unit Says* (Jan. 8, 2018), https://news.delaware.gov/2018/01/08/cryptocurrency/.

102   *See* Karl Baker, *Delaware Eases Off Early Blockchain Zeal After Concerns over Disruption to Business*, DELAWAREONLINE (Feb. 1, 2018), https://www.delawareonline.com/story/news/2018/02/02/delaware-eases-off-early-blockchain-zeal-after-concerns-over-disruption-business/1082536001/.

103   *See id.*

104   Kyle Torpey, *Chicago's Cook County to Test Bitcoin Blockchain-Based Property Title Transfer*, BITCOIN MAGAZINE (Oct. 6, 2016), https://bitcoinmagazine.com/articles/

The CCRD issued the Blockchain Pilot Program Final Report in May 2017. CCRD concluded that it would continue to explore ways in which aspects of blockchain or distributed ledger technology could be used to improve recordkeeping and to work with technology partners interested in finding a distributed ledger structure that made sense for government. But CCRD determined not to move the land-records system fully onto the blockchain at that time. CCRD stated that "[b]lockchain is not an all-or-nothing approach; aspects of the component technology can be implemented individually or selectively to improve recordkeeping outcomes."[105] According to the report, CCRD would "work with the industry to develop future-case functionality and toward a stronger and more logical public land record."[106]

(ii) Illinois Blockchain Initiative

In December 2016, Illinois announced that four state agencies and CCRD would partner together to launch the Illinois Blockchain Initiative (Initiative). The participating state agencies were the Illinois Department of Commerce & Economic Opportunity (DCEO), Illinois Department of Financial and Professional Regulation (IDFPR), Illinois Department of Insurance (IDOI), and Illinois Department of Innovation & Technology (DOIT). The Initiative would collaboratively explore opportunities to use blockchain technology and distributed-ledger technology. The Initiative's focus included "ensuring a welcoming regulatory environment for innovative digital currency and blockchain companies wanting to do business in Illinois"[107] and creating "a public/private collaborative platform for developing specific blockchain and distributed ledger applications and prototypes for use in Illinois government."[108] Alongside the announcement of the Initiative, Illinois took three steps:

- The IDFPR announced that it would release for comment its proposed Digital Currency Regulatory Guidance.

---

chicago-s-cook-county-to-test-bitcoin-blockchain-based-public-records-1475768860/.

105 John Mirkovic, *Blockchain Pilot Program Final Report*, COOK COUNTY RECORDER OF DEEDS (May 30, 2017), http://cookrecorder.com/blockchain/.

106 *See id.*

107 *Illinois Announces Initiative to Grow Innovation Sector*, THE ILLINOIS BLOCKCHAIN INITIATIVE (Dec. 2, 2016), https://illinoisblockchain.tech/illinois-announces-initiative-to-grow-innovation-sector-ccf13e460287.

108 *Id.*

- Jennifer O'Rourke, Assistant Deputy Director of Entrepreneurship, Innovation and Technology, was named as Illinois's first Blockchain Business Liaison.
- The DOIT released a Request for Information seeking input and feedback from the blockchain-technology community on developing and implementing blockchain applications in government.[109]

In March 2017, the IDFPR announced that it would join the distributed-ledger group created by R3, an enterprise software firm. The IDFPR was the first state-level regulator to join this collaborative initiative, which included over eighty of the world's largest financial institutions. "Members work closely with R3 to continue the development of Corda, an open source distributed ledger platform for recording, managing and synchronizing financial agreements."[110] The other member agencies of the Initiative have continued to join various blockchain and distributed ledger collaboration groups, including Linux Foundation's Hyperledger Project[111] and the Enterprise Ethereum Alliance.[112]

At the DC Blockchain Summit in March 2017, the Initiative gave a presentation on the progress it had made to date. The Initiative reported that its ranks were growing—another department, the Illinois Pollution Control Board, had joined. To date the Initiative had launched, had issued digital currency guidance, had opened a Request For Information for blockchain applications, had partnered with R3, and had opened the Blockchain Center. The Initiative announced that it would move forward with launching proofs-of-concept, holding a blockchain code-a-thon, forming an advisory committee, and releasing a white paper.[113]

---

109   *See id.*

110   Emily Rutland, *Illinois Becomes First State Level Regulator to Join R3 Distributed Ledger Group*, R3 (Mar. 16, 2017), http://www.r3cev.com/press/2017/3/21/illinois-becomes-first-state-level-regulator-to-join-r3-distributed-ledger-group.

111   Press Release, *Illinois Blockchain Initiative Joins Hyperledger Project—Hyperledger Adds Seven New Members*, ILLINOIS BLOCKCHAIN INITIATIVE (Apr. 26, 2017), https://illinoisblockchain.tech/illinois-blockchain-initiative-joins-hyperledger-project-731b50427f8c.

112   Press Release, *State of Illinois Joins the Enterprise Ethereum Alliance—Enterprise Ethereum Alliance Expands Dramatically Announcing 86 New Members*, ENTERPRISE ETHEREUM ALLIANCE (May 22, 2017), https://illinoisblockchain.tech/state-of-illinois-joins-the-enterprise-ethereum-alliance-2c8871dc1751.

113   Jennifer O'Rourke (presenter) and Cab Morris (slide deck author), *Insights, Progress & Horizon Scanning*, ILLINOIS BLOCKCHAIN INITIATIVE (Mar. 16, 2017), https://illinoisblockchain.tech/illinois-blockchain-initiative-insights-progress-horizon-scanning-61e25a51e345.

In August 2017, the Initiative announced that it would partner with Hashed Health to create a pilot program focused on using blockchain technology in the Illinois medical credentialing process. IDFPR secretary Bryan Schneider stated that the pilot program had goals for the short term and for the long term: "In the short-term we anticipate this pilot will show how distributed ledger technology can help reduce the complexity of interstate licensing processes in Illinois."[114] Looking to the long term, the pilot would lead to "a secure, privacy-enhancing way in which state licensure boards can efficiently manage credentialing at national scale, while also presenting health payers and provider networks a 'single source-of-truth' to improve the veracity of provider directories and claims adjudication processes."[115]

Also in August 2017, the Initiative announced that it would partner with Evernym to explore the use of distributed-ledger technology in creating and launching a birth registration pilot program. This program would "create a secure, 'self-sovereign' identity for Illinois citizens during the birth registration process."[116] Jennifer O'Rourke, Blockchain Business Liaison for the Initiative, observed that "Government has an important role to play in the development of any digital identity ecosystem. Identity is not only foundational to nearly every government service, but is the basis for trust and legitimacy in the public sector."[117]

Illinois's progress in these areas has been well received. As one commentator noted, "[t]he five pilots undertaken by the state include the areas of land title registry, academic credentials, health provider registries, energy credit marketplaces and vital records. The state's idea is that if it can figure out blockchain, there are a lot of record keeping and transaction processes that can be made more secure and more reliable."[118]

---

114 *Illinois Opens Blockchain Development Partnership with Hashed Health*, The ILLINOIS BLOCKCHAIN INITIATIVE (Aug. 9, 2017), https://illinoisblockchain.tech/illinois-opens-blockchain-development-partnership-with-hashed-health-fe3891e500bb.

115 *Id.*

116 *Illinois Partners with Evernym to Launch Birth Registration Pilot—Illinois Blockchain Initiative and Self-Sovereign Identity Leader Evernym Partner to Develop Secure Identity Solutions on Distributed Ledger Technology*, THE ILLINOIS BLOCKCHAIN INITIATIVE (Aug. 9, 2017), https://illinoisblockchain.tech/illinois-partners-with-evernym-to-launch-birth-registration-pilot-f2668664f67c.

117 *Id.*

118 Colin Wood, *Illinois State Government Is Embedding Itself in the World of Blockchain Tech*, StateScoop (Aug. 2, 2017), http://statescoop.com/illinois-state-government-is-embedding-itself-in-the-world-of-cryptocurrency.

(iii) Illinois Legislative Blockchain and Distributed Ledger Task Force

In June 2017, Illinois adopted House Joint Resolution 25, creating the Illinois Legislative Blockchain and Distributed Ledger Task Force. This resolution defined blockchain as "distributed databases and ledgers protected against revision by publicly-verifiable open source cryptographic algorithms, and protected from data loss by distributed records sharing."[119] In creating the legislative Task Force, the state reasoned that blockchain technology could lead to "more efficient government service delivery models and economies of scale."[120] In particular, the technology could "facilitat[e] safe, paperless transactions, and permanent recordkeeping immune to cyber-attacks, and data destruction."[121] The resolution also focused on blockchain's potential to "reduce the prevalence of government's disparate, computer systems, databases, and custom-built software interfaces, reducing costs associated with maintenance and implementation and allowing more regions of the state to participate in electronic government services."[122]

Because the Illinois Initiative was well underway, there was an established history of "collaborative regulatory exchange with technology firms, software developers, and service providers."[123] The Task Force could leverage this background in drafting regulations (if needed) that would be "the product of a collaborative . . . approach, with the goal of encouraging economic development through innovation."[124]

The Task Force—comprised of seventeen members appointed by the legislature, the CCRD, the Cook County Clerk, and many state agencies— was to research, analyze, and consider:

- Opportunities and risks associated with using blockchain and distributed ledger technology;
- Different types of blockchains, both public and private, and different consensus algorithms;
- Projects and use cases currently under development in other states and nations and how those cases could be applied in Illinois;
- How current state laws can be modified to support secure, paperless recordkeeping;

---

119   H.J. Res. 25, 100th Gen. Assemb., 1st Reg. Sess. (Ill. 2017).
120   *Id.*
121   *Id.*
122   *Id.*
123   *Id.*
124   *Id.*

- The state Public Key Infrastructure and digital signatures; and
- Official reports and recommendations from the Illinois Block-chain Initiative.[125]

The Task Force presented its findings and recommendations in a Final Report to the General Assembly on January 31, 2018.[126] In a symbolic gesture, this report was the "first official government report in Illinois to be permanently certified in a public blockchain."[127] The Task Force found that blockchain technology could "facilitate highly-secure methods for interacting with government and keeping paperless records, increasing data accuracy and providing better cybersecurity protections for Illinois residents."[128] Although blockchain technology still needed refinement, the Task Force saw an opportunity for government "to help shape and adopt innovative solutions."[129] The report discussed the challenges and risks associated with the technology, expounded upon the government's role in leveraging new technologies to improve services and data security for its citizens, and explored future opportunities for the state to use blockchain and distributed-ledger technology in conjunction with other developing technologies such as the Internet of Things and autonomous vehicles. The report concluded with eight legislative recommendations[130] to facilitate the state's future use of blockchain technology, especially for property law and public recording.

---

125 *Id.* In addition to the Illinois House and Senate representatives and Cook County, the participating state agencies were the Division of Banking, the Secretary of State, the DCEO, the DOIT, the IDOI, and the IDFPR.

126 *Final Report to the General Assembly*, Illinois BLOCKCHAIN AND DISTRIBUTED LEDGER TASK FORCE, (Jan. 31, 2018), https://www2.illinois.gov/sites/doit/Strategy/Documents/BlockchainTaskForceFinalReport020518.pdf; *see also* Press Release, *State of Illinois Releases Blockchain Task Force Report—Distributed Ledger Technology Poised to Strengthen Security and Bring Economic Opportunities*, IL DOIT (Jan. 31, 2018), https://www2.illinois.gov/IISNews/15316-DoIT_Blockchain_Task_Force_Report.pdf.

127 *Id.*

128 *Id.* at 5.

129 *Id.*

130 *Id.* at 18, 30–32 (Appendix A). These recommendations include (1) reconciling the Illinois digital signature laws with the Uniform Electronic Transactions Act; (2) modernizing notarial statutes; (3) allowing self-notarization, rather than certification, of public blockchain records; (4) clarifying the Illinois conveyance and recording statute to make it a "pure notice" statute; (5) requiring claims against real estate to be publicly recorded; (6) allowing direct submission of plain-text data for a transaction into the public record; (7) modernizing the submission of omnibus real estate records to shift away from paper-based modes; and (8) adopting a standard to give every parcel of real estate a unique identifying number, similar to the VIN system for automobiles. *See id.*

(c) Vermont Blockchain Studies

In Vermont, the state legislature authorized two studies to look into block-chain technology and to make recommendations about its potential benefits to the state.

The first of these studies was published in January 2016. The secretary of state, the state's attorney general, and the state Commissioner of Financial Regulation (in consultation with the Center for Legal Innovation at Vermont Law School and Vermont's delegates to the National Conference of Commissioners on Uniform State Laws) were to report their "finding and recommendations on the potential opportunities and risks of creating a presumption of validity for electronic facts and records that employ block-chain technology and addressing any unresolved regulatory issues."[131]

The conclusions of this first study were lukewarm toward the benefit of new blockchain-related legislation. The study concluded that Vermont already offered a hospitable environment for businesses associated with blockchain, even without specific statutory recognition of the technology. It observed that blockchain technology was already being used in the private sector, although its use was not yet widespread. Legislative efforts would not necessarily serve to further attract this industry to the state. Perhaps most significantly, the study concluded that even if state agencies were to adopt blockchain technology, the benefit to the state would not justify the costs related to implementation.[132]

Considered in its totality, the study appeared to conclude that blockchain-related legislation was unnecessary—either to regulate the technology's use in the private sector or to incorporate it into government practice. Notwithstanding that first study's conclusions, the legislature adopted a statute that authenticated blockchain records as evidence in Vermont courts, much like the legislative starting point identified in the study.[133]

A year later the Vermont Legislature commissioned a second study to prepare itself to address opportunities and concerns in the rapidly expanding and developing field of financial technology.[134] This time the Legislature charged the Center for Legal Innovation at Vermont Law School with the task (in consultation with some of the government entities that had been charged with the 2015 study). The bill authorizing this second study leaves

---

131   S. 138, 2015–16 Leg. Sess., § A.3 (Vt. 2015).

132   James Condos, et al., BLOCKCHAIN TECHNOLOGY:, OPPORTUNITIES AND RISKS 19–20 (Jan. 15, 2016), https://legislature.vermont.gov/assets/Legislative-Reports/blockchain-technology-report-final.pdf.

133   See the discussion of section 1913 *in* Section 2(a) of this chapter.

134   S. 135 2017–18 Leg. Sess., § G.1 (Vt. 2017).

the distinct impression that its impetus was to position Vermont to compete for financial benefits with those states already adopting blockchain legislation.[135] Indeed, the 2017 report from this second study offered a final caution: "If Vermont wishes to pursue FinTech initiatives, it would be wise to proceed with reasonable speed. Other states are picking up various pieces of the puzzle."[136]

In this second Vermont study, the Center for Legal Innovation at Vermont Law School identified a number of areas in which Vermont could legislate blockchain-related technologies in order to invite businesses (and increased tax revenue) into the state. These included identity trust companies, insurance products, e-banking, safe harbors for financial trustees, digital property transfers and registries, and autonomous agent corporations.[137] The study also determined that it would be worth revisiting whether blockchain technology would be valuable in conducting state business; it went on to suggest some ways in which the technology might benefit the work of various government programs.[138]

In January 2018, Senator Alison Clarkson introduced a new bill relating to blockchain, cryptocurrency, and financial technology. Addressing some of the issues highlighted in the Center for Legal Innovations' December report, the bill's purpose is "to implement strategies relating to blockchain, cryptocurrency, and financial technology" in order to serve the goals of regulatory efficiency, better business and government structures that expand opportunities in financial technology, and the adoption of financial technology by both government and business.[139]

As introduced, the bill would have authorized several new types of business entities geared to blockchain and virtual currency and also ordered an ambitious series of studies, reports, and summits. But as of March 2018, the bill is more limited: it would authorize personal information trust companies with fiduciary obligations and place them under the regulatory supervision of the State Department of Financial Regulation. The bill would also require the department to study and report on the potential

---

135   *See id.*

136   *Financial Technology Report,* Center for Legal Innovation of Vermont Law School 8 (Dec. 7, 2017), https://legislature.vermont.gov/assets/Legislative-Reports/Vermont-Report-Final-Version-December-7.pdf.

137   *See id.* at 26–37.

138   *See id.* at 37–38.

139   S. 269, 2017–18 Leg. Sess. (Vt. 2018) (introduced Jan. 3, 2018). Specifically, the bill seeks to implement blockchain strategies to "promote regulatory efficiency; enable business organizational and governance structures that may expand opportunities in financial technology; and promote education and adoption of financial technology in the public and private sectors." *Id.*

application of blockchain technology to insurance and e-banking. Finally, it would authorize a FinTech Summit to be held under the auspices of state agencies and universities in consultation with the private sector.[140]

(d) Arizona "Sandbox"

After first passing legislation to authorize blockchain records as electronic records and to authorize smart contracts,[141] Arizona later authorized a "sandbox" program, administered by the attorney general, to test innovative financial products or services.[142]

The first blockchain statute in Arizona reportedly passed with difficulty because the technology was so new that lawmakers had a hard time understanding exactly what it was they were legislating.[143] The bill's sponsor, Representative Jeff Weninger, said that he shared TED Talks with his colleagues to help them understand the importance of the new technology.[144] But blockchain legislation has now gathered momentum in Arizona. Recognizing the high financial costs and long regulatory delays inherent in starting up a financial technology company, Attorney General Mark Brnovich proposed in September 2017 that Arizona create a sandbox for FinTech start-ups.[145] Sandboxes, already encouraged in the United Kingdom, Singapore and Australia, allow "startups [to] launch products on a limited scale to real consumers without incurring the regulatory costs that would otherwise be imposed."[146] In March 2018, the Arizona legislature enacted such "sandbox" legislation. The new statute authorizes the attorney general to establish a regulatory program in which approved participants will provide innovative financial products or services that are available to a limited number of consumers, subject to specific dollar caps,

---

140   *See id.* For the current status of the Vermont bill, *see* https://legislature.vermont.gov/bill/status/2018/S.269.

141   *See* Section 2(b) of this chapter.

142   The new law both amends Title 41 of the Arizona Revised Statutes and adds a new chapter. To see these changes, see https://legiscan.com/AZ/text/HB2434/id/1769899/Arizona-2018-HB2434-Chaptered.html; see also H. 2434, 53rd Leg., 2nd Reg. Sess. (Ariz. 2018).

143   *See* Nathan Fish, *Arizona Edges to Front of States Eyeing Blockchain Technology*, Tucson.com (Aug. 18, 2017), http://tucson.com/business/arizona-edges-to-front-of-states-eyeing-blockchain-technology/article_be68d42f-ddb5-5650-9a04-97915b22bf24.html.

144   *Id.*

145   *See* Mark Brnovich, *BankThink Regulatory Sandboxes Can Help States Advance FinTech* (Sept. 5, 2017), AMERICAN BANKER, https://www.americanbanker.com/opinion/regulatory-sandboxes-can-help-states-advance-fintech.

146   *Id.*

and free from certain state regulatory laws that would otherwise apply.[147] The statute also provides consumer protections, mainly in the form of mandatory disclosures, and gives the attorney general authority to impose reporting requirements, remove participants from the sandbox, and take other regulatory actions.[148] By law, the sandbox program will expire on July 1, 2028.[149]

5. CONCLUSION—A WORD ABOUT THE FUTURE

The application of blockchain and distributed ledger technology is changing rapidly in the financial, manufacturing, retail, and service sectors of the economy. But even as the technology becomes more widespread, its potential to transform business and government is only beginning to be understood. It comes as no surprise then that legislative and regulatory responses to blockchain technology can be fast moving as well. In this chapter, we have described a wide range of perspectives on how state (and even local) governments have addressed this new technology. Although this chapter provides a guide to the various state approaches as of early 2018, it will remain important to take another look at the rapidly changing legislative and regulatory environment before doing business in a particular state in the future. As one blockchain-sector advisor has described it, state legislative adoption of blockchain technology is "a relay race, not a sprint," and innovation moves onward as one state "take[s] the baton" from another.[150]

---

147 *See* H. 2434, 53rd Leg., 2nd Reg. Sess. (Ariz. 2018).

148 *See id.*

149 *See id.*

150 Gary Miller, *Blockchain Valley: Wyoming Is Poised to Become the Cryptocurrency Capital of America*, Newsweek (Mar. 2, 2018), http://www.newsweek.com/wyoming-cowboy-state-poised-today-become-blockchain-valley-828124 (quoting Andrea Tinianow, former director of the Delaware blockchain initiative).

CHAPTER 8

Disputes, Liability, and Jurisdiction in the Blockchain Era

Joseph Melnik
Bradley W. Harrison

Although blockchain technology, like other disruptive technologies that have come before, may minimize or even eliminate many types of disputes arising from traditional ways of doing business, new types of disputes will inevitably arise, including many that have been discussed extensively in earlier chapters. This chapter outlines various considerations of blockchain-related dispute resolution. We begin with an identification of the various parties in the world of blockchain technology and some of the complexities arising from them with regard to dispute resolution. From there, we discuss ways that disputes among these parties may be conceptualized and addressed. We then turn to jurisdictional issues arising from the world-wide use of blockchain technology. Finally, we discuss issues associated with enforceability of court orders on blockchain companies and assets.

1. IDENTIFYING AND ALLOCATING RISK AND RESPONSIBILITY FROM THE USE OF BLOCKCHAIN TECHNOLOGY

(a) Blockchain Participants

Before discussing the issues surrounding blockchain-technology dispute resolution, it is critical to understand the various participants in a blockchain. For any market participant (in the most general sense of the word), depending on the specific circumstances, there may be some potential for responsibility and liability should a dispute arise. As blockchain technology and the law surrounding it becomes more widespread and develops, careful consideration must be paid to whether an individual or entity is an appropriate target of a lawsuit or other dispute resolution mechanism, including, among other things, (a) whether the individual or entity can be identified,[1] (b) what role a particular individual or entity played in the dispute, and (c) whether the target is a "juridical entity," recognized under the law as being capable of being sued. Below is a brief, nonexhaustive summary of typical participants in the more common blockchain-use cases and some of the aspects of their existence and participation that must be considered within any dispute resolution framework.

Platforms. These are the blockchain systems, infrastructures, networks, software, and protocols that are the foundation of blockchain technologies. Examples include IBM Blockchain,[2] Bitcoin Core,[3] and Ethereum Project.[4] These are the building blocks for blockchain applications and include the networks on which the applications are run.[5]

Among the questions relating to potential platform liability, which courts ultimately will have to resolve, is whether decentralized blockchain platforms, like Bitcoin, are juridical entities that can sue or be sued separate and apart from the users of the platform.[6]

Application developers. Applications are those programs designed to take advantage of blockchain technology and built to operate on platforms. Individuals or entities develop and release these applications.

Hardware entities. Because blockchain operates in a virtual world, computers and other devices are needed to enable a blockchain and its use by potential blockchain participants. Various entities develop, market, and sell this hardware.

---

1   Although the public and private key systems on blockchain are designed to encourage anonymity, that is not always the case, which is discussed in more detail in Chapters 1 and 4. *See generally*, Steve Goldfeder, Harry Kalodner, Dillon Reisman, & Arvind Narayanan, *When the Cookie Meets the Blockchain: Privacy Risks of Web Payments via Cryptocurrencies* (2017) (unpublished manuscript available at https://arxiv.org/pdf/1708.04748.pdf).

2   IBM Blockchain, https://www.ibm.com/blockchain/.

3   Bitcoin, https://bitcoin.org/en/bitcoin-core/.

4   Ethereum, https://www.ethereum.org/.

5   *See* Chapter 1 for a discussion of blockchain operation.

6   *See, e.g.*, Bitcoin, *About bitcoin.org*, https://bitcoin.org/en/about-us ("Bitcoin is controlled by all Bitcoin users around the world.").

ICO issuers and cryptocurrency entities. Currently the most recognized participants in blockchain technology are those individuals and entities involved in the issuance of various cryptocurrency coins or tokens and entities involved in cryptocurrency transactions and exchanges (be it currency-to-cryptocurrency exchanges, cryptocurrency-to-currency exchanges, or cryptocurrency-to-cryptocurrency exchanges).[7]

Blockchain participants/nodes. These are the end-users of blockchain technology. This includes holders of tokens or cryptocurrencies, parties to smart contracts, users of blockchain applications—essentially, all parties transacting on the blockchain. This also involves individuals or entities in clearing or validating transactions on the blockchain.[8] The composition and fundamental makeup of the participants/nodes in a blockchain will be technology- and platform-specific.

Blockchain participants/nodes may not always be known. For *permissionless blockchains*, any member of the public may effect and verify changes to the ledger. As described in Chapter 1, to prevent the possibility of double spending, transactions on permissionless blockchains are announced publicly and each blockchain node typically includes a complete record of all transactions. These permissionless blockchains may provide some semblance of anonymity for the participants, severing the link between the digital signatures on the blockchain and the identities of the people actually involved in the transactions. This raises the specter of being unable to trace or, at least, being very difficult to trace the identity of a particular participant/node (a potentially liable party in a dispute).[9]

Blockchain participants/nodes may be known. A network of nodes running a blockchain need not be publicly accessible or involve anonymous participants/nodes. *Permissioned blockchains*, or blockchain networks with limitations placed on access or availability of information, are also employed. The operators of a network can limit access to previously identified, authorized individuals or entities. Only authorized participants

---

7   These entities, and their potential responsibilities, are discussed in greater detail in Chapters 3 and 6.

8   As discussed in Chapter 1, a key feature of blockchain is consensus and proof of work and validation by nodes on the distributed ledger.

9   This is not to say that permissionless systems create intractable problems and true anonymity: there are often ways to identify the people even when it is permissionless. Information on "anonymous" blockchain applications like Bitcoin can often be tracked back to real people. For example, many Bitcoin holders make frequent use of financial institutions for services such as exchanging bitcoins for fiat currencies or laws and regulations require disclosure to the financial institutions of the holders' real identity. *See generally*, Chapter 6.

or "trusted nodes" may have permission to create records and verify changes to the ledger. Different participants may have distinct authorizations and specialized responsibilities, including different rights to read, write, and/or delete data.

The structure of the blockchain and the roles and responsibilities of its participants are likely to influence the potential responsibilities of the participants and the corresponding potential liability should a dispute arise.

(b) Means of Resolving Disputes Arising from the Use of Blockchain Technology

Disputes among the various blockchain participants have already occurred and are certain to happen in the future. The variation of the inevitable disputes is likely as broad as the potential uses of blockchain technology itself. Accordingly, it would be both premature and futile to speculate how the various disputes will be handled and resolved. But that does not preclude discussion of the issues surrounding blockchain-related dispute resolution and envisioning the various frameworks through which blockchain disputes could be addressed. It is imperative that blockchain participants consider and address how disputes might be handled.

(i) Existing Law

Although disputes arising from the use of blockchain technology may present some unique challenges, it can be reasonably expected that courts will look to familiar legal paradigms as they consider disputes arising from the use of blockchain technology. Familiar contract, tort, and existing statutory law are likely to be applied to disputes involving blockchain technology.[10] Indeed, as discussed in Chapter 4, this is already being seen in cybersecurity and "hacking" cases. Also, as discussed in Chapter 2, federal and state governments have adapted existing securities law to blockchain technology. These adaptations likely foreshadow civil litigation between private parties dealing in blockchain-based securities and the application of existing law to these disputes.

And, certainly, just because a dispute "involves" blockchain does not mean the dispute is "about" blockchain; thus, existing laws would likely be applied. Over the past several years, disputes have arisen from the alleged failure of a supplier to timely deliver Bitcoin mining computers, where

---

10 *See, e.g.*, Gordon v. Dailey, No. 14-7495, 2016 WL 3457003, at *1 (D.N.J. June 21, 2016) (amended complaint asserting breach of contract and unjust enrichment claims in connection with bonds issued by Bitcoin mining company).

aggrieved parties assert that time is often of the essence because "Bitcoin mining computers lose their value at a rapid rate due to the fact that more powerful computers are needed to effectively 'mine' for Bitcoins as time goes on."[11]

Even as some of the novel aspects of blockchain technology take hold, existing law may provide the dispute framework and guiding principles. For example, a supply chain that is organized on a blockchain may automatically track shipments and may even trigger automatic receipts and payments through a smart contract upon delivery of a shipment. Nonetheless, a party may still commit a traditional "breach of contract" by failing to deliver goods on time or otherwise as agreed to. Although involving blockchain technology, the dispute would likely remain a traditional breach of contract action and fall within existing law.

Accordingly, to the extent that disputes arising from the use of blockchain technology may fall within existing law (or interpretative expansion of existing law), practitioners should not abandon the developed law. New technologies, like blockchain, inevitably lead to development of new law for blockchain. But the transactions and business practices to which blockchain may be applied, nonetheless, are often familiar and should be expected to be governed by familiar law.

The application of existing law will have limits. How blockchains are set up, how various transactions on a blockchain are characterized, and how transactions are ultimately completed will impact how and to what extent existing laws may apply. It may be the case that certain aspects of blockchain technology, including its distributed-ledger configuration and proof-of-work clearing process, will pose courts significant difficulty.

Even if it is envisioned that existing laws may be appropriately applied to a blockchain dispute, there remains a significant question of what law to apply. Distributed-ledger technology, by its very nature, and the use of blockchain present unique choice-of-law challenges that may affect which and to what extent traditional bodies of law and legal rights governing the allocation of liability will apply.

---

11 *See* Morici v. Hashfast Techs LLC, No. 14-cv-00087, 2014 WL 4983854, at *1 (N.D. Cal. Oct. 6, 2014); Bevand v. BF Labs Inc., No. 16-cv-1115, 2017 WL 4273308, at *1 (W.D. Mo. Sept. 26, 2017) (asserting RICO, breach of contract, violations of state unfair practices law, conversion, and unjust enrichment in connection with Bitcoin mining machines that were never received); Lenell v. Advanced Mining Tech., Inc., No. 14-cv-01924, 2014 WL 7008609, at *1 (E.D. Pa. Dec. 11, 2014) (putative class action arising from an alleged failure to deliver mining computers to customers as ordered or as advertised).

As more blockchain-based disputes arise, it will be important to monitor how courts are applying existing laws to those disputes.

(ii) Contractual Options for Allocating Liability

In the absence—or uncertainty—of existing law to govern a dispute involving blockchain technology, contractual options may provide an alternative means of addressing disputes. As discussed above, there are a number of blockchain participants and the technology builds on itself. Accordingly, there may be numerous opportunities to create contractual dispute resolution mechanisms and rules.

Platform agreements. Blockchain platforms and application developers may utilize end-user license agreements and/or terms of service, in the same manner as virtually all traditional online platforms (e.g., Twitter, Facebook) have. These platform agreements may create a set of predictable rules governing the relationship between the blockchain service provider and end users. They further allow their proponents to place limitations on liability, describe the scope of the services, and impose privacy policies and security measures. Perhaps most important, platform agreements may include provisions aimed at resolving disputes and allocating liability, including mandatory arbitration agreements, class-action waivers, and governing-law provisions prescribing the jurisdiction whose substantive and procedural law will govern the rights, remedies, and obligations of the parties. In all cases, users could be required to sign up to specific terms of service or similar agreements before being granted access to the blockchain.[12]

Platform constitutions and "laws." In place of traditional terms of service, proponents of blockchain technology have proposed a decentralized peer-to-peer approach to securing user rights and enabling dispute resolution. Under these so-called blockchain constitutions, users of a blockchain platform establish overarching rules for recognizing the rights and obligations of each user and establishing procedures for resolving disputes. Piggybacking on smart contracts, blockchain constitutions can provide an automated process for implementing, enforcing, and amending rules governing the use of a platform. Blockchain constitutions may be drafted as simple multiparty contracts executed by virtue of using a particular platform. They also can take advantage of the platform to serve notice of

---

12   *See, e.g.,* Blockchain Luxembourg S.A., *Terms of Service and Use,* https://www.blockchain.com/legal/termshtml; Chain.com, *Terms of Services,* https://chain.com/legal/.

disputes and may provide a basis for prosecuting and defending disputes in a pseudo-anonymous fashion.

Transaction agreements. Transaction agreements are an alternative to one-size-fits-all agreements imposed on all users of a platform. In transaction agreements, counterparties to a blockchain-enabled transaction negotiate the terms of the transaction and allocate liability risk as one facet of a mutually beneficial contractual arrangement. Transaction agreements are effectively contracts negotiated between sophisticated business entities.

Smart contracts. No discussion of contractual allocation is complete without mentioning smart contracts. Distributed ledgers can incorporate computer code that runs on a blockchain and specifies self-executed consequences once certain conditions are met. As discussed in more detail in Chapter 3, the extent and requirements for whether this "smart code" constitutes a legally binding contract alone or in combination with traditional forms of contractual documentation need to be addressed. Nonetheless, smart contracts have the potential to mediate relationships across several categories of platforms that rely on blockchain technology. Smart contracts may also have the potential for allocating liability and dispute resolution through self-enforcement or traditional court/arbitration enforcement, depending on the content of the agreements and the preferences of the contracting parties. For example, a smart contract may self-execute a "remedy" if a specified set of conditions constituting a "breach" occurs; alternatively, it could render moot the very notion of "breach" in certain situations by making nonperformance an impossibility. Smart contracts could also specify particular forms of mediation or arbitration. Smart contracts may raise unique dispute resolution considerations where traditional court intervention is sought. For example, because smart contracts are self-executing, a court may have to grapple with how to unwind or alter the smart contract after it has been executed.

(iii) Developing New Laws

In addition to existing law and contractual allocation of responsibility and means of dispute resolution, new laws are being and will likely continue being developed. These new laws can address the peculiar features of blockchain technologies and, like securities laws, identify specific instances and bases for liability by different market participants. Legislatures might enact new statutes aimed at these technologies, or regulators could try to shoehorn regulation of blockchain technologies into existing laws. As seen in Chapters 2, 6, and 7, these undertakings are already underway.

Like legislatures and regulators, the judiciary will likely also create novel legal concepts to address the peculiarities of blockchain technology. At the level of the judiciary, application of law to blockchain disputes will inevitably occur, which will create an emerging body of law to be applied to blockchain transactions. Thus, even absent legislative or regulatory action, new law will develop around blockchain as disputes wend their way through state and federal courts.

2. NATIONAL AND STATE JURISDICTION ISSUES ARISING FROM BLOCKCHAIN USE

Jurisdictional issues are threshold considerations for any civil action in the United States. A court must determine both if it has personal jurisdiction over the defendant and if it has jurisdiction over the subject matter of the dispute.[13] In recent years, with the advent and expansion of technologies such as the internet, these core jurisdictional requirements have been stretched to fit the unique challenges raised by the new technology.[14] Blockchain and distributed-ledger technologies, which are frequently deployed across state and national boundaries, will further challenge traditional jurisdictional concepts. Litigants and courts will be forced to face even more novel jurisdiction questions such as: How do you sue an anonymous party involved in a blockchain-based transaction? Can you establish jurisdiction over the participants in a decentralized blockchain? How does one establish "minimum contacts" with a forum for blockchain-based activities, which often are not directed at any physical location? There are no clear-cut answers to any of these questions, leaving courts to grapple with them as blockchain technology becomes more commonplace.

(a) Traditional Ideas of Jurisdiction

(i) Creation of Law

There are many sources of law in the United States. Lawmaking is divided between the states and the federal government, in accordance with the

---

13   This section is designed to address jurisdictional issues in civil disputes in the United States, not criminal or regulatory actions, nor actions brought in countries other than the United States.

14   "The Internet . . . has allowed businesses and other organizations previously viewed as local to reach out across the nation and around the world, thus increasing the possibilities of conflict between parties who are physically distant." Stephen J. Newman, *Proof of Personal Jurisdiction in the Internet Age*, 59 Am. Jur. Proof of Facts 3d 1 (2017).

system of federalism outlined in the U.S. Constitution.[15] The states also have their own constitutions that outline lawmaking and rights within their borders. Federal and state legislatures create law, but so do courts and administrative agencies.

As new technologies unconstrained by state or national borders proliferate, federal and state governments will likely wrestle over who has the authority to legislate in relation to it. For example, the internet is considered an instrument of interstate commerce and thus the federal government has jurisdiction to regulate it.[16] But using their constitutional police power, states have attempted to impose regulations on the internet, such as protection of minors from sexual predators.[17] Courts have struck down many of these state regulations, relying on principles such as the Dormant Commerce Clause[18] and federal preemption,[19] finding that those state regulations impacted use of the regulated technology beyond the borders of the state. "The borderless world of the Internet raises profound questions concerning the relationship among the several states and the relationship of the federal government to each state, questions that go to the heart of 'our federalism.'"[20] Similarly, blockchain technology promises to elevate those, and potentially many other, problems beyond state borders.

---

15   U.S. Const., amend. X ("The powers not delegated to the United States by the Constitution, nor prohibited by it to the States, are reserved to the States respectively, or to the people.").

16   "[U]nder the Commerce Clause, Congress 'is empowered to regulate and protect the instrumentalities of interstate commerce, or persons or things in interstate commerce, even though the threat may come only from intrastate activities.'" Wash. v. Guillen, 537 U.S. 129, 147, 123 S. Ct. 720, 731 (2003) (quoting United States v. Lopez, 514 U.S. 549, 558, 115 S.Ct. 1624, 1629 (1995)); United States v. Faris, 583 F.3d 756, 759 (11th Cir. 2009) ("The internet is an instrumentality of interstate commerce.") (quotation omitted); Utah Lighthouse Ministry v. Foundation for Apologetic Information, 527 F.3d 1045, 1054 (10th Cir. 2008) ("We agree that the Internet is generally an instrumentality of interstate commerce."); United States v. Sutcliffe, 505 F.3d 944, 953 (9th Cir. 2007) (holding that the internet is a channel and instrumentality of interstate commerce); United States v. MacEwan, 445 F.3d 237, 245 (3d Cir. 2006) (same).

17   *See, e.g.,* WASH. REV. CODE § 9.68A.104 (West 2012); TENN. CODE ANN. § 39-13-315 (West 2012); N.J. STAT. ANN. § 2C:13-10 (West 2013).

18   *See* Backpage.com, LLC v. Cooper, 939 F. Supp. 2d 805, 841–45 (M.D. Tenn. 2013); Backpage.com, LLC v. McKenna, 881 F. Supp. 2d 1262, 1285–86 (W.D. Wash. 2012); Backpage.com, LLC v. Hoffman, 13-CV-03952, 2013 WL 4502097, at *11–12 (D.N.J. Aug. 20, 2013). The Dormant Commerce Clause achieves "the Constitution's special concern both with the maintenance of a national economic union unfettered by state-imposed limitations on interstate commerce and with the autonomy of the individual States within their respective spheres." Healy v. Beer Inst., 491 U.S. 324, 335–36, 109 S. Ct. 2491, 2499 (1989).

19   *See Cooper,* 939 F. Supp. 2d at 823–27; *McKenna,* 881 F. Supp. 2d at 1271–75; *Hoffman,* 13-CV-03952, 2013 WL 4502097, at *5–7; 47 U.S.C. § 230.

20   Am. Libraries Ass'n v. Pataki, 969 F. Supp. 160, 168 (S.D.N.Y. 1997) (citing Younger v. Harris, 401 U.S. 37, 44, 91 S. Ct. 746, 750–51 (1971)).

(ii) Personal Jurisdiction

Personal jurisdiction ensures that it is fair and just for the state to exercise power over a defendant based on the individual's contact with the state.[21] The Supreme Court's landmark decision, *International Shoe Co. v. State of Washington*, addressed the historical formulation of personal jurisdiction—the presence within the boundaries of the state—and whether that was consistent with modern concepts such as "service of summons or other form[s] of notice[.]"[22] In *International Shoe*, the Court divided personal jurisdiction into "general" and "specific" jurisdiction. [23] These notions of general and specific jurisdiction were further developed and elaborated on throughout the remainder of the twentieth century.[24] Under current formulations, general jurisdiction exists where a defendant's contact with the state is so "continuous and systematic" that he can be sued there for any action, even those not connected with his activities in the forum.[25] Specific jurisdiction is limited to actions based solely on a defendant's contact with the given state and instances where a defendant "purposefully directs" his conduct to the forum.[26]

These concepts are more complex when applied to corporations. A corporation is only sufficiently "at home" to warrant general jurisdiction if, generally speaking, the forum is either its place of incorporation or the

---

21 "[D]ue process requires only that in order to subject a defendant to a judgment in personam . . . he have certain minimum contacts with it such that the maintenance of the suit does not offend 'traditional notions of fair play and substantial justice.'" Int'l Shoe Co. v. State of Wash., 326 U.S. 310, 316, 66 S. Ct. 154, 158 (1945) (citing Milliken v. Meyer, 311 U.S. 457, 463, 61 S.Ct. 339, 343 (1940)). Whether there is personal jurisdiction over a defendant also requires analyzing the state's long-arm statute, but "[w]hen a state's long-arm statute reaches as far as the limits of the Due Process Clause, the two inquiries merge and the court need only determine whether the assertion of personal jurisdiction . . . violates constitutional due process." Intera Corp. v. Henderson, 428 F.3d 605, 616 (6th Cir. 2005) (quotation omitted). Because most states have enacted long-arm statutes that reach as far as the Due Process Clause allows, this section focuses solely on the constitutional analysis. *See* Newman, *Proof of Personal Jurisdiction in the Internet Age* at 1.

22 *Int'l Shoe Co.*, 326 U.S. at 316, 66 S. Ct. at 158.

23 *Id.* at 317, 66 S. Ct. at 159.

24 *See, e.g.*, Burnham v. Superior Court of California, 495 U.S. 604, 110 S. Ct. 2105 (1990); Asahi Metal Indus. Co. v. Superior Court of Cal., 480 U.S. 102, 107 S. Ct. 1026 (1987); Burger King Corp. v. Rudzewicz, 471 U.S. 462, 105 S. Ct. 2174 (1985); Helicopteros Nacionales de Colombia, S.A. v. Hall, 466 U.S. 408, 104 S. Ct. 1868 (1984); World-Wide Volkswagen Corp. v. Woodson, 444 U.S. 286, 100 S. Ct. 559 (1980).

25 *Helicopteros Nacionales de Colombia, S.A.*, 466 U.S. at 416, 104 S. Ct. at 187.

26 *Burger King Corp.*, 471 U.S. at 473, 105 S. Ct. at 2182.

location of its principal place of business.[27] But in deciding whether specific jurisdiction is appropriate, courts primarily look at the burden that litigating in the forum state places on the defendant.[28] To a lesser degree, courts also consider the interests of the forum state and its relationship with the plaintiff.[29] "In order for a court to exercise specific jurisdiction over a claim, there must be an affiliation between the forum and the underlying controversy, principally, an activity or an occurrence that takes place in the forum State."[30]

The Due Process Clause contemplates whether it is reasonable to submit a defendant to the U.S. judicial system.[31] In interpreting the constitutional limits of personal jurisdiction, the Supreme Court places "significant weight" on protecting those who are defending themselves in an alien jurisdiction.[32] But even if technology were to make litigating in a foreign country easier, personal jurisdiction will still exist to limit the power of individual states and the federal government.[33] Thus, even as technology and the economy become global, such as with more efficient and reliable blockchain-based transactions, personal jurisdiction will still need to be considered.

When personal jurisdiction over a defendant is not possible, a plaintiff may be able to establish *in rem* or *quasi in rem* jurisdiction over the subject of the litigation. *In rem* jurisdiction is jurisdiction over property that is located within a state.[34] *Quasi in rem* jurisdiction is based on the court seizing property within the jurisdiction to establish personal jurisdiction, without reference to an individual defendant's contacts with the state.[35] The key difference between *in rem* and *quasi in rem* jurisdiction is whether an individual will ultimately be the subject of the judgment.[36] In a pure *in rem* action, the judgment is over the property itself; however, in a *quasi in rem*

---

27 Goodyear Dunlop Tires Operations, S.A. v. Brown, 564 U.S. 915, 924, 131 S. Ct. 2846, 2854 (2011).

28 Bristol-Myers Squibb Co. v. Superior Court of Cal., 137 S. Ct. 1773, 1780 (2017) (citations omitted).

29 *Id.*

30 *Id.* at 1781 (citing *Goodyear*, 564 U.S. at 919, 131 S. Ct. at 2851).

31 *Asahi Metal Indus. Co.*, 480 U.S. at 114, 107 S. Ct. at 1033.

32 *Id.*

33 *See* Hanson v. Denckla, 357 U.S. 235, 250-51, 78 S. Ct. 1228, 1238 (1958).

34 Pennoyer v. Neff, 95 U.S. 714, 722 (1878).

35 Shaffer v. Heitner, 433 U.S. 186, 196, 97 S. Ct. 2569, 2575 (1977).

36 Hanson v. Denckla, 357 U.S. at 246 n.12, 78 S. Ct. at 1235.

action, the court uses the defendant's property to get jurisdiction over the defendant and can ultimately seize the property to satisfy the judgment.[37]

(iii) Subject-Matter Jurisdiction

Subject-matter jurisdiction assesses the powers of government and whether a sovereign has authority to regulate the particular conduct at issue. In the United States, federal courts are courts of limited subject-matter jurisdiction, meaning that they can only hear those claims for which they have been granted authority to adjudicate by Congress or the Constitution.[38] Aside from federal courts established under Article III of the U.S. Constitution, Congress has created additional federal courts with even more limited jurisdiction, such as bankruptcy courts that can only adjudge disputes under the Bankruptcy Code.[39] The subject-matter jurisdiction of the state courts in the United States is generally broader than that of federal courts, but some matters do fall within the exclusive subject-matter jurisdiction of the federal courts.[40] Additionally, U.S. statutes and regulations, even federal ones, generally only apply domestically.[41]

Alternatively, even when there is no federal law or right at issue, federal courts still can have subject-matter jurisdiction where diversity jurisdiction exists. Diversity jurisdiction arises from a federal statute that gives federal courts original jurisdiction over matters where the amount in controversy exceeds $75,000 and the parties to the dispute are citizens of different states or nations.[42] The $75,000 amount in controversy is calculated based on the date that the plaintiff files the complaint, and if some claims are dismissed after filing, resulting in claimed damages being less than $75,000, there is still federal subject-matter jurisdiction.[43] Given that there are no blockchain-specific federal statutes that create federal jurisdiction, if a litigant wants to avail itself of federal court, it would likely need to establish diversity jurisdiction, which requires a good faith pleading that

---

37 *Id.*

38 *See, e.g.,* 28 U.S.C. § 1331 (federal question); 28 U.S.C. § 1333 (admiralty); 28 U.S.C. § 1334 (bankruptcy); 28 U.S.C. § 1337 (federal commerce and antitrust); 28 U.S.C. § 1338 (federal patents, copyrights, and trademarks); 28 U.S.C. § 1345 (U.S. is a plaintiff).

39 11 U.S.C. §§ 101 *et seq.*

40 18 U.S.C. § 1338 (granting exclusive federal court jurisdiction over "patents, plant variety protection, copyrights and trademarks"); 28 USC §1337 (same for antitrust).

41 "United States law governs domestically but does not rule the world." Microsoft Corp. v. AT&T Corp., 550 U.S. 437, 454, 127 S. Ct. 1746, 1758 (2007).

42 28 U.S.C. § 1332.

43 Hall v. EarthLink Network, Inc., 396 F.3d 500, 506–07 (2d Cir. 2005).

the amount in dispute exceeds $75,000 and that the parties to the dispute are geographically diverse.[44]

(b) Assumptions of Traditional Judicial Jurisdiction That May Not Be Present for Blockchain

Blockchain, by its nature, is capable of operating across jurisdictional boundaries. Courts have yet to grapple with the jurisdictional issues related to blockchain technology. Traditional notions of jurisdiction, grounded in the physical connections with the forum, are difficult to reconcile with actions and injuries that occur in the virtual realm.[45] Since the advent of the internet and the explosion of social media, courts have increasingly faced the challenge of determining jurisdiction over virtual activities and injuries.[46] A court faced with the novel task of determining jurisdiction in a blockchain-related dispute may turn to internet-related jurisdiction cases for guidance.

One of the seminal cases in the area of personal jurisdiction over the internet was decided in 1997 by the Western District of Pennsylvania. In *Zippo Mfg. Co. v. Zippo dot com*, 952 F. Supp. 1119 (W.D. Pa. 1997), the court attempted to apply the traditional jurisdictional standards to the then newly emerging internet. In the *Zippo* case, the court posited that the commercial nature and interactivity of a website can measure contacts

---

44 Alternatively, a federal statute that is not blockchain-specific can get a blockchain-based dispute into federal court. For example, a shareholder derivative lawsuit can be brought pursuant to Sections 10(b) and 20(a) of the Exchange Act against the board members of a blockchain securities company. Complaint, Takata v. Riot Blockchain, Inc., No. 3:18-cv-02293 (filed Feb. 17, 2018) (citing 15 U.S.C. §§ 78j(b) and 78t(a); 17 C.F.R. § 240.10B-5); *see also* Complaint, Berk v. Coinbase, Inc., No. 4:18-cv-01364 (filed Mar. 1, 2018) (same pursuant to the Class Action Fairness Act, 28 U.S.C. § 1332(d)).

45 Wulf A. Kaal and Craig Calcaterra, *Crypto Transaction Dispute Resolution*, 73 Bus. Law. 109, 113 (2017) ("While personal jurisdiction would technically still apply to parties engaging in encrypted, distributed smart contracts, enforcement is impossible because of the separation of physical identifiers and encrypted, distributed smart contracts."); *see generally* Chapter 4 regarding anonymity and blockchain transactions.

46 In 1957, the Supreme Court acknowledged that its personal jurisdiction jurisprudence was affected by the economic and technological transformation that made transactions across state lines easier and more prevalent. McGee v. International Life Ins. Co., 355 U.S. 220, 222-23, 78 S. Ct. 199, 201 (1957) ("Today many commercial transactions touch two or more States and may involve parties separated by the full continent. With this increasing nationalization of commerce has come a great increase in the amount of business conducted by mail across state lines. At the same time modern transportation and communication have made it much less burdensome for a party sued to defend himself in a State where he engages in economic activity."). The spread of blockchain technology promises further evolution in the doctrine.

and purposefulness and created essentially a sliding scale where a passive website would not be enough to establish jurisdiction, while an interactive website coupled with actual contemplated sales in a forum would be sufficient.[47] The *Zippo* case was influential in the realm of personal jurisdiction over internet-related claims and has been adopted in several Circuits.[48] Other Circuits have relied on *Zippo* but have required "something more" to establish jurisdiction in the internet context.[49] Still other Circuits have developed an analysis focused on whether the defendant "purposefully availed" itself of the forum through its internet activity.[50]

The court's analysis in *Zippo* on the interactivity of a website may inform how courts would analyze jurisdictional issues in blockchain-related disputes. Where a website is largely interactive, such as one where users can download information and create contracts, a court will generally find that jurisdiction is proper under the Due Process Clause.[51] And where there is an exchange of information between the host and the website's users, personal jurisdiction is generally considered appropriate when that exchange is of a commercial nature.[52] But a passive website—one where there is no exchange of information but rather it communicates information to viewers—is generally not sufficient for minimum contacts and personal jurisdiction.[53] Some of the various uses of blockchain technology can fit into this framework. For example, a smart contract,[54] which allows blockchain-platform participants to interact with each other to craft an agreement that will automatically execute, is likely to be viewed as analogous to an interactive website which, under *Zippo*, would support personal jurisdiction. Even where a court does not apply the *Zippo* test, a smart contract may still give rise to specific personal jurisdiction if, assuming that

---

47   Zippo Mfg. Co. v. Zippo Dot Com, 952 F. Supp. 1119, 1124 (W.D. Pa. 1997).

48   *See* Inc. v. Imago Eyewear Pty, 167 Fed. Appx. 518, 522–23 (6th Cir. 2006); Lakin v. Prudential Sec. Inc., 348 F.3d 704, 711 (8th Cir. 2003); Neogen Corp. v. Neo Gen Screening, Inc., 282 F.3d 883, 890 (6th Cir. 2002).

49   *See* Toys "R" Us, Inc. v. Step Two, S.A., 318 F.3d 446, 452–54 (3d Cir. 2003) (citation omitted); ALS Scan Inc. v. Digital Serv. Consultants, 293 F.3d 707, 714–15 (4th Cir. 2002)

50   *See* Louis Vuitton Malletier, S.A. v. Mosseri, 736 F.3d 1339, 1355 n.10 (11th Cir. 2013); Pervasive Software, Inc. v. Lexware GmbH & Co. K.G., 688 F.3d 214, 227 n.7 (5th Cir. 2012); Illinois v. Hemi Group LLC, 622 F.3d 754, 758 (7th Cir. 2010); Best Van Lines v. Walker, 490 F.3d 239, 252 (2d Cir. 2007); Cybersell, Inc. v. Cybersell, Inc., 130 F.3d 414, 418–19 (9th Cir. 1997).

51   Lifestyle Lift Holding Co., Inc. v. Prendiville, 768 F. Supp. 2d 929, 934 (E.D. Mich. 2011).

52   *Id.*

53   *Id.*

54   *See* Chapter 3 for discussion of smart contracts.

the plaintiff knows the defendant's identity,[55] the defendant's contact with the forum is sufficient under the traditional Due Process Clause analysis.[56] However, most cases will not be as clear-cut, and courts will need to apply these standards in a case-by-case approach, just as they have had to do in an earlier era with websites.[57]

Blockchain and its myriad of uses pose even further challenges to the traditional notions of jurisdiction than the internet did. Although a website must be hosted on servers that will have a discrete location, blockchain technology is decentralized. No single or discrete location exists at which the blockchain is located or hosted as there is with a website. In fact, a fundamental precept of blockchain technology is that there is no central blockchain node that that participates in all blockchain transitions.[58] As a result, it is difficult to ascertain where a blockchain is "located" for purposes of applying traditional jurisdictional rules. Additionally, participants and users of blockchain may be anonymous (and, indeed, some proponents of the technology hail this anonymity as a benefit to the technology), which again is inconsistent with jurisdiction based on identity and location. When the identity of the defendant and its location are unknown, then traditionally accepted notions of jurisdiction tethered to geographic location are not available. And while an analogy to internet jurisdiction may seem convenient to the courts, a blockchain may not be of the same character as commercial websites; blockchain technology does

---

55　In some instances, anonymous parties will enter into a smart contract. If there is a breach, the nonbreaching party may then try to bring a claim against a "Doe" defendant to ascertain the defendant's identity through limited discovery. But the plaintiff in that case would still need to "have at least a good faith belief that such discovery will enable it to show that the court has personal jurisdiction over the defendant." *Caribbean Broadcasting System, Ltd. v. Cable & Wireless PLC*, 148 F.3d 1080, 1090 (D.C. Cir. 1998); *see also AF Holdings, LLC v. Does 1-1058*, 752 F.3d 990, 994–96 (D.C. Cir. 2014) (holding that there was no good faith belief in personal jurisdiction when the plaintiff sued over 1,000 individuals and did not tailor its request for ISP numbers to those who had downloaded illegal content in the forum).

56　*See generally* Picot v. Weston, 780 F.3d 1206, 1213 (9th Cir. 2015) (noting that courts will look at whether the forum state holds a "special place in [the defendant's] performance under the agreement as a whole").

57　*See, e.g.*, Fenn v. Mleads Enterprises, Inc., 137 P.3d 706, 715 (Utah 2006) (single e-mail advertisement was insufficient contact with the forum under the Due Process Clause's personal jurisdiction analysis); Doe v. Ciolli, 611 F. Supp. 2d 216, 223–24 (D. Conn. 2009) (postings on a website were sufficient to satisfy personal jurisdiction burden); *Lifestyle Lift Holding Co.*, 768 F. Supp. 2d at 936 (finding that the website did not satisfy minimum contacts because it was passive); Cohen v. Facebook, Inc., 252 F. Supp. 3d 140, 153–54 (E.D.N.Y. 2017) (holding that the website's minimum contacts in the United States were sufficient under the Antiterrorism Act).

58　*See* Chapter 1.

not always target or direct itself to a given forum, and sales are often not consummated in a specific forum. Further, the nature of blockchain's code may not fit cleanly within a traditional civil litigation framework.[59]

(c) Options to Address Jurisdictional Concerns

(i) Contract/Transaction

An obvious solution to the above issues is for the parties to agree at the outset of a transaction where jurisdiction can be asserted for disputes. Such clauses could be included in documentation related to smart contracts and/or terms of use to access to the blockchain. Courts generally enforce such forum selection clauses unless there is evidence of bad faith.[60] In analyzing these clauses, courts look to three principles:

1. "whether the clause was reasonably communicated to the party resisting enforcement";[61]
2. "whether the clause is mandatory or permissive, i.e., whether the parties are required to bring any . . . dispute to the designated forum or simply permitted to do so";[62] and
3. "whether the claims and parties involved in the suit are subject to the forum selection clause."[63]

If the forum selection clause was properly disclosed, a presumption arises that it is enforceable.[64] This presumption can be overcome by demonstrating that "enforcement would be unreasonable or unjust, or

---

59 "Because of the emphasis on code for computer programming (and artificial intelligence), courts may not be able to hypothesize a reasonable human's interpretation of a given smart contract." Wulf A. Kaal and Craig Calcaterra, *Crypto Transaction Dispute Resolution*, 73 BUS. LAW. 109, 136 (2017). Additionally, remedies may not be feasible. "If a transaction in a smart contract fails to be completed or is partially completed but not added to the blockchain, it is unclear how liability will be allocated if those eventualities have not been accounted for in applicable code." *Id.* at 137.

60 "[F]orum-selection clauses contained in form passage contracts are subject to judicial scrutiny for fundamental fairness." Carnival Cruise Lines, Inc. v. Shute, 499 U.S. 585, 595, 111 S. Ct. 1522, 1528 (1991).

61 Martinez v. Bloomberg LP, 740 F.3d 211, 217 (2d Cir. 2014) (citing Phillips v. Audio Active Ltd., 494 F.3d 378, 383 (2d Cir. 2007)).

62 *Id; see also* Autoridad de Energia Electrica de Puerto Rico v. Vitol S.A., 859 F.3d 140, 145 (1st Cir. 2017).

63 *Martinez*, 740 F.3d at 217.

64 *Id.*

that the clause was invalid for such reasons as fraud or overreaching."[65] A court also may disregard a forum selection clause where its enforcement would violate public policy.[66] But where there is notice, a party seeking to avoid a forum selection clause is subject to an arduous burden.[67] This is true even if the designated forum is in another country,[68] which may often be the case in disputes arising from worldwide blockchain-related smart contracts.

Nonetheless, notice may be difficult in the context of online contracts.[69] Although a forum selection clause may be included in "terms and conditions" that must be accepted before proceeding with a transaction, such clauses may ultimately become the subject of litigation.[70] These critical clauses, such as submission to jurisdiction, must be "clear and unambiguous," which may require bold and capitalized headings, large font, separate e-mails containing the terms, and the ability for consumers to read those terms and conditions after accepting them.[71]

Alternatively, for private blockchains that are hosted by an intermediary, that intermediary could craft its own dispute resolution mechanism. There are many proposals for these systems, although they are still developing. One such application is "The Aragon Network," which would include anonymous judges and regulators that govern blockchain-based dispute resolution.[72] Disputes would be addressed once a party posts a bond and argues its case in a brief, which the judges evaluate.[73] Those judges must also post bonds that they forfeit if they do not decide with the majority.[74]

---

65 *Id.*; *see also* Feggestad v. Kerzner Int'l Bahamas Ltd., 843 F.3d 915, 918 (11th Cir. 2016).

66 *See, e.g.,* Doe 1 v. AOL LLC, 552 F.3d 1077, 1084 (9th Cir. 2009) (invalidating a forum selection clause where it violated California's public policy of applying its consumer protection laws); M/S Bremen v. Zapata Off-Shore Co., 407 U.S. 1, 15, 92 S.Ct. 1907 (1972); *but see* TradeComet.com LLC v. Google, Inc., 435 Fed. Appx. 31, 37 (9th Cir. 2011) (rejecting the plaintiff's argument to set aside a clause where "Google's forum selection clause [was alleged to be] contrary to public policy favoring enforcement of antitrust laws by private parties").

67 *Carnival Cruise Lines,* 499 U.S. at 595, 111 S. Ct at 1528.

68 "[I]nternational forum-selection clauses are prima facie valid, especially when freely negotiated between private parties." 1st Source Bank v. Neto, 861 F.3d 607, 612 (7th Cir. 2017) (citing M/S Bremen, 407 U.S. at 10, 92 S. Ct. at 1907).

69 *See, e.g.,* Starkey v. G Adventures, Inc., 796 F.3d 193, 197 (2d Cir. 2015).

70 *Id*; *see also TradeComet.com* LLC, 435 Fed. Appx. at 34.

71 *See, e.g., Starkey,* 796 F.3d at 197.

72 Wulf A. Kaal and Craig Calcaterra, *Blockchain Technology's Distributed Jurisdiction,* Medium at 10 (June 20, 2017), https://medium.com/@wulfkaal/blockchain-technologys-distributed-jurisdiction-a2177c244538.

73 *Id.*

74 *Id.*

Another proposed option is "CrowdJury," which hopes to put a virtual version of the justice system on a blockchain.[75] "Think transparent processes with crowdsourced discovery, crowdsourced analysis, and crowdsourced decision making and presto—you get an accurate outcome in a much shorter time frame and at a vastly reduced cost."[76] A final example is "an open-source platform ecosystem of smart contracting dispute resolution that allows users to opt in to conflict resolution mechanisms that simultaneously could enable more nuanced crypto solutions and produce greater (legal) certainty."[77] However, the larger the role played by the intermediary, the increased potential for liability assumed by the intermediary. Additionally, requiring an intermediary to administer a dispute resolution process could increase transactions costs (both in terms of money and time), which undermines some of the benefits of employing blockchain technology.

Attempts to fill the jurisdictional void either through contract clauses or at a platform level although appropriate for both pemissionless and permissioned blockchains, may have greater potential for permissioned blockchains. Permissionless, public blockchains raise jurisdictional challenges of anonymous users and decentralized systems without necessarily providing a mechanism to address those challenges.

(ii) Developing Laws

Another possible mechanism to address the jurisdictional issues raised by blockchain is to legislate jurisdiction. For example, the Anticybersquatting Consumer Protection Act (ACPA) was passed during the advent of the internet to keep people from registering domain names and then charging exorbitant prices for them to companies that want to use them.[78] In domain name cases under the ACPA, the domain name is itself the subject of the litigation and the court has *in rem* jurisdiction over the name rather than over the individual defendant.[79] The ACPA model does not necessarily address all blockchain jurisdictional concerns, since not all blockchain disputes will be focused on the blockchain itself, but may involve the users

---

75 CrowdJury: A Justice System for the Internet Age, https://www.crowdjury.org.

76 Don Tapscott and Alex Tapscott, Blockchain Revolution 220 (2016).

77 Wulf A. Kaal and Criag Calcaterra, *Crypto Transaction Dispute Resolution*, 73 Bus. Law. 109, 148 (2017).

78 15 U.S.C. § 1125(d).

79 Mattel, Inc. v. Barbie-Club.com, 310 F.3d 293, 301 (2002) (noting that Congress "establish[ed] a circumscribed basis for in rem jurisdiction that is grounded in the "nexus" provided by the registrar or other domain-name authority having custody of the disputed property").

of the blockchain. But what the ACPA example does demonstrate is that creative legislative solutions, taking into account blockchain technology, may be able to ameliorate the jurisdictional issues raised by blockchains.

State legislatures have been active in developing laws regulating blockchain technology. Arizona has recently passed a law granting bringing smart contracts or anything else "secured through blockchain technology" under the ambit of Arizona's Electronic Transactions Act, which, among other things, gives smart contracts the same legal effect, validity, and enforceability as their standard contract counterparts.[80] Other states have proposed or adopted legislation that gives blockchain transactions legal force.[81] Unfortunately, none of the state statutes to date contain any jurisdictional provisions. This could be considered a lost opportunity to create an important framework for the orderly and predictable resolution of disputes. But as seen in the internet context, state statutes that attempt to broadly regulate blockchains might not survive constitutional scrutiny.[82]

Although a federal blockchain law might survive constitutional scrutiny, it still might not be able to address all of the jurisdictional issues raised by blockchains. Any federal law addressing blockchain must consider its extraterritorial application, as blockchain users are found not only in the United States.[83]

3. ENFORCEMENT OF COURT JUDGMENTS IN BLOCKCHAIN DISPUTES

For disputes that may arise in the context of commercial blockchain applications, enforcing a court's judgment will present issues similar to those in a traditional commercial case. For example, if a corporation obtains a

---

80 Craig A. de Ridder, Mercedes K. Tunstall, & Nathalie Prescott, *Recognition of Smart Contracts in the United States*, 29 No. 11 INTELL. PROP. & TECH L.J. 17 (2017).

81 These states include Arizona, Delaware, Nevada, and Vermont. ARIZ. REV. STAT. ANN. § 44-7061 (2017) (giving blockchain-based signatures and contracts legal validity); Act of Aug. 1, 2017, Sen. Bill 69 (amending sections of the Delaware code to govern storing information on blockchains); 2017 NEV. REV. STAT. §§ 719.240–719.350 (recognizing blockchain as an untaxable electronic record); Vt. Stat. Ann. Tit. 12 § 1913 (West 2016) (making blockchain-stored information admissible in court) *See generally* Chapter 7.

82 *See Cooper*, 939 F. Supp. 2d at 84; *McKenna*, 881 F. Supp. 2d at 1285; *Hoffman*, 13-CV-03952, 2013 WL 4502097, at *12.

83 *See* Morrison v. National Australia Bank Ltd., 561 U.S. 247, 269–70, 130 S. Ct. 2869, 2885–86 (2010). In *Morrison*, other countries filed amici curiae briefs that "complain[ed] of the interference with foreign securities regulation that application of § 10(b) abroad would produce, and urge[d] the adoption of a clear test that will avoid that consequence." *Id.*

judgment against a foreign-based platform provider, the plaintiff may need to enforce that judgment in the provider's home country. Accordingly, this section reviews the general framework for recognition and enforcement of (1) foreign judgments in U.S. courts and (2) judgments from U.S. courts in foreign countries. The section then discusses some of the enforcement mechanisms that networks have developed to address the unique enforcement issues that can arise for blockchain technology where participants remain anonymous.

(a) Recognition and Enforcement of Foreign Judgments in U.S. Courts

The United States is not a party to any international treaty or other agreement that would control enforcement of judgements abroad.[84] For a judgment to be enforced by a court in the United States (state or federal), the judgment generally first must be recognized.[85] Whether a foreign judgment will be recognized, in turn, is governed by the law of the state (whether in state court or in federal court on diversity jurisdiction) in which the party brings the recognition action.[86] Virtually all of the states follow either the Restatement (Third) of Foreign Relations Law or one of the two uniform acts on recognition and enforcement of foreign judgments—the Uniform Foreign Money-Judgments Recognition Act and the Uniform Foreign-Country Money Judgments Recognition Act.[87]

Although not identical, the Uniform Acts and the Restatement are similar enough to discuss them together.[88] The general rule is that a foreign

---

84   *See* U.S. DEP'T OF STATE, ENFORCEMENT OF JUDGMENTS, https://travel.state.gov/content/travel/en/legal/travel-legal-considerations/internl-judicial-asst/Enforcement-of-Judges.html.

85   Ronald A. Brand, *Federal Judicial Center International Litigation Guide: Recognition and Enforcement of Foreign Judgments*, 74 U. PITTSBURG L. REV. 491, 499 (2013) ("Recognition of foreign judgments and enforcement of foreign judgments are separate matters."); RESTATEMENT (THIRD) ON FOREIGN RELATIONS LAW § 481, cmt. a ("The judgment of a foreign state may not be enforced unless it is entitled to recognition.").

86   In cases in federal court on federal-question jurisdiction, federal common law governs. And federal common law on recognition of judgments follows the principles set forth in Hilton v. Guyot, 159 U.S. 113 (1895) or the Restatement. *See* Brand, *Recognition & Enforcement*, *supra* note 85, at 494 (Restatement); Saskatchewan Mut. Ins. Co. v. CE Design, Ltd., 865 F.3d 537, 541 n.1 (7th Cir. 2017) ("The leading federal case on recognition and enforcement of foreign-country judgments remains *Hilton* . . .").

87   Specifically, thirty-five states have adopted one of the Uniform Acts. *See* Haig, 3 BUS. & COM. LITIG. FED. CTS. § 21:109 (4th ed.).

88   Walter W. Heiser, *The Hague Convention on Choice of Court Agreements: The Impact of Forum Non Conveniens, Transfer of Venue, Removal, and Recognition of Judgments in United States Courts*, 31 U. PA. J. INT'L L. 1013, 1025 (2010). For purposes of this chapter, citations to "Uniform Act" refer to the Uniform Foreign-Money Judgments Recognition Act.

judgment that is conclusive and enforceable where it was rendered "is conclusive between the parties to the extent that it grants or denies recovery of a sum of money." Uniform Act §§ 2, 3; *Restatement (Third) of Foreign Relations Law* § 481 (1987). That general rule is modified by two mandatory and discretionary exceptions. The mandatory exceptions are circumstances in which the court *cannot* recognize the judgment. A court may not recognize a judgment if "the judgment was rendered under a judicial system that does not provide impartial tribunals or procedures compatible with due process" or where the foreign court did not have personal jurisdiction over the defendant (*Restatement* § 482(1); Act § 4(a)(1)) and, under the Uniform Act, where the court did not have subject-matter jurisdiction. The discretionary exceptions, on the other hand, permit a court to decline to recognize the judgment for a variety of reasons. A court "need not" recognize the judgment if, among other things, the defendant did not receive sufficient notice, the judgment was obtained by fraud, the judgment conflicts with another final and conclusive judgment, or the judgment is based on a claim that "is repugnant to the public policy" of the particular state.[89] Additionally, some states permit courts to refuse recognition in the absence of reciprocity—i.e., if the foreign country would not recognize a similar judgment from the state.[90]

There are procedural issues to consider too. Many states require that the party seeking recognition of the foreign judgment establish that the court have personal jurisdiction over the defendant, such as sufficient minimum contacts or assets in the state.[91]

Once a U.S. court recognizes the foreign judgment in a recognition proceeding, the foreign judgment in effect becomes a domestic or local judgment. In other words, the judgment becomes fully enforceable in that state and entitled to full faith and credit in other state and federal courts.[92]

---

89   *See* Uniform Act § 4(b); Restatement § 482(2).

90   *E.g.*, Fla. Stat. § 55.605(2)(g); *see also* Brand, *Recognition & Enforcement*, at 507 (identifying states with a reciprocity requirement).

91   Brand, *Recognition & Enforcement*, *supra* note 85, at 505–06 (discussing variation in states' jurisdictional requirements for enforcement).

92   Brand, *Recognition & Enforcement*, *supra* note 85, at 495; Yuliya Zeynalova, *The Law on Recognition and Enforcement of Foreign Judgments: Is It Broken and How Do We Fix It?*, 31 Berkeley J. of Int'l L. 150, 156 (2013); *e.g.*, Fla. Stat. § 55.604(5) ("Upon entry of an order recognizing the out-of-country foreign judgment, or upon recording of the clerk's certificate set forth above, the out-of-country foreign judgment shall be enforced in the same manner as the judgment of a court of this state.").

(b) Recognition and Enforcement of U.S. Judgments in Foreign Courts

The general perception is that it is more difficult to enforce judgments from U.S. courts in foreign countries than it is to enforce foreign judgments in U.S. courts.[93] Because the United States is not a party to any international agreement regarding reciprocal recognition of judgments, whether a foreign court will enforce a judgment from the United States depends on the laws of that country.

These laws will, of course, vary, but there are some general principles. In deciding whether to enforce a judgment from a U.S. court, a foreign court will consider whether the court had jurisdiction, whether the defendant received proper notice, whether the proceedings were tainted by fraud, and whether the judgment is contrary to the country's public policy.[94] Jurisdiction and public policy issues often come into play. Because the United States has a more expansive view of jurisdiction than do many other countries, the foreign court may conclude that the defendant was not subject to jurisdiction under its own standards.[95] Public policy concerns, moreover, may lead the foreign court to reject a judgment that includes punitive damages or treble (or other multiple) damages.[96] Other reasons a foreign court may reject a judgment from the United States include the absence of reciprocity, the lack of a treaty governing judgment recognition, or a conflict between the judgment and a proceeding in the foreign country.[97]

(c) Application to Blockchain Technology

In many commercial applications of blockchain using permissioned networks—e.g., where actors in a supply chain enter secure transactions into a blockchain system to track products—enforcement issues unique to

---

93 *See, e.g.,* Zeynalova, *The Law on Recognition and Enforcement of Foreign Judgments, supra* note 92, at 153, 163; Richard W. Hulbert, *Some Thoughts on Judgments, Reciprocity, and the Seeming Paradox of Int'l Comm'l Arbitration,* 29 U. Pa. J. Int'l L. 641, 646–47 (2008).

94 U.S. State Dep't, https://travel.state.gov/content/travel/en/legal/travel-legal-considerations/internl-judicial-asst/Enforcement-of-Judges.html; *see also* Zeynalova, 31 Berkeley J. of Int'l L. at 165–68.

95 Committee on Foreign and Comparative Law, Association of the Bar of the City of N.Y., Survey on Foreign Recognition of U.S. Money Judgments 4 (2001); *see also* 3 Bus. & Com. Litig. Fed. Cts. § 21:109 (4th ed.); U.S. State Dep't, *Enforcing Judgments,* https://travel.state.gov/content/travel/en/legal/travel-legal-considerations/internl-judicial-asst/Enforcement-of-Judges.html.

96 Survey on Foreign Recognition at 9–13; *see also* 3 Bus. & Com. Litig. Fed. Cts. § 21:109 (4th ed.), U.S. State Dep't, *Enforcing Judgments,* https://travel.state.gov/content/travel/en/legal/travel-legal-considerations/internl-judicial-asst/Enforcement-of-Judges.html.

97 *See generally* Survey on Foreign Recognition *supra* note 96, at 4–23.

blockchain are less likely to arise. That is because the various participants contributing to the blockchain (e.g., the manufacturer, the supplier, the retailer) are known companies (rather than anonymous actors) and have real-world assets. Likewise, in disputes against providers of blockchain platforms or service providers helping companies integrate blockchain,[98] the enforcement issues will likely be similar to those in a traditional legal dispute. The same may hold true for many permissionless blockchain applications. Even where a defendant cannot be identified at the outset of the litigation, the defendant may be sued as a fictitious defendant or "Doe defendant."[99] So if the defendant is identified during the litigation and substituted for the fictitious or "Doe defendant," then enforcement would proceed in the same manner as in a traditional lawsuit. There will, of course, be situations where a defendant cannot be identified, which raises its own set of concerns—for both enforcement and jurisdictional considerations.

It is not hard to imagine potential cases involving blockchain technology that could present difficult enforcement issues. Judgements awarded in cryptocurrency provide one example. If the cryptocurrency coins are backed by real-world property, the plaintiff may have better luck enforcing the judgment by asking the court to seize the real-world assets rather than attempting to obtain the cryptocurrency. A cryptocurrency with only "intrinsic" value, like Bitcoin, would not provide that option. Bitcoin and other intrinsic-value tokens may present other issues. Consider a case in which a court awards the plaintiff a certain amount of Bitcoin. If the relevant jurisdiction does not consider Bitcoin "money,"[100] but instead treats it as analogous to a tangible piece of property, that could affect the judgment creditor's ability to garnish wages or go after bank or other deposit accounts.

In sum, certain applications of blockchain like Bitcoin may require use of novel enforcement mechanisms; however, for disputes arising out of business uses of blockchain involving permissioned networks, companies are likely to face enforcement issues similar to those in traditional litigation. Because the United States is not a party to any treaty or other international agreement, the standards governing whether a judgment will be enforced often will depend on the local law of the recognizing jurisdiction. To the

---

98 Elena Mesropyan, *30 Companies Providing Enterprise-Grade Blockchain Solutions*, Medici (Feb. 19, 2017), https://letstalkpayments.com/companies-providing-enterprise-grade-blockchain-solutions/.

99 *E.g.*, Federal Procedure, § 1:192 (state court); Federal Procedure, § 62:109 (federal court).

100 *See* Chapter 6.

extent cross-border enforceability is a concern, parties may consider arbitration as a dispute-resolution mechanism. An arbitral award rendered in the United States generally will be easier to enforce abroad than a court judgment from the United States.[101] That is because the United States is a party to the "New York Convention," the 1958 United Nations Convention on the Recognition and Enforcement of Foreign Arbitral Awards.[102]

---

101   Brand, *Recognition & Enforcement, supra* note 85, at 526; Zeynalova, *The Law on Recognition and Enforcement of Foreign Judgments, supra* note 92, at 153, 163 ("Transnational litigants are therefore more likely to encounter difficulties enforcing their foreign court awards than parties seeking to enforce their foreign arbitral awards."); *see also* Hulbert, *Some Thoughts on Judgments, supra* note 93, at 648 ("American judgment creditors never have access to the simpler, cheaper, quicker avenues for enforcement provided by treaty.").

102   *See* 9 U.S.C. § 201.

Table of Cases

Index